PARADISE DIVIDED

PARADISE DIVIDED

The changes, the challenges, the choices for Australia

Paul Kelly

Allen & Unwin

First published in 2000

Copyright ©Paul Kelly 2000

Index by Geraldine Suter

Allen & Unwin
9 Atchison Street, St Leonards NSW 2560 Australia
Phone: (61 2) 8425 0100
Fax: (61 2) 9906 2218
E-mail: frontdesk@allen-unwin.com.au
Web: http://www.allen-unwin.com.au

National Library of Australia
Cataloguing-in-Publication entry:

Kelly, Paul, 1947– .
  Paradise divided: the changes, the challenges, the choices
  for Australia.

  Includes index.
  ISBN 1 86508 291 0.

  1. Globalization. 2. Australia—Social conditions—1990– .
  3. Australia—Civilization—1990– . 4. Australia—Politics
  and government—1990– . I. Title. II. Title: Australian
  (Canberra, A.C.T.)

306.0994

Set in 11/13pt Janson by DOCUPRO, Sydney
Printed and bound by Griffin Press, Adelaide

10 9 8 7 6 5 4 3 2 1

CONTENTS

INTRODUCTION

AUSTRALIA IS AT the cutting edge of globalisation, which it both celebrates and shuns. The nation is beset by the contradictions of globalisation—a rapid take-up of new technology, an embrace of the Internet, a new economic confidence amid growing personal insecurity, family breakdown, broken trust and complaints that Australia has lost control of its destiny. Australia is a laboratory in which to study the impact of globalisation. With their pragmatic instinct, Australians demanded the advantages of globalisation while their political system soon incorporated its divisive consequences.

For Australia the phenomenon of globalisation coincided with a series of millennium debates about identity. Should Australia become a republic? How can reconciliation with the Aboriginal people be achieved? How does Australia see itself at its centenary as a nation? Can Australia combine a quest for excellence with its common man heritage? After the East Timor crisis, how does Australia interpret the idea of its engagement with Asia?

The two politicians who dominated the 1990s and offered different answers to the issues of globalisation and identity were Paul Keating and John Howard. While the Keating–Howard differences were real, they were inflated by personal antagonism. Keating and Howard both supported Australia's economic opening to the world but they had contrasting perspectives on the nation's future.

Australia, in effect, was having two debates: how to define itself and how to relate to the world. The agendas involved taxation, capital flows, economic growth, immigration, trade, foreign policy, the greenhouse effect, technology, community values and the trade-off between the Australian tradition and irresistible international pressure to change.

The over-arching theme of Australian politics in the 1990s has been the clash between the economic imperative of globalisation and the community demand for reassurance. The same struggle has been repeated throughout the democracies. That is why the experience of Bill Clinton in the US and Tony Blair in Great Britain has relevance for Australia.

As a process, globalisation is both empowering and mesmerising. It is destroying the old barriers that divided and defined national life. It accelerated with the demise of the Cold War. It continues through the revolutions in finance, technology and communication which make the world smaller, faster and more integrated. No nation or people is immune from this process. Globalisation has its own winners and losers. The greatest losers have been those Asian nations who fell victim to the late 1990s financial crisis.

The consequences of globalisation are still hardly grasped. Will it destroy Australia's egalitarian ethic? Is Australia becoming two nations along a new divide? Can democratic institutions survive the free market? Will Australia emerge stronger or weaker from the new international system? Will the model of free financial flows ultimately self-destruct?

Globalisation has created fantastic wealth. It has generated a schism between the newly empowered 'knowledge workers' and the victims of those industries in decline. It has enhanced the cult of individualism by creating vast new opportunities for self-realisation, thereby making political compromise harder to achieve.

This book is about all these issues. It is a collection of articles and commentaries from the 1990s during my time as Editor-in-Chief of *The Australian* and then as the paper's International Editor. It is opinionated, doesn't pretend to be consistent and is highly selective. It begins with a series of 'snapshot' pieces and then has sections dealing with the Howard government, the culture of the 1990s, the international scene, the republic debate and our future as an immigrant nation. The articles and speeches are published in the original, but edited for brevity and to avoid repetition.

PART I

SNAPSHOTS

FOR MOST PEOPLE in the 1990s life got a lot better and also far more complex. But it has become an embarrassment to tell the truth—that most people are better off and some are a lot better off.

The pace of change is intellectually stimulating yet destructive of historical memory. In a media saturated society the images now flicker faster than ever. But their meaning is often lost. A man in Britain whose wife died the same week as Princess Diana reported that he grieved more for the princess he never knew than the wife who shared his life.

Beneath the prosperity of the 1990s were two concerns—that individual wellbeing was dependent upon a worthwhile social order and a degree of spiritual meaning. These 'discoveries' often presented as 1990s revelations are ancient truths. But they helped to create the ambivalence of the decade. The 1990s saw the creation of new wealth, new ways of working and living, more options for individual self-fulfillment but generated alarm because in some parts of Australia the social order was degenerating.

The first snapshot deals with Australia's main challenge—to avoid a split into two nations. That demands a better integration of economic and social policy which, in turn, means a political system that works. But the omens from the 1990s are not favourable for the political system. The melodrama involving Bill Clinton and American democracy, the second snapshot, reveals politics succumbing to culture of trivia. Is this the direction in which Australia is headed?

Australia, of course, has the common man as prime minister, the argument of the next snapshot. This is John Howard's political strength but it will impose a time limit on his tenure. The next piece provides a contrast with Howard, an account of British prime minister Tony Blair's 'Third Way'. Snapshot five deals with national memory. Australia's centenary as a nation is on 1 January 2001. The public will celebrate an event it has all but forgotten or never learnt about.

This piece is followed by an exercise in nostalgia, 'Coffee with Gough', which reminds us how sweeping have been the changes of the past 25 years. Whitlam the modernist is now a museum piece. 'Howard Florey, our tallest poppy' is about the most famous Australian of all time whose excellence has rarely been recognised. It is a parable for our decade, the difference between the hero and the celebrity.

The 1990s ended with the East Timor crisis, an event that shattered the myths about Indonesia by which Australia has lived for too long. The year 1999 also saw Australia confront and retreat from its destiny as a republic. There are many ways of interpreting this event. I see it as a test and a failure of Australian conservatism. Finally, these snapshots deal with how those great ideas of liberty and equality have been re-intepreted in Australia today.

AUSTRALIA IN THE
GLOBAL ECONOMY

SOCIAL POLICY IN Australia today should not be a secondary priority. Social policy isn't just an afterthought of economic policy, it is an indispensable companion. Social and economic policy must go together. Unless we accept this, then market-based economics won't survive, let alone advance. The ultimate guarantee of this is the ballot box. Australia is a compulsory voting democracy. Everybody has to vote. The vote of the battler is worth the same as a millionaire. Unless the community is given a stake in the new economic system, then it will vote against the system and against its political champions.

Last year we saw an epic event in Asia. Market forces terminated the Asian economic miracle. It was frightening to watch. John Howard said Asia got worse than it deserved. He said the global financial system failed it. What the markets did to Indonesia became divorced from the merits or otherwise of Indonesia's economy. Markets aren't necessarily wise or moral or geared to the public good. They lack democratic legitimacy. They can be an invaluable benefit to society but they can destroy. Capitalism is a process of creative destruction.

There are two messages from the Asian crisis. First, nations must get the economic fundamentals right and the sanctions against a mistake are greater than ever. Second, the power of the market must be qualified and limited.

The cost of social dysfunction is rising today in all its manifestations. In recent times in both Colorado and Port Arthur, we have seen terrible massacres, events baffling but somehow a combination of alienation, culture and guns. The symbolic message from these tragedies is the vulnerability of society to acts of solitary recklessness and the destructive power which a tiny minority can deploy against an entire community. The trademark of the current age, in fact, is that rapid change is both empowering people and demoralising them.

The combination of open financial flows and technological change has put a hurricane in the sails of capitalism. The post-Cold War period represents a capitalistic revolution, the full magnitude of which we can't quite perceive at this stage. We've seen the creation of wealth on a fantastic scale, but the more capitalism creates, the more it destroys. This is true from the village to the nation-state. Creation and destruction are the bed companions of capitalism. There is an evil embedded in the genius of the market-place. This worries all sorts of people from the Pope to George Soros to Dr Mahathir to Alan Greenspan. Not surprisingly, they have different solutions. The problem has different dimensions.

A new economy is being created on the shoulders of the old economy. Agriculture and manufacturing are shrinking in relative terms while the services, information and technological sectors are exploding. The message is that those who can adapt will succeed and those who can't adapt will struggle.

Australia has taken the historic decision to be an open economy. It was taken in the 1980s and it means we accept the discipline of the international marketplace. The consequences of this are a loss of national economic sovereignty and the imperative to compete internationally. It is like being in a permanent Olympics. It's on all the time; it doesn't stop and, once you open your economy, you must change your way of life. This process is still at an early stage in Australia.

Globalisation and market outcomes promote a growing inequality of income and assets amid greater prosperity. So far, Australians have tolerated this, but what are the limits to such tolerance? Recent studies by Access Economics show that the top 10 per cent of Australian income units owned 48 per cent of the wealth compared to 43 per cent just five years ago. Share market wealth is highly concentrated despite its nominal expansion. The top 10 per cent of income units own 90 per cent of share wealth. What sort of society will we become in another 25 years if these trends continue without offsetting action?

The paradox is that people have never been so well off materially, if simultaneously, so unhappy about their lot. The overwhelming majority of people are better off than they were before—GDP, per capita income, real wages, have all risen in the 1990s. If people were transported back 40 years and had to live without television, videos, the Internet, jumbo jets, freeways, mobile phones, modern contraception, wines, refrigeration and sewerage, they would be in shock therapy. But gains are taken for granted and expectations merely move to a new level.

The search today is for individual fulfilment through career, recreation, travel, relationships, entertainment, religion. These ambitions were inconceivable when the challenge was material survival. The search, in fact, is for personal fulfilment, but this often breeds endless dissatisfaction because personal fulfilment is an illusive concept. If we don't get it, the tendency is to blame somebody—somebody else.

I suggest that internationalisation and the momentum for economic reform is in its early stages. This great new phase of history is probably just beginning. There are enormous sections of the Australian economy that are still underperforming. The benefits for Australia from running a comprehensive and truly efficient economy are enormous—many rewards are waiting to be reaped in the future. But how do we sustain the economic changes necessary to realise such rewards? What are the benchmarks for social policy?

I suggest we need a new politics and we need a much greater integration of economic and social policy. I want to put forward six benchmarks.

First, we need an over-arching commitment to social inclusion as the basis for a successful 21st century society. There are many reasons we need this, both in its own right but also because of other benefits social inclusion gives. Policies of social inclusion buy leaders economic policy manoeuvrability. The socially inclusive leader can get away with much tougher economic reforms than a socially divisive leader. There is no place in the 21st century for the leader who refuses to champion the cause of social inclusion. Social inclusion is tied to the idea of interdependence. It is not just a moral requirement; it is a practical need. It flows from the recognition that in today's society we are more interdependent than ever. You can't have one section or several sections of the community alienated and expect to have a harmonious society. It just won't work. Social inclusion is based upon recognition of the strength of diversity, but also on an acceptance that diversity must operate within limits. It means that the leader must serve as a role model. The essence of contemporary leadership lies in the power of example. I am reminded of the National Economic Summit in 1983, an event which changed the atmospherics of public life in Australia and made possible outcomes which otherwise would not have been possible. The main requirement for such tasks, of course, is trust, since no group can expect to have all its demands satisfied. Community tolerance is based on social compromise.

My second point is that the community's participation in an ownership of the new economy needs to be maximised. In a democracy this is the key to the success of the new economy. The real reason why socialism was defeated in Australia 50 years ago is that the majority of families became property owners and small time capitalists. Governments and corporations must now tackle this issue jointly.

There is a divide in Australia today between the elite who rightly applaud the Australian economic miracle of the late 1990s, and the bulk of the community who merely ask 'What miracle?'. These people don't have a sense of ownership of the process. There needs to be a much deeper commitment from the government to economic justice and involving the community in the new sources of wealth creation in the marketplace. No nation as yet has stumbled upon the ideal solution to this conundrum. But in Australia, it involves many things. A strong, transparent and universal superannuation system. A tax system which seeks to balance incentive and fairness. Putting intergenerational equity squarely onto the political agenda. Corporate policies that empower the individual with a stake in his or her company. Policies to generate an investment culture at the individual, family and small business level.

My third point is a need for a genuine full employment strategy. Unemployment is probably the greatest source of inequity and social dislocation. For Australia, this means seeking its own solution, presumably a midpoint between European social regulation and United States labour market deregulation. It means keeping a social safety-net but seeking a more flexible labour market above this—a better integration between tax and welfare payments. Above all, it means a political campaign to seek a coordinated policy package to achieve 5 per cent unemployment for the health of individuals, families and society at large.

Fourth, there needs to be a new commitment to individual self-realisation through a knowledge-based society. In Australia, education is far from a fashionable value. There is now growing evidence that our education system is sliding down the international comparison ladder. Australian universities pitching for overseas students have a crisis of conscience in promoting their quality profile. We hear a lot today about how Australia must have a world-best tax system. Whoever talks about a world-best education system? There needs to be a re-think in policy, priority and finance in terms of a commitment to education. The value of knowledge in this community and in our university sectors is being debased. Australia isn't doing well enough in job training and retraining and in equipping its workforce for the information industries of the future.

Fifth, we need to be able to simultaneously applaud winners and rehabilitate losers. The community understands this and will support it. Structural change is greater than ever before, yet its victims tend to be found in particular locations, regions and suburbs. Welfare benefits aren't enough. A third generation of unemployment beneficiaries now exists. A combination of new strategies is needed—a proactive approach to welfare designed to get people back to work, effective relocation and retraining schemes and a greater role for community groups. The commitment needs to be firm and it will cost a lot of money. Structural change that benefits the community overall must be underwritten by policies that improve the plight of the losers.

Finally, we must ensure that parliamentary democracy survives globalisation. It may be a close-run thing. This demands a very different and new approach to governance. There is a crisis in existing institutions everywhere; some have lost their relevance, others require reinvention—notably political parties, the trade unions, the *Women's Weekly*, the RSL, the Boy Scouts, the Church, the Rugby League, even the Olympics, the public utilities, and above all, the government and the Parliament. Parliamentary democracy is an idea derived from another age altogether, symbolised by calling people honourable and ringing bells. Its essence is gradualism and compromise and interest group driven third-best outcomes. Compared to speed of decision-making in the marketplace, parliamentary democracy is hopelessly old-fashioned. The business community gets more and more irritated by the political system, yet the political system is expected to do too much at the very time when globalisation is weakening the power of government. The State's capacity to help individuals is in decline, necessitating a redefinition of the relationship between the individual and the State.

We need, in fact, a new strategic role for government which can revive confidence and faith in representative institutions. Governments should define the rules of the marketplace; they should not run businesses whether they be a bank, an airline or a phone company. Governments need to privatise and to outsource. They need to redefine and focus on what they do best. Their new responsibilities and challenges will be immense. They are about getting markets to work for the community. That means: competition policy, reliance on institutions such as the ACCC to hold the line against monopolies and undesirable mergers, using the Productivity Commission to provide a transparent analysis of economic resources and performance, negotiating regional and global arrangements to help keep a viable international system. Governments need to be able to convince their people of the vast opportunities offered by the marketplace, yet signal their willingness to hold the line against a new market-imposed tyranny. It is a difficult policy and rhetorical balance to strike. Integral to this is getting a better balance between the expectations of government and the more limited capacity of governments to deliver.

This, in turn, is tied to the need to redefine individual rights and responsibilities. Most individuals will have to accept a greater responsibility for their own fate, whether it is meeting some of their education costs, preparing for retirement, managing job and career change, or accepting obligations for government benefits. I have often written that the Howard government's strength is economic policy, and its weakness is social policy. My whole argument today is that unless you put the two together and make the combination work, then economic policy will unravel. The challenge, in reality, is a new politics. Its essence is managing a faster pace of change than we have ever seen before.

The most difficult aspect is the cultural one, because it means when people ask you, 'When will the reform be over?', the answer is: 'It won't, since change is permanent.'

Speech to the Australia Unlimited Conference, 1999

BILL CLINTON AND
AMERICAN DEMOCRACY

THE INTERACTION BETWEEN Bill Clinton and the American public is pivotal to understanding not just why his presidency has survived but how Western democracy is being transformed.

The powers of the US presidency have long possessed a metaphysical as well as a constitutional dimension. The metaphysical was once related to that 'aristocracy of virtue and talent' so beloved by Thomas Jefferson. But Clinton, in effect, has redefined the metaphysical element and has brought to its zenith a new dialect of politics—the fusion of Washington and Hollywood.

This is where his victory over his critics has been comprehensive. Clinton is a master interpreter and manipulator of the moods, values and emotions of the new politics. The American people, despite their dismay over his lies and cover-ups, stubbornly refused to eliminate the presidential perjurer.

The tragic Clinton–Lewinsky farce has a multiple of meanings. It is not just a defining clash between the legislature and the executive, between the Republicans and Democrats, between the libertarian and religious traditions in American culture. It is all these and something more complex and subtle—it is a revelation of the transformed nature of leadership and democracy.

The symptoms are most advanced in the US, as usual, but they are also pronounced in the UK in the court of Tony Blair. The only issue is how long before they overwhelm Australia.

Paula Jones and Monica Lewinsky had no worthwhile contribution to make to public life yet they became for a year the most important story in the world, around which the presidency revolved. American historian Arthur Schlesinger Jr surely got it right when he branded the Clinton case one of 'low crimes and misdemeanors'.

What was your reaction to Clinton's impeachment? If you felt unease, what was the source of the problem? For many people it was the point raised by Schlesinger—the gulf between the gravity of the process and the mundane cheapness of the crime. Did you want to destroy a president on the grounds of a cover-up post-fellatio?

The American people didn't. They refused to buy the Republican proposition that Clinton was guilty of 'high crimes' and there is no reason to believe they are fooled by the Republican Party's rationalisation of its failure; namely, that the constitutional system, when tested by legislators of courage, worked beautifully, undermined only by a lack of party numbers in the Senate.

Nor is there any reason to believe the American public fell for Clinton's declarations of innocence. They would probably endorse the view of former political insider and famous *Washington Post* editor Ben Bradlee, who said: 'There isn't a person in the House or Senate who believes the President told the truth.' This distrust has deepened further since the 56-year-old Juanita Broaddrick came forward alleging that Clinton raped her 21 years ago. Her story adds a monstrous and serial element to perceptions of Clinton's sexual behaviour.

A rough averaging of the polls suggests that 75 per cent wanted Clinton to remain as president but only 20 per cent believed his story. It was the Constitution's threshold, a two-thirds Senate majority, that made a conviction so difficult, but it was the sentiment of the American people that made a conviction untenable, a sentiment that infuriated the President's self-appointed executioners.

One of his most ideological critics, William J. Bennett, author of *The Death of Outrage: Bill Clinton and the Assault on American Ideals* (Free Press), maintained his own rage, declaring: 'At every critical juncture during this scandal, when it seemed some damaging new revelation would lead to the downfall of the President, public opinion rescued him.'

Ah, public opinion. Yet the US was founded on Jefferson's assertion that a ploughman had better political judgment than a professor.

Clinton, like all politicians riding high, exalted his masters. 'The American people get it right, all the time,' he said. In public, this sounded like a compliment; in private, it could only have been a joke. Clinton was both victim and manipulator of these events.

Jones and Lewinsky are famous for being famous. Their public roles are devoid of worth. They became famous because of their association with the President. Yet such encounters, of no intrinsic worth, have been transformed by the US political process into not just the biggest entertainment on Earth but the greatest political story.

It is the debasement of politics to soap opera; the triumph of entertainment over ideology. The US has always been ambivalent about its political soul, cast between Jefferson's noble ideals in the Declaration of Independence and the backrooms where money, extortion, false ballots, FBI phone taps and crooks from Joe Kennedy to LBJ plied their trade. Yet the cultural war over Clinton gives debasement a whole new meaning.

American scholar Daniel J. Boorstin says: 'The fact that Congress made a president's [survival] turn on a relationship with an intern is quite remarkable—astonishing, disturbing. These are not the kinds of great issues that have engaged us in the past.'

The *Wall Street Journal* identified Aldous Huxley's *Brave New World* as the prophetic document for the times. On page one, it featured Neil Postman, from the department of culture and communication at New York University, who wrote a book more than a decade ago about the competing visions of Huxley and George Orwell. Postman wrote in 1985: 'Orwell feared that the truth would be concealed from us. Huxley feared that the truth would be drowned in a sea of irrelevance. Orwell feared that we would become a captive culture. Huxley feared that we would become a trivial culture . . . this book is about the possibility that Huxley, not Orwell, was right.'

Clinton's impeachment vindicates Huxley's insight. The US, with its enormous intellectual resources, is drowned in trivia. Its political system has lost the ability to discern value. Gold is abandoned amid the chaff. The US is a political system losing its power of discernment. Yet this did not happen by accident.

There are, clearly, institutional and social forces at work. Three can be readily identified.

First, there is the decision of the Republicans to make Clinton a morality test. They decided to accept the political invitation offered by Clinton's sexual self-indulgence to prosecute him. This was never just a cool decision based on detached self-interest. It was also a hot decision, driven by passion and denunciation and a view of Clinton as a man of corruption and decadence. This was the culture war. It was a pursuit that alienated the Republicans from the voters since the dominant value of a diverse society is tolerance and the Republicans appeared in their quest to be intolerant.

Second, it was driven by the commercial power and cash flow of the intersecting entertainment-media industry. This was the ultimate sex and power story. It was a non-fiction version that dwarfed the imaginative resources of the fictional library, though the film *Wag the Dog* proved prescient. Often the unfolding sex story was broken by the new media, with the Internet leading the way. The distaste for the story held by some of the established political journalists was swept away by the news momentum it generated.

Finally, it was about the corruption of the individual by the celebrity cycle. The best exposition of this ghastly descent came from the *Financial Times* correspondent Gerard Baker. He reviewed, then dismissed, the two stereotypical versions of the impeachment—that it was a brave attempt to remove a corrupt president and that it was a conspiracy to overturn a national election result. Baker looked deeper to find a political version of Tom Wolfe's *Bonfire of the Vanities*: 'A story with no heroes, no morals, no lessons, just self-obsessed individuals in a fight for survival; a vast landscape painting of life as it truly is in Washington at the turn of the millennium, a Guernica of overfed egos.'

It is a picture of a relentless competition for attention, with the prize being celebrity, sex, power, money or fame for fame's sake. But riding the waves was the master mariner.

There are two moments in this battle, destined to be immortalised, that capture the essential Clinton, stunning and shocking. During his State of the Union address this year, dedicated to defying his critics by ignoring them, Clinton at one point paused, looked at Hillary and, before a television audience of millions, said: 'I honour her.'

So the most publicly betrayed woman in history is honoured by her betrayer. This is an event of psychological complexity and political audacity. Clinton is nothing if not brazen! Where did the politician end and the actor begin? The mix is perfect; the fusion is complete.

The second event was Clinton's brief White House appearance after his acquittal. For those who watched the orchestration of this event, it was sheer Hollywood. For those who studied the message, it was about a president, amid such disunity, preaching unity. He was 'humbled and very grateful', appreciative of 'the prayers I have received from millions of Americans' and dedicated to the process of 'reconciliation and renewal'.

The paradox of Clinton is that he is a president who has purported to show moral leadership while his immorality is the issue. No leader has tried this before with such sincerity. During his presidency, Clinton has made the apology into an art form on behalf of reconciliation. But the ultimate apology was for himself and his actions. It was a political necessity and the ultimate emotional engagement. Clinton showed the American people how to seek forgiveness for the sin to which all people succumb, if only in their hearts. They were appalled by him, yet drawn to his dramatic predicament. Clinton suffered for the ignominy of his sin, but saved his political neck by a plea for forgiveness. Don't think for a moment it was other than a professional exercise. 'I beat the odds' was his private boast.

Clinton is the perfect leader for the relativist age. He is no hero, but he doesn't pose as a hero. He identifies with the people; he presents himself as a man of the people who grasps their problems because he is both a leader and, like them, a sinner. A leader and a man. Clinton's consummate performance helps the American people to accept that the leader can be capable while the man can be flawed.

Clinton is the classic 'end of innocence' leader because he operates in an age when the privacy of the public man is shattered. The American people never knew JFK as they know Clinton. They discovered the private Kennedy only later and realised that their image of Kennedy had been a caricature. Clinton teaches the need for a separation between the public and private.

But such ability would count for nothing and all Clinton's efforts would be worthless if not for the fact that he is, in the domain of politics and not sex, a successful president for his time. This is the final but decisive part of the story.

Clinton is the arch interpreter of the politics of soft power—the new medium by which influence is transmitted and wealth accumulated. Soft power is about culture, values, entertainment, media image, financial flows, community reconciliation, technology and the Internet. Soft power encapsulates the mood and content of the 1990s. It is closely tied to the rise of the information age, the decline of national sovereignty, the loss of governmental influence, community disorientation at the pace of change, disillusionment with politics, the destruction of the barriers between news, politics and entertainment, and the phenomenon of nineties American triumphalism whose real dynamic is creativity and innovation. In his style and policy, Clinton is the authentic voice of soft power and a model for aspiring leaders the world over, a status he shares with Blair.

It is easy to forget how much the contours of politics have changed in just ten years. The foundations of the politics of hard power have all but collapsed. Hard power was based upon ideological conflict, external enemies, military might, manufacturing muscle, Keynesian stabilisation policies and, above all, leadership authority. The paradigm was the strong leader as deliverer and protector. The styles varied from the rough and tumble Harry S. Truman to the calm and controlled Dwight D. Eisenhower to the youthful glamour of JFK, but the message stayed the same. This leadership ethic was defined, above all, by Winston Churchill and Franklin Delano Roosevelt during World War II. From Roosevelt onwards to Ronald Reagan, the same rules applied.

Each and every president was a war leader; each was an ideological warrior of distinct hue; each defended the US against a foreign foe; each embodied in his persona the hope of the democratic or free world against the fascists or communists or the anti-Christ; each bore the ultimate responsibility of nuclear deterrence and the nuclear button; each assumed, or pretended to assume, a degree of command over the US economy inconceivable in the market-globalism of the nineties, where US

Federal Reserve boss Alan Greenspan warns of the irrationality of market excesses; each operated closer to the iron and steel age than the information age of today's high-tech stocks; each was a believer in US might and presidential 'can-do' power.

But these hard-power props have been stripped from the arsenal. Traditional politics went with them. The politics of the missile gap, Star Wars and the Soviet menace have gone, along with the Soviet Union. The terrorists are just as likely to be in Oklahoma as in Baghdad. Government's role as an economic manager essentially runs to balancing the budget, hiring the best central banker in town, educating the kids, reskilling the workforce, reforming the 'passive' welfare State, keeping tax rates low and competitive, and cheering the entrepreneurial spirit.

The US is the sole superpower. But it is more admired for its creative impulse. Hollywood and the Internet have finally eclipsed the Pentagon and the Marines as the dominant symbols of the US abroad.

Clinton redefined his presidency after the 1994 congressional election scare. The story is told by his former aide and pollster Dick Morris (who quit after being caught telling secrets to a prostitute) in his book *Behind the Oval Office*. Morris sold Clinton on 'triangulation', which is another name for Blair's 'third way'. Morris drew the idea from Euclid's geometry, invoking it to 'create a new position' above the orthodox political spectrum. Clinton, Morris argued, should not just move to a middle position on the spectrum between the Republicans and old Democrats. The task was to transcend the old debate and constitute a third force on another axis.

Clinton has largely accomplished this feat. He stands for market economics, social inclusion and a better society. He is neither old Democrat nor Republican but styles himself a New Democrat. He knows that Republican individualism and Democrat interventionism are no longer credible platforms in their own right.

So Clinton champions a balanced budget and accepts the limits to government implied by financial markets. His aim is to encourage the animal spirits of a market-oriented economy. He supports a flexible economy, the dynamic of new technology and the US entertainment culture. He grasps the political fact that tax cuts must never be presented as a bribe but as a reward for responsibility and an incentive for opportunity.

Clinton knows from the polling that the nineties community realises self-interest isn't enough anymore. The average American, as Morris said, 'felt that his or her personal wellbeing was impaired more by the dysfunction of society as a whole than by a lack of money for themselves in particular'. So Clinton pitched to these worries—crime, the evils of tobacco, youth discipline, television violence, drinking, drug use, a safe environment, the affordability of college, sexual and racial justice, and an end to the passive welfare State. He has made improvements to the health system and school system. His proposals have been modest but practical. It is the perfect script for a time of prosperity, though it will need revision when this business cycle expires—that's when economic policy will return to primacy.

In the post-1994 period, Clinton exploited the extremes of Newt Gingrich's 'Contract with America' to reposition his administration in the shifting middle ground, putting an added emphasis on values as substitute for a diminished role for government. Morris believes that Clinton's dialogue with the American people really connected at the time of the Oklahoma City bombing. This is when he spoke directly as a spiritual leader, met the victimised families and responded at an emotional level to the emotions he felt from others.

Clinton, in fact, has played down the expectations about government and played up the aspirations for community. He understands that the modern leader is no longer primarily an economic manager or a commander-in-chief but an interpreter of the nation's mood to itself. He is a therapist, a performer, a spiritualist—as well as a president. The evidence is irresistible—the people think he has been a good, perhaps a very good, president.

Although Clinton is a masterful exponent of soft power, he cannot arrest the malaise in American democracy. This has two manifestations, which are both relevant to Australia.

First, the voter turnout continues to fall. It was below 50 per cent at the last presidential election. The US, in truth, is a flawed democracy; a half democracy. The impeachment process in its totality—Clinton's behaviour, the sexual politics, the Ken Starr investigation, the Republican-driven trial—reveals a gulf between the people and the Washington elite. The elite wanted the trial; the people did not. It is a chasm between the representative institutions and the public.

Of course, the historians may be right. Each cycle of US polity may surrender to a counter-cycle. Yet this theory is too convenient. The fresh defects in US democracy arise from social changes that won't easily be deflected. Clinton both embodies these defects and disguises them. His role, as usual, is riddled with ambiguity.

Second, Clinton's impeachment reveals the old-fashioned defects of the US separation of powers as opposed to our Westminster system. No Australian leader could be put on trial by the legislature. This is because, under our system of responsible government, the party caucus applies a swifter and cleaner political solution. The leader is replaced or confirmed by his own party. How bizarre that in Australia's republican debate so many people favour the US model and want to 'Clintonise' our system.

The Australian's Review of Books, *14 April 1999*

THE COMMON MAN AS
PRIME MINISTER

THE PARADOX OF John Howard's 25 years as a political warrior is that it oscillates between denigration for his lack of vision and hostility towards the reforms he has championed.

Howard is a peculiar mix of economic libertarian, social conservative and a Joe Lyons-style common man. It is a combination that infuriates the progressive intelligentsia that dominates Australia's opinion-making and which is sceptical of the market and traditional social values.

Howard's skill is his grasp of the sentiment of Robert Menzies' 'forgotten people' two generations beyond Ming. Australia has changed greatly since the 1950s but the family-based, suburban property-owning and aspiring middle class still constitutes the reduced backbone of the country.

These people and their values are the bedrock of Howard's power. Their concerns are family, security, order, decency, economic growth, social unity, individual responsibility and suspicion of special deals for minorities, from Aborigines to drug addicts.

It is the tune Howard plays and often overplays. Two blunders mark his career: opposition to Asian immigration in the late eighties and appeasement of Pauline Hanson in the late nineties. The former was instrumental in costing him the leadership and the latter threatened his prime ministership.

But Howard has never fitted the 'born to rule' leadership ethic embedded within the Liberal Party and much of its business base. The complaints about him are legion: a small man, no projection, no deep thinking, poor people-management and little capacity to influence opinion.

Named Winston after Churchill and sitting at Menzies' old desk, his political life is in permanent shadow from the giants he admires but against whom he can never compare. Yet he is constantly underestimated. Slated as a weak leader, Howard has won two of the three elections he has contested as leader.

It is typical of perceptions of Howard's leadership that, having won the 1998 election on a comprehensive GST-led tax reform package (an international first), the failure of the Senate to pass his package is seen as merely another Howard defect rather than the breach of a democratic mandate by the Senate.

There is in Howard a battler, a sense of the Anzac, a stubborn righteousness, a stamina, a determination and a Mark Taylor-like ability to play the next delivery on merit, having just been beaten.

Howard's political range is shaped by the parameters of his own life. A government-school boy from an anti-Labor, small business, Methodist background who did law but not arts at Sydney, nursed cricket as his lifelong hobby, married a Young Liberal and became a North Shore lawyer as a prelude to an inevitable political career. The key to Howard's success lies in his own deep commitment to this life experience. It is both his strength and his limitation.

Short of imagination, creativity and the skill to empathise with a culturally diverse Australia, Howard has been strong on political debate, basic faiths and interpreting that deep strand of middle-class conservatism that Australian intellectuals under-rate. He is proud of his ability, like that of Bob Hawke, to discern the electorate's mind.

The furore over Howard has revolved around his qualities as leader. There has never been any doubt about the high calibre of his all-round political strengths. They were recognised early by Malcolm Fraser. Having been elected to Parliament on 18 May 1974, Howard was treasurer by late 1977 and deputy leader in 1982. A rapid advance.

The major evolution in his thinking was his gradual conversion at Treasury to market economics, an event that brought him into confrontation with Fraser. But it gave him intellectual leadership of the Liberal Party in the eighties as Howard became a champion of economic liberalism: tax reform, a freer industrial system, privatisation and deregulation.

In February 1981 he unsuccessfully took to Cabinet a sweeping proposal for a broadly based indirect tax with cuts in personal rates. With the Coalition then controlling the Senate, Howard came close to securing eighteen years ago the tax reform for which he strives now.

In 1985 he became, in effect, the first pro-market Liberal leader, a turning point for the conservative Coalition. But Howard's four bitter, frustrating years as leader saw him under assault from the Left and Right of non-Labor politics in a phase of internal suicide.

His overthrow as leader in May 1989 was shattering for both Howard and his wife Janette, with ambition buried in tears. But Howard had no other career; he stayed, while believing the prime ministership was lost forever.

When the party finally returned to Howard six years later, he felt it was time. He campaigned with skill in 1995 and 1996 to prevail against his old nemesis, Paul Keating. Howard PM was different—a harder, more cynical and far more political leader. Having declared in 1985 it was better 'to be right than popular', Howard now concluded there was no substitute for winning.

So Howard defined his new political persona as an election winner, not as a policy man. But the ghosts returned: a revolt from the Hansonite Right, ministerial resignations, and lots of grumbles about lack of vision.

Sensing trouble, Howard reverted to instinct. He re-dressed as the reformer and stepped onstage for the final, dramatic tax campaign.

Howard's 1998 victory was the authentic win of his career— on his own agenda, securing his own mandate. That is why he would have found Brian Harradine's veto last week so shattering. But Howard will cut his package to the Senate's numbers. Don't misjudge his ability to seal a Coalition–Democrat (tax) package that strengthens his own position.

The Australian, *19 May 1999*

TONY BLAIR'S THIRD WAY

I'm worried about that young man. He's getting awfully bossy.

—Margaret Thatcher, speaking of British Prime Minister
Tony Blair

*The ideological differences between me and many of the Liberal
Democrats are pretty small.*

—Tony Blair in January

As THE LABOR Party in Australia prepares for a battle over its
future, British Labour, led by Tony Blair, is engaged in a
reinvention to exploit both the Thatcher legacy and find a new
role for social democracy.

Blair believes the Labour Party tradition is obsolete; that
modern leadership is about creating the mood in which government and people interact; and that the presidential model must
be incorporated into Westminster.

Blair is deeply influenced by Margaret Thatcher. But their
differences are sharp: Thatcher governed by ideology and conviction; Blair governs through the image and strategy of New
Labour, which he manipulates.

The true story told in Whitehall is that, in the early days
of Blair's government, one of his aides told a meeting: 'You may
see a change from a feudal system of barons to a more Napo-
leonic system.'

Blair is a contradiction. His political personality is open, pluralistic and democratic, but he runs his government through 10 Downing Street with an addiction to command and control. Outgoing Liberal Democrat leader Paddy Ashdown branded Blair's style that of a 'control freak'.

Professor Peter Hennessy, one of Britain's leading political analysts, says that under Blair, Cabinet meetings have been downgraded, that key policy is simply brokered between Blair and Chancellor Gordon Brown and that ministers are under firm instructions to have Downing Street vet all their important speeches and announcements.

Blair is presiding over two revolutions. He is redefining the purpose of Labour in power and he is terminating Britain's long twentieth century ideological struggle over economic policy.

This is packaged as the Third Way, which is both a process and a strategy. It is a surface ideology for a party that had lost its real ideology. Above all, it is a recipe for electoral victory. It is a device Blair has used to hold Labour to policies of economic growth, redistribution and social inclusion.

Australia's reaction to Blair is an amalgam of insisting the Poms can't teach us anything, that Blair is playing catch-up with the Hawke–Keating product, that he's too religious and that he can't last.

Well, he probably won't last, at least not much beyond a decade or so. At present he is utterly dominant. The Third Way is flawed, perhaps deeply flawed, but that's because it is experimental (Blair calls it 'a work in progress'). Anybody studying how to reconcile globalisation with community values will know that easy solutions don't exist.

What exactly is the Third Way? 'The Third Way is not an attempt to split the difference between right and left,' Blair says. 'It is about traditional values in a changed world. And it draws vitality from uniting the two great streams of left-of-centre thought—democratic socialism and liberalism—whose divorce this century did so much to weaken progressive politics across the West.'

This is an amazing statement from a Labour leader. But Blair means what he says: that British Labourism must merge with liberalism (to marginalise the Tory opposition). He seems to have a 'ground zero' belief that much of Labour's past is an aberration. Contrary to claims that he stands for nothing, Blair, judged by his words, stands for the end of the old Labour Party. His internal opponents take his words with a deadly intent; they wait to strike against Blair when he stumbles. The backlash from the Left is inevitable. When it comes, it will be fierce.

Blair has created a close working relationship with the Liberal Democrats, the heirs of the old great Liberal Party. The Tories watch most of this agog. One of the senior Tories told me: 'Blair is obsessed about coalition-building on all fronts, the Right, the Centre, the moderate Left. He puts no limit on trying to win new voters.'

Blair says of his philosophy: 'It is a third way because it moves decisively beyond an Old Left preoccupied by State control, high taxation and producer interests, and a New Right treating public investment, and often the very notions of "society" and collective endeavour, as evils to be undone.'

The Third Way repudiates the class struggle and its language (the rationale for the creation of Labor parties); it repudiates the weapons of intervention Labour has used for a century: nationalisation, high taxes, big spending.

Blair is a myth-maker, aware that modern culture thrives on the destruction of memory. He paints the past as failure, the responsibility of both Tory and Labour governments equally. He has a different language from any previous Labour leader: 'My politics are rooted in a belief we can only realise ourselves as individuals in a thriving civil society, comprising strong families and civic institutions buttressed by intelligent government.'

Many British columnists of the old Labour and libertarian right variety hate Blair. They struggle with the bizarre mix of influences that make his persona—a Thatcherite family background, religious faith, an actor's instinct and Labour Party careerism. When Blair became leader, he knew the party was ready for stealing, so he stole it.

Blair's technique is to disguise his pragmatism with values— 'equal worth, opportunity for all, responsibility and community'. (Who would not vote for such virtues?) He declares his policy technique is 'permanent revisionism', by which he means a search for whatever works to advance these values.

The Third Way, in effect, falls under three headings: economy, society and government. Blair's impact is distinct in each and dramatic in the last, where he reverses Thatcherism.

Economic policy rests upon the market but cushioned at the margin, pushing the new 'knowledge-based' sector and vesting monetary policy in the Bank of England—which is probably delivering a soft landing for an overheated economy.

Economic growth is projected to be 1–1.5 per cent this year, rising to about 3 per cent in 2001. A budget surplus is predicted for the next five years, inflation is at 2.5 per cent, unemployment is at 6.25 per cent, public borrowing is low and public debt is falling. The Blair–Brown ship is tight.

It tries to be proactive in building a culture of information technology, entrepreneurship and higher productivity (in ways that outshine the Howard government). For small companies, there will be a new 10 per cent corporate tax rate. The recent budget offers tax credits and incentives to promote research and development, venture capital, employee share ownership, IT and science infrastructure. Blair talks about the need to create 'serial entrepreneurship'.

On society, Blair and Brown have pursued two somewhat conflicting aims: a national minimum wage to combat exploitation at the bottom end of a relatively free labour market and a 'welfare to work' strategy as part of a larger redesign of the welfare State.

Blair's Social Security Minister Alistair Darling says: 'We will end the something-for-nothing approach that has characterised the past . . . people have a clear responsibility to help themselves.'

Blair has achieved a new threshold in the welfare debate. The aim is not to destroy the social safety net but, as Darling says, 'to confront the causes of failure [since] benefits cannot remove the causes of poverty'. Blair says: 'In recent decades, responsibility and duty were the preserve of the Right. They are no longer and it was a mistake for them ever to become so. For too long, the demand for rights from the State was separated from the duty of citizenship and the imperative for mutual responsibility on the part of individuals and institutions.'

Yet Blair's family focus is different from that of John Howard: 'To emphasise the importance of the family is not to believe that we can recreate a nostalgic version of family life in the fifties,' he says.

'This is unreal and misguided . . . the politics of "us" rather than "me" demands an ethic of responsibility as well as rights . . . some marriages and relationships will not be for life. But people's need to be able to make commitments, and to abide by them, has not changed.'

The Weekend Australian, *3–4 April 1999*

THE FORGOTTEN
CENTENARY

AUSTRALIANS TEND TO take the past for granted, worry about the present and postpone the future. If this is right, it might be the virtue of a still young country. But we take too little note of political history, seeing war, military history and sport as closest to our identity.

I think there is a bigger market for Australian history than most publishing houses would believe.

Angle and promotion are, of course, the keys. In the 1970s we found on the late *National Times* a tremendous interest among our readers in contemporary Australian history. In the 1990s as Editor-in-Chief of *The Australian*, I devoted considerable resources to historical themes—a tribute to the 1950s, a commemoration of the 50th anniversary of John Curtin's death, an historical special on the paper's 30th birthday, the Beatles' trip to Australia, the post-war immigration program, the 25th anniversary of that famous year 1968, the Republic debate and many others. These themes were popular because they worked for the paper in circulation terms, disproving the view of those who dismissed contemporary history as a point of genuine interest. A spin off was that we involved prominent Australian academics writing at length for the newspaper.

As we approach the centenary of Federation the issue of what it means and how it should be commemorated will press upon us. Federation, I think, has had a bad press for too long. It is an idea and a movement which is more powerful than is commonly depicted.

In the dying pages of his six-volume *History of Australia*,

Manning Clark declared: 'In the second half of the twentieth century Australians lived in a country when neither the historians, the prophets, the poets nor the priests had drawn the map . . . the people turned to the worship of the Golden Calf . . . of all the dreams of those Europeans of what Australia might be—all that seemed to survive was the idea of Australia as a place of "uncommonly large profit".'

Clark's genius was as a storyteller and a myth-maker. But Clark fell victim to the spell of his own vision. He accepted, fully, the choice which Henry Lawson put to the young nation— that it must choose between the Old Dead Tree and the Young Green Tree.

What choice did Australians make? They declined to choose. They insisted on both. They said Lawson's was a phoney choice. They wanted lord and empire and imperial security and bourgeois society but they wanted a new democracy, social justice, equality of opportunity and recognition of their native ability. The people were smarter than Lawson and they outsmarted Clark, dooming him to disappointment. They elected Bob Menzies, the ultimate symbol of Clark's Old Dead Tree and they elected John Curtin, who to Clark was the embodiment of Lawson's Young Green Tree.

Australians, in fact, display an aversion to political poets and ideologues and they have a penchant to purchase off the shelf what works best according to the times. Our political tradition is anchored in rule of law, representative democracy, stubborn egalitarianism, a pragmatic search for self-interest and an astute recognition of the need to balance individualism against State intervention. Our self-consciousness means that we don't wave flags, sing national anthems outside sporting arenas, recite or even possess a constitutional declaration of common beliefs.

In his great book *Cycles of American History*, Arthur Schlesinger Jr identifies what he calls the tradition and counter-tradition in US history. The tradition is the theory of America as an experiment undertaken in defiance of history, brave but risky. George Washington himself described the American republic as an 'experiment'. The counter-tradition is America as the elect nation, the redeemer nation based partly on the hallucination of America as the new Jerusalem, obsessed about salvation at home and then salvation abroad.

Does Australia have a tradition and counter-tradition?

I think two competing streams are apparent though we have never had the utopian idealism and economic options of the US. Founded in despair, authority and a battling evolving capitalism, Australians have fluctuated between believing in themselves on the one hand, and, on the other, a lack of self-confidence driven by deference to imperial power and a native-born inferiority complex.

Our history, in turn, is divided into periods of national confidence and pessimism. In those periods of confidence Australia can transcend the inferiority complex implanted at its origins or the debilitating paralysis of its internal divisions and move forward decisively.

There are many examples. Federation is an instance; another is the great nation building period between 1901 and 1914; the first AIF is another example; so is the creation of arbitration; further instances are post-World War II reconstruction, the launch and development of the post-war immigration program, the creation of ANZUS, our support for Indonesian independence, the Japan trade relationship, the phasing out of the White Australian Policy, the opening up of our economy in the 1980s, the Mabo case and Aboriginal reconciliation.

Yet between and almost matching these bursts of progress and national renewal are long periods in the 1920s, '30s, '50s, '70s and '90s when the nation appears chronically divided or decalmed or hostage to leadership inertia; these are times of missed opportunity when the nation is too prey to mediocrity and too frightened of what occurred in its immediately preceding period of confidence. It is a 'stop and start' history.

Federation's place in this story is clearly on the positive side of the balance sheet. However, it is disappointing that there is not a greater awareness of or enthusiasm for the centenary of Federation. Working in the media it is impossible not to draw a contrast between the massive preparation for the coverage of the Sydney Olympic Games in September 2000 and the relatively low preparation profile to mark the centenary of Federation itself.

How should we see Federation? Firstly we should see it as a major achievement of political leadership. The Colonies were divided by distance, outlook and political temperament. Deakin, Barton, Kingston, Reid, Griffith, Forrest and others were practical politicians forced to cut deals to resolve differences as they headed towards the ultimate objective. There are many defects in the Constitution but the Federation was realised. The Colonies surrendered powers to a new Commonwealth. There was a political entity created and a new nation that reflected the optimism of the leaders, their nationalism and, ultimately, their capacity to resolve differences. These leaders deserve to be remembered and they deserve a better recognition than what they have so far received in this country.

Secondly, our Federation is unique. While its architects drew upon or declined to draw upon the models in Great Britain, the United States and Canada, the finished construct is a unique product of Australia's own circumstances and its democracy. It is a true federation, neither a mere confederation nor an absolute unification. The States are subject to an overseeing authority in matters of common concern. Australia became a Commonwealth, which means a body founded to advance the common good. I think we should give far more attention these days to the use of the word 'commonwealth'. At the time of Federation it won general acceptance and it has remained popular over the last hundred years. It is noteworthy that in the debate about the transition to a republic the word 'commonwealth' will be retained. It is a word which sums up our commitment to each other and a commitment to the common good of Australia.

Thirdly, Federation was an example of people power, a point well known among historians but I assure you that the community is almost in total ignorance of this fact. The Constitution was adopted by popular vote in all Colonies. It has a democratic legitimacy rare in the world. Yet this link between the people and the Constitution has long since collapsed. Half of today's Australians don't even know that we have a constitution. The challenge of 2001 is to rebuild the link between the people and the Constitution. This can only be done by dialogue, convention and referendum.

Finally, an opportunity to focus on both Federation and the nation will come in 1999 when there will be a referendum to create an Australian republic and to agree on a new constitutional preamble. This debate will create division but it is important to press ahead. It was clear on the last day of the February Constitutional Convention that Prime Minister John Howard believed, possibly for the first time, that these debates could be advanced without significant damage to national unity. I think it is very important for non-politicians and community organisations to become involved in this process. I am sure that they will. The key to the public's favourable response to last February's Constitutional Convention was the introduction of non-politicians as delegates, the liberation of the assembly from party discipline and the role of persuasion. It was a meeting where arguments actually mattered and delegates did change their mind in response to argument and debate. If the 1999 referendum is defeated that should not be the closing of the issue, merely the opportunity for its reinvention in another way.

Will the next few years, according to my paradigm, fall into a period of national confidence or paralysis?

On the last page of *The Coming Commonwealth*, Sir Robert Garran wrote, 'When a constitution has been framed and adopted, the work of the Australian union will have been begun, not finished. The nation will be a nation, not of clauses and sub-clauses, but of men and women; and the destiny of Australia will rest with the Australian people rather than with the Australian constitution. The work now at hand—the making of a constitution—is great and important, but it is the beginning, not the end'.

Address to the Bendigo Federation History Conference, June 1998

COFFEE WITH GOUGH

GOUGH WHITLAM IS undaunted, unchanged and unapologetic. He waits upon history confident that the ultimate judgment on his government will be one of vindication. It is twenty years, two recessions and three prime ministers since Whitlam's famous 1972 'It's Time' election win—the point of generational change in Australia's post-war politics. Whitlam's victory terminated the twilight of the Menzian Age. It saw an influx of baby boomers commit to Labor because of Whitlam.

Gough, now 76, more florid than before, slower and with less of the old Whitlam panache, remains a beacon of consistency and constancy. He has outlived Kerr, seen Hawke's humiliating ejection as prime minister, and delivers cautious praise for Keating.

Whitlam is Labor's father figure—the man who saved the party from self-destruction in the sixties; the leader who won the support of a new generation of politically aware students from the same decade; and the prime minister whose reformist audacity and impatience produced an infuriating government whose grand achievements were undermined by an equally grand folly.

Talking to Whitlam twenty years later, one is struck by his dogmatism and his refusal to buckle to fashion. It is hard to imagine Whitlam as a popular hero. He is utterly out of touch with the slick public relations that dominate today's politics and it is inconceivable that he could succumb to it. In the sixties, the media saw Whitlam as modern, sophisticated and practical—but a return visit to the great man provides a reminder that while he is unchanged, our politics are faster and looser, with a shorter attention span than during Gough's reign.

Whitlam is an intellectual, a passionate reformer and a professional observer of today's issues. Unlike Hawke, he was never a populist and, in fact, was a popular leader only very briefly. Hawke appealed to the common man where Whitlam appealed to the new class.

One of my most vivid recollections of Whitlam was during the 1974 election campaign, when he addressed an evening meeting at Miranda shopping mall in Sydney. A huge crowd had gathered, waiting to be inspired by Whitlam's rhetoric. But Whitlam refused to indulge them and delivered instead a 50-minute lecture on constitutional referenda to his frustrated followers. Whitlam the politician was a schoolmaster, not a conjurer.

When I ask Whitlam what was his greatest mistake, he replies: 'I suppose I should have concentrated on the national rehabilitation and compensation proposals as far as they concerned road accidents and I wouldn't have broadened it to disabilities.' Of course, it is exactly what I am thinking!—as distinct from Khemlani, Kerr, Cairns, unemployment and inflation. This is the typical Whitlam with his obsession about structure, legalisms and community delivery.

In some ways Whitlam is an old-fashioned politician—he insisted upon keeping his promises, implementing his agenda despite economic conditions, and never succumbing to the status quo. In the famous remark explaining his philosophy of reform Whitlam declared: 'When you're faced with an impasse, you've got to crash through or you've got to crash.' Whitlam correctly rejects the criticism of his government that it tried to do 'too much, too fast'. The negative, of course, was its style and economic ineptitude.

Whitlam himself was a domineering political freak, a creative politician with vision, passion and energy, possessed of a grip on history from King David onwards and interested in providing sewerage to Australia's suburban sprawl. He pioneered a new approach to policy by the consistent application of greater federal government power to improve the lives of the people.

What does Whitlam do now? It's a silly question, really. He maintains a disciplined schedule and works from his Sydney office surrounded by his Hansards and his records. Above all, Whitlam still pursues the Whitlam program.

The real message from morning coffee with Gough is that the program still lives. The program is the blueprint carefully devised by Whitlam in the pre-1972 period by which he wanted to transform the lives of Australians. I remember the program from a thousand speeches, rallies, press conferences and briefings. The program was to deliver equality of opportunity to all Australians through a greater role for the federal government in education, health, welfare, justice, the environment, transport and human rights as applied to Aborigines, voters and women.

Whitlam is confident of the verdict of history, since like Churchill, he has taken no chances and written it himself (*The Whitlam Government*, published in 1985 and running to 787 pages).

The program did not die with Gough's defeat. It is a living agenda for which Whitlam agitates and propagandises and by which he judges all his successors. Asked about Australia's national progress since he lost office in 1975, Whitlam declared that it's 'very disappointing'. Why? 'Because Fraser dismantled as much as he could of the issues we put on the agenda—and Hawke never put them back.' But he has great hopes for Keating since Keating can adapt and 'he realises that to survive he has to embrace the Whitlam government programs'.

The Whitlam era began with an amazing two-man government—Whitlam and his deputy Lance Barnard, who took 40 decisions in twelve days—and finished in Whitlam's dismissal by the Governor-General whom he had appointed and had trusted. From first to last, it was a government that broke tradition and precedent.

The two-man government was an intoxicating entrée—it abolished conscription, withdrew the remaining troops from Vietnam, banned sporting teams from South Africa, changed Australia's votes in the UN on racial issues and negotiated diplomatic relations with China. Australia's international image was transformed almost overnight. Some of the duumvirate's moves were small but symbolic—lifting the ban on the advertising of contraceptives in Canberra.

The two-man government exaggerated the ease of change and captured the enthusiasm which many Australians experienced, called by author Robert Drewe the 'new nationalism'.

The Whitlam government used *Advance Australia Fair* as the national anthem, inaugurated the Order of Australia, changed the Queen's title to 'Queen of Australia', introduced FM radio, colour TV, appointed the Australia Council, and laid the foundation stones for the Australia National Gallery and the High Court building.

Gough says that 'before us, the State galleries would just buy British'—a reminder that Whitlam restored, perhaps created, a sense of national pride and confidence. He is convinced that Australia will soon become a republic: 'I think 2001 is a practical timetable. Becoming a republic doesn't mean that we have to leave the Commonwealth.'

Whitlam offered a new deal for pensioners, migrants, women, Aborigines and students. Three great achievements were Medibank, education funding to schools on a 'needs basis', which ended a century of sectarian dispute over State aid, and the assumption of responsibility for universities. Whitlam appeared to be a contemporary prime minister dealing direct with the community. His weak suit was Bob Hawke's subsequent strength—business and unions. In the early seventies Prime Minister Whitlam and ACTU president Hawke were conspicuous for their public brawls.

Asked how much of his program was implemented Whitlam says: 'A great deal was irreversibly enacted or installed—one vote, one value. We expanded the federal agenda, by earmarking grants to the States and in that way we took over tertiary education and expanded secondary and technical education. Other instances commenced but not fulfilled were urban affairs. Medibank was a reform of national standards. There are two other areas where we expanded federal jurisdiction by applying the Constitution with respect to external affairs—the environment, where we ratified the world heritage convention [in connection with Lake Pedder], and human rights, with the *Racial Discrimination Act*, relied upon international conventions.'

Whitlam says that one of his chief aims now is to see that the federal government ratifies relevant UN conventions—what he calls 'best national and international standards' and he lectures that 'human rights and the environment are now international issues'.

The program was the inspiration of a legal mind and a practical politician who understood the Constitution and had a faith in Canberra, where he was raised as a boy. Whitlam once said that he was a 'small-town prime minister'. His political consciousness was formed in the war and post-war period, when faith in government had reached its zenith. Whitlam said of himself: 'My role in the Labor Party has been that of innovator . . . I am the first member of this parliament who has suggested the significance of federal government action in a whole range of domestic concerns.'

This insight is the true Whitlam memorial. The Whitlam era was filled with drama, excess and excitement. 'People got excited because things were finally being done', says Whitlam. 'Many of the things we did should have been done long before— the Gallery, the Film and Television School, the novels. The 1967 referendum had given the federal government responsibility for Aborigines—but not a single act was passed before we came in. Overseas we were messing around over what was the real government of China.'

When Whitlam took office, unemployment was 2 per cent— a figure seen as unacceptably high—and inflation was 7 per cent. Far from being economically indolent, Whitlam advanced an unusual agenda—a 25 per cent tariff cut and the start of a reordering of federal spending priorities which finished in a massive spending blow-out in 1974 which, along with severe miscalculations by the Reserve Bank, saw Australia beset by a chronic stagflation.

But Whitlam is quick to defend his government against the 'economic incompetence' tag. He says that high inflation was 'universal' in the early seventies; his government, through the Coombs task force, eliminated a lot of rorts; and finally, that national debt was $3 billion in his time, while it is now 50 times that level.

Whitlam promotes his government as a champion of micro-economic reform, which will surprise many—he points to the tariff cut, the takeover of State railways, new urban plans with the States, modernisation of the rail systems in Sydney, Melbourne and Brisbane, and criticises his successors for the failure to tackle Sydney airport. He says that 'Keating is the first PM since me to have spoken on coordination of the modes of transport in Australia'.

During his first year, Whitlam was Foreign Minister as well as Prime Minister, and he dominated foreign policy during the entire period. Many press gallery members declared that, for the first time, they were travelling overseas with a leader of whom they felt proud, not ashamed.

The upshot was that Papua New Guinea became independent in 1975; Australia launched a protracted campaign against French nuclear tests in the Pacific; and in his first year, Whitlam visited China, India, Indonesia and Japan, our largest neighbours.

Prompted about the mistakes, Whitlam has his explanations ready; Kerr—'I didn't assess his character strictly enough. When he was appointed, it was universally applauded'; Jim Cairns as Treasurer—'Cairns was making utterances on economic affairs so I told him to accept responsibility [become Treasurer] or shut up . . . Finally, of course, I had to get rid of him and I then got the best Treasurer of the last twenty years in Hayden'; Khemlani, the loan middleman—'No funds were raised. There was no illegality or impropriety. If one looks at the things Rex Connor proposed for the spending, it's obvious that they were wise initiatives'.

Where did Whitlam falter? I think primarily in three areas. First, Whitlam's timing was wrong since he was elected on a program of public sector expansion on the eve of the 1973 OPEC shock and the international stagflation of the seventies— a challenge for which he was quite unprepared. Second, Whitlam and his team lacked the discipline and professionalism for office. Despite their achievements, Frank Crean, Jim Cairns, Rex Connor and Clyde Cameron were overwhelmed by events. Too many errors were made in political appointments, personal indulgence and public relations. Whitlam himself was determined to be prime minister on his own terms, not the more limited terms set out by the electorate.

Finally, Whitlam was subject to a political sabotage through the Senate which destroyed him. History was cruel in that Whitlam won two House of Representatives elections—1972 and 1974—but never controlled the Senate. Labor was not swept into office in 1972. Its win was limited with a nine seat majority. Labor never had effective power. The Senate forced the 1974 election and then the 1975 constitutional crisis which culminated in Kerr's dismissal of Whitlam and Fraser's election victory.

Whitlam's achievements are immense—he remodelled Labor

in the sixties; his 1972 victory was the first since 1929 that brought Labor from opposition to power; his government changed Australia's international stance and the role of federal administration forever. As leader, Whitlam dominated his team— as he once said: 'I don't care how many prima donnas there are in the Labor Party, as long as I'm the prima donna absoluta.'

The Australian Magazine, *28–29 November 1992*

HOWARD FLOREY, OUR TALLEST POPPY

TODAY WE CELEBRATE, or perhaps fail to celebrate, the birthday of the Australian who has done most to improve the lot of mankind. An authentic hero; a model for the century; and an Australian who is almost unknown.

Such obscurity rules out Bruce Ruxton, Kate Fischer, Elle Macpherson, Alan Jones or John Farnham. Nor is our candidate Sir Donald Bradman, possibly the most famous of all Australians, whom John Howard has called the 'greatest living Australian'.

Today is the 99th anniversary of the birth of Howard Walter Florey, in Malvern, Adelaide, the youngest of five children and only son of a bootmaker, who in 1945 won the Nobel Prize jointly with Alexander Fleming and Ernst Chain for his development of penicillin.

On Florey's death in 1968, Lord Blackett, then president of the Royal Society, and Dr H.C. Coombs, chancellor of the ANU, wrote: 'Millions of human beings have since owed their lives or their health to treatment with penicillin and related antibiotics whose production became possible as a result of Florey's pioneering work. The consequences for the good of mankind even today have yet to be fully realised, and Florey is rightly honoured throughout the world as Jenner, Pasteur and Lister were honoured before him.'

But has this prophecy at Florey's death been realised over the past 30 years? Has Florey been honoured in his own country? Is he a source of inspiration? Have your children heard his name?

The answers are obvious.

Perhaps we should listen to ALP president and international biography authority Barry Jones: 'On the most conservative estimates Florey's work saved 50 million lives. He may be responsible for the population explosion and the greenhouse effect too.'

The Jones' list of the ten greatest figures of the twentieth century—defining 'greatest' solely as 'influential'—includes Mao, Hitler, Stalin, Gandhi, Henry Ford, Franklin Roosevelt, Freud, Picasso, Einstein and Florey.

What sort of man was Florey? Read this tribute to him penned by Sir Robert Menzies, originally for *The Lancet*: 'He had the essential attributes of greatness: courage, integrity, tremendous drive and an unswerving sense of direction. Lack of any one of these often renders high intellectual achievements, even genius, ineffectual . . . It was Florey's courage which made penicillin therapy an actuality. Undaunted by his failure to get enough penicillin produced commercially for a therapeutic trial, he turned a university department into a factory against every sort of difficulty and in the middle of a world war . . . He was completely free from cant, humbug and pretentiousness . . . If he did not know something he said so, and he was equally ruthless towards the ignorance of others.'

How good was Florey? One of our leading scientists, Sir Gustav Nossal, says: 'Sixty years ago Florey displayed all the characteristics which Australia is now desperate for in a medical academic. A combination of originality with the entrepreneurship to do something about it. He bridged the gap between academia and industry long before his time. That was his genius.'

Florey was educated at St Peter's College and the University of Adelaide, became a Rhodes scholar, and pursued an academic career in Oxford, Cambridge and London. In 1935, aged 37, he became head of the Sir William Dunn School of Pathology at Oxford where he worked with a small team to develop the work of Alexander Fleming that certain bacteria were destroyed by a mould that had contaminated one of his cultures of staphylococci. Florey believed that penicillin was an antibacterial agent that could be applied for clinical use.

In his biography of Florey, *Rise Up To Life*, Lennard Bickel described the world that the Australian helped to transform: 'At least one-half of the recorded deaths under the age of six were attributed to infectious diseases. In adult life the toll was almost as heavy . . . Like a wet sponge on a blackboard, penicillin and the subsequent antibiotics wiped away the dread of pneumonia, meningitis, tuberculosis, anthrax, septicaemia, syphilis and the feared childbed fever.'

Unlike his counterpart Fleming who had a flair for promotion, Florey shunned the media and personal publicity with the consequence that there was little public, as distinct from professional, awareness of his contribution.

The chair of the Australian Institute of Political Science, John Best, says: 'Florey was very reserved, yet is probably the greatest Australian who has ever lived. It is time this country celebrated his contribution to ourselves, a contribution which has spanned the socio-economic fabric of the globe.'

Irreverence has been a healthy Australian characteristic. Yet if irreverence converts into lack of interest or appreciation of national achievement and genuine heroes it becomes corrosive.

The lapsed memory of Florey betrays an apathy in the public imagination about science and a failure of national self-esteem which, in turn, feeds the reluctance to value our own history. It is illustrative of another malaise—the persistence of the tall poppy syndrome.

It is useful to note Florey's 99th anniversary because this day next year will be his centenary. It is a centenary that should become an event. That is the intention of Health Minister Michael Wooldridge, who says the centenary should be used to promote science and has asked Best to coordinate these efforts.

'We aren't good at making heroes of our scientists,' Wooldridge says. 'They should have the same place as our sporting heroes.'

Best's aim is to do this and more. 'We've linked Florey to the tall poppy,' he says. 'We want to say to Australians it's time to celebrate the tall poppy, not cut them down. After all, he's our greatest Australian.'

Not cut them down! That implies a cultural revolution! So does giving recognition to achievers rather than celebrities. This sounds like an attack upon our values and our distorted concept of success. Of course, there's a bigger message here—using the 2001 centenary of Federation as an occasion to identify and celebrate the real Australian achievers of the past century.

The Australian, *24 September 1997*

AUSTRALIA, INDONESIA AND EAST TIMOR

THIS WEEK AUSTRALIANS faced the contradiction between wanting to rescue the East Timorese from slaughter and our military and political inability to save them.

As Dili burned, Australia faced possibly its worst foreign policy failure since the Indonesian incorporation of East Timor in 1975. But this is not just a humiliation for the Howard government—it represents a much deeper failure by Australia as a society.

The Howard government never expected a slaughter on this scale, or that the Indonesian military would be so brazen and brutal. The revelations in coming days will be truly horrific.

John Howard and Alexander Downer trusted President B.J. Habibie too much and underestimated his weakness; they misjudged the Indonesian nationalistic bent to hold on to East Timor; they misread the risk in seizing the opportunity for a ballot this year; they failed to run a specific strategy focused on the military; and they should have mounted an international effort at an earlier stage in case a peacekeeping force was needed immediately post-ballot. Many of these are judgments in retrospect.

There is one great plus—the East Timorese voted for their own independence and the world must honour this choice for which so many of them have paid with their lives.

Australia faces a disastrous scenario—a scorched-earth East Timor; a fracture with Indonesia; a need to reappraise the US alliance; and still no solution to the political and humanitarian crisis just off Darwin.

In the East Timor debacle the myths of the Left and Right have been exposed. A nation that suffers from multiple delusions will eventually fall victim to them, and that has happened to Australia.

Myth one is that Australia could save East Timor from Indonesian military force. It could not in 1975, and it could not in 1999. When will this lesson ever be learned? The Australian public deludes itself. It is unwilling to sustain even an adequate defence budget, and when there is a regional crisis it complains that Australia lacks the power to act decisively.

Asked whether Australia had the military capability to intervene unilaterally in East Timor, our leading defence strategist, Dr Paul Dibb, says: 'Absolutely not. We currently spend 1.7 per cent of gross domestic product on defence. That is the lowest level since the late 1930s. We would have trouble sustaining a brigade for six months in the field of combat. The contrast with Britain is illuminating. Britain spends 2.9 per cent of GDP on defence and it [had] a credible expeditionary force to send to the Gulf and Kosovo. Australia doesn't have a credible force.'

There are now 25 000 Indonesian troops and police in East Timor. This is more than five times the size of the 4500 troops slated for Australia's UN contribution. The head of the Catholic Church, Cardinal Edward Clancy, is right that Australia has a moral obligation to act. But moral obligations have to be redeemed by military force. Indonesia has told Australia it would regard any unilateral Australian military action as a hostile act. It would be an act of war.

If Australia wants to be a significant regional player—often the key to humanitarian efforts—then it needs to possess more military force in its own right. That means reviving the notion of strategic interest as the guiding star of the public debate about foreign policy.

Myth two is that the rest of the world has been agitating to liberate East Timor. Most nations are reluctant to help when a real sacrifice is needed. Take the Americans. Their attitude this week is a watershed for Australia. It will shatter another set of delusions.

A fortnight ago one of the most experienced political journalists in the US told his Australian friends: 'East Timor isn't on America's radar screen.' Ten days ago the chairman of the congressional committee on the Asia–Pacific, Doug Bereuter, told Downer that Congress wouldn't support US troops going to Timor. The Pentagon has firmly opposed the idea. The US has never raised the idea of troops at ministerial level with Australia. The Clinton administration, it seems, prefers to make a logistical contribution to a UN force rather than troops. At the Australia–US dialogue a fortnight ago the US message was manifest: Australia can 'look after' this part of the world.

Howard and Downer are deeply frustrated with the US. This is the first time in the 50-year history of the alliance that Australia has actually asked the US for troop support for a regional exercise we are leading. The US is not being unfriendly; it is merely saying that Timor is our problem.

Howard knows this. Australia has promised to lead the UN force; it has pledged its own troops; it is lobbying other nations to contribute. But it wants a bigger US effort.

By the week's end Howard was openly criticising Clinton: 'I don't think the Americans have yet put as much pressure on as we would like.' He would have been dismayed by Clinton's instinctive reach for tokenism—suspending military ties with Jakarta but declining to pledge troops.

Clinton knew of Australia's agitation. By yesterday he was praising Howard's leadership as 'very strong, very impressive'.

But the generation of Howard and John Moore, let alone the public, cannot grasp that US policy has been transformed by the end of the Cold War. The Australian–US alliance has reached a crossroads. It will only work in future if Australia grasps that it must assume more responsibility in this region.

Within Asia, East Timor has scarcely been an issue. The Association of South East Asian Nations has backed Jakarta on East Timor over the 1975 incorporation and ever since. The recent ASEAN position is that it wouldn't have an independent East Timor as a member. Malaysia and Thailand would never dream of sending troops in a UN force without Jakarta's consent. For China, given its sensitivity over Taiwan, the principle of non-interference is sacrosanct. Timor was always a wedge between Australia and Asia.

Australia now faces the reality that building a 'coalition of the willing' over East Timor is a very hard slog. It is not an international priority. It is not a problem the Asian region has aspired to solve. It is not an issue on which the Asia–Pacific

Economic Cooperation forum can do much. The UN machinery is slow and cumbersome. People who rely upon the UN to save their lives will die.

Myth three was that Australia could establish strategic solidarity with Indonesia by pioneering a close military-to-military relationship. This idea has been dominant for a decade. Its appeal was that in Indonesia the military had two roles—national defence and running the country. It was the most important institution. It still is. But in this crisis the military relationship has been useless for Australia and it is a national embarrassment. Australian forces have trained some of the Indonesians who planned and conducted this week's operation.

The director of the Asia–Pacific security program at the Australian National University, Alan Dupont, says: 'The defence relationship can't survive in its present form. The lesson is that shared values are important in security and military relationships. You can't fabricate them when they don't exist. We need to rethink this process.'

Bob Lowry, a retired army officer and expert on the Indonesian military, highlights another bizarre Australian failure: 'About 99 per cent of these events are the responsibility of General Wiranto. He's gone out on a limb. But our misjudgment is that we didn't grasp the military was the key to this entire process. We didn't devise a tactic to target the military to try to achieve our policy.'

Myth four is that Australia, via some magical process, exerts a decisive influence over Indonesian behaviour. It didn't in 1975 and it doesn't in 1999. Will this lesson finally be absorbed?

This is the myth on which the appeasement theory is based. It asserts that somehow Australia could have persuaded or intimidated Indonesia against the 1975 invasion (which had the acquiescence of the US and Dr Henry Kissinger, who told the US ambassador to stop sending him so many cables about a crisis as unimportant as East Timor).

The most recent variation is ALP spokesman Laurie Brereton's insistence that Australia could have persuaded Indonesia to accept a UN peacekeeping force to supervise the East Timor ballot. This is another delusion, dangerous because it derailed so much of the recent debate. It assumes that Indonesia is not only poor but that it has no pride. Indonesia's military tolerated Habibie's ballot but they would never have tolerated foreign troops on the soil where they had shed their own blood in the cause of incorporation.

Howard put this issue directly to Habibie earlier this year; so did a delegation of Australian editors. His answer was a non-negotiable 'no'. If the price for the ballot was a UN force, there would have been no ballot. Can anybody doubt this after the events of the last week?

There are now calls for Australia to bring pressure against Indonesia by cutting trade or aid links. There are arguments for this—but any claim that such retaliation would influence Jakarta is laughable. Australia has no such leverage. We delude ourselves in thinking that we do. Indeed, it is highly debatable whether the international community has much leverage. Indonesia has just sustained the greatest loss of GDP of any country this century and the pain threshold has little meaning.

Myth five is that Australia had a special obligation to solve the East Timor problem. This has become part of our political culture created by a unique coalition of the RSL, the Catholic Church, a media much influenced by the deaths of five journalists, the Timor lobby, and people genuinely appalled by the injustice of the Timor situation. During the past year the ALP has been lashing itself for its 'sins' of the past. The national guilt runs deep. Australian opinion has decided that East Timor was its problem.

It is idle to believe this sentiment did not influence Howard and Downer. Their historic change of policy late last year and their joining with Habibie in backing his ballot was always a great gamble. They were seduced by the prize—the prospect of resolving the Timor issue and the kudos this would carry in Australia in domestic and diplomatic terms. They saw the chance to cure the national neurosis that plagued the Indonesian relationship, achieve independence for East Timor and take much of the international credit.

The historical question here is whether Howard and Downer pressed too hard for independence at the wrong time. It is still too early to make a final judgment here, but the number of dead East Timorese will probably be conclusive. Former ambassador Dick Woolcott says: 'The timing was foolish. It would have been far more sensible to defer the UN role until there was a constitutionally elected new government in Jakarta whose writ ran wider.'

On the other hand, this was a window-of-opportunity situation. There was no guarantee that a new president such as Megawati Sukarnoputri would have called a ballot. So the issue is whether Australia should have supported Habibie's ballot or told him to wait. The truth is that any Australian government that asked Habibie to defer the ballot would have been crucified politically.

The fact remains that if Australia hadn't tried to do the right thing, if it hadn't tried to support the ballot, if it had opposed the ballot, then many dead Timorese would be alive today. Bishop Carlos Belo warned earlier this year that East Timor's best option was autonomy for an extended period and then independence. This was also the option put by Howard to Habibie last December in a letter that triggered Habibie's more radical policy of a 1999 ballot.

Howard and Downer gambled the entire Australian–Indonesian relationship on Timor; they gambled that Indonesia could simultaneously make its own traumatic transition and handle the loss of East Timor—and it appears they lost.

But Howard and Downer were merely the principal players in Australia's sentimental national delusions about Timor that have trapped our minds and weakened our judgment. They are still fighting desperately to salvage their policy—to persuade Indonesia to permit peacekeepers, to ratify the ballot and to give East Timor its independence.

The Weekend Australian, *11–12 September 1999*

WHAT THE
REPUBLIC NEEDS

THE ISSUE AUSTRALIANS have to decide in the republican referendum is what sort of president they want—an impartial constitutional umpire or a strong politician involved in running the country.

The model proposed at the November referendum has been designed to preserve Australia's current system of government—in effect, to move from a Westminster monarchy to a Westminster republic.

The signs now are that most of the Liberal Party ministry will reject this transition—and that rejection might even defeat the referendum. If so, it will be a pyrrhic victory.

The Liberal Party, in reality, is marching towards a debacle on this issue. It is lining up at the dawn of the new millennium to affirm Australia as a constitutional monarchy. That is the Liberal view of Australia's future; under John Howard it may become the party's great achievement for the millennium. If so, the monarchical brand name will be stamped on the Liberal Party for decades, long after Australia is a republic. This tag will stick.

The government's justification has been enunciated frequently by Howard—that the Australian people aren't really interested in this issue. It is totally contradicted by the turnout in Corowa last Sunday, when a diligent audience crammed the courthouse for three hours for the first town debate on the republic sponsored by this newspaper. These people cared very much.

But a victory for the No case on the back of a Liberal

government will have even greater consequences than affirming the monarchy. It will mean a rejection of the Westminster republic model. So what other model does the Liberal Party think it wants for an Australian republic?

A No victory will inevitably turn the Labor Party and the Australian Republican Movement towards a popular-election model and a radical change in the system of government. At the Constitutional Convention, Howard said it 'is hard to see how such a system' was compatible with 'the Australian version of Westminster' and that an elected presidency 'seems to me to be a sure way of politicising the office and creating unparalleled tensions'.

The dilemma for the Liberals is that a No victory will come only at the price of promoting the popular-election model which Howard says will imperil our Westminster system.

The republicans supporting the referendum model are regularly accused of being elitist, out of touch, chardonnay drinkers and contemptuous of the wishes of the people. What utter fools they must be!

Why would they embark on the apparently suicidal course of supporting a republican model with parliamentary election of the president rather than the more popular direct election?

There is no secret to this. It is to guarantee a non-partisan president who acts as a constitutional umpire. It means the president will have the same powers and function as the governor-general. The presidency will inherit the constitutional tradition of impartiality invested in the office of governor-general.

Let's be honest: it is a decision inspired by conservatism. It also had another motive: the belief that this was the best way to win the Liberal Party to the republic.

Now it may be that Australians don't want this model. It may be that Australians, ultimately, will only settle for a republic with a popularly elected political president. So be it.

Elections, of course, create politicians—that is their purpose. Once Australians elect their president then the old office of governor-general is transformed beyond recognition—it becomes partisan. Elections are contests; they involve competing candidates; the candidates offer different programs; they try to discredit their rivals; they conduct media and advertising campaigns; and, for the victorious candidate, there is an office that combines the powers of the Crown and a popular mandate exceeding that of the prime minister.

Let's not fool ourselves. Popular election means the president will be a politician. Constitutional umpires such as Sir Zelman Cowen, Sir Ninian Stephen, Sir John Kerr and Sir William Deane would never have stood for popular election. Have an elected presidency and you rule them out. Exit the umpire.

There is a very good reason for the current referendum. Australia should be given the opportunity to keep its Westminster system in the transition to a republic. It should have the opportunity to endorse a cautious change that preserves the current system of government. It should be given the chance to become a republic without having to adopt the US system—a true disaster—or the French system, or to launch into some other radical experiment.

Claims that the current model greatly strengthens the prime minister's power are wrong. Under the present system, the prime minister chooses the governor-general. He doesn't ask the people, the Parliament or the Opposition. He runs the decision past his Cabinet and then advises the Queen.

Under the republic model, the president is appointed on the nomination of the PM, seconded by the Opposition leader and affirmed by a two-thirds majority of federal Parliament. Each step is written into the Constitution. So, on appointment, the PM manifestly has less power in the republic model than he enjoys now.

On removal, the PM can now remove the governor-general any time, for any reason. The Queen acts on this advice and, if so advised, would act. The difference in the model is that the PM could remove the president immediately but then has to call either an election or get the House to endorse the decision within 30 days.

The arrangement is workable but far from the optimum. Yet it is no worse than the current system. Of course, if the Liberals were seriously worried about the removal provisions, they would seek to amend the bill to improve them!

The Liberals' present stance seems calculated to keep the monarchy for the time being but promote the non-Westminster republic forces. Whatever happened to intelligent conservatism?

The Australian, *4 August 1999*

LIBERTY AND EQUALITY

WHAT DOES LIBERTY mean today? It was the American philosopher Michael Novak who quoted Lord Acton that true liberty is the liberty to do what you ought to do, not merely to do what you wish.

That is, liberty was not licence but was intimately associated with the notion of obligation. Humans live by reason, not just by instinct. Liberty is informed by reason and, as a result, liberty should advance the grandeur of the individual and of society. Liberty recognises that the distinguishing feature of mankind is his capacity to make moral choices.

Does this accord with our view of liberty today?

Frankly, I have some doubts. I suggest that the idea of liberty has been incorporated into our culture and then regurgitated in the form of escalating claims for greater freedom. The right to be free of racial vilification, the right to welfare, a job and free tertiary education, the right to privacy, the right to be liberated from censorship, the right of children to be free from parental demands—despite the potential contradictions between such demands. The defect with our current practice is that liberal societies define liberty as an end in itself. Perhaps this has always been the case. The present condition of liberty was summarised by Francis Fukuyama, pessimistically but with insight:

> Beyond establishing rules for mutual self-preservation, liberal societies do not attempt to define any positive goals for their citizens or promote a particular way of life as superior or

desirable to another. Whatever positive content life may have
has to be filled by the individual himself. That positive content
can be a high one of public service and private generosity, or
it can be a low one of selfish pleasure and personal meanness.
The state as such is indifferent . . . government is committed
to the tolerance of different 'lifestyles' except when the exercise of one right impinges upon another. In the absence of
positive 'higher' goals what usually fills the vacuum . . . is the
open-ended pursuit of wealth . . .

If this is an approximate version of the reality, then it portrays
the deeper crisis of Western liberalism, a crisis inherent in the
idea.

Our present liberal inheritance rests upon two great divorces
over the last millennium—the separation of Church and State
and the separation of scientific progress from religious belief.
The first separation is political and the second is intellectual. It
is these two epic events which have determined the character
of the twentieth century liberal State.

The formal separation of Church and State meant, by definition, that the State vacated any claims to a theology for its
citizens. This step is fundamental to the triumph of liberty. It
guarantees freedom of religion and confirms that the State
passes no judgment on the relations or absence of relations
between its citizens and God.

The parallel development was the destruction of the long
compact between Christianity and scientific progress. It was the
advance of science from Newton to Darwin to Einstein which
increasingly drove a wedge between the realms of faith and
reason. With each step science successively undermined the
notion of biblical revelation, man as the centre of the universe
and the story of mankind as a function of God's design. The
sophistication of scientific technique meant that the Christian
view came to be seen as falling outside the scope of scientific
explanation. This, in turn, meant that the Christian faith lost
its primacy within society and much of its legitimacy, since
scientific reason became the new test of intelligence and the
entry to influence.

This leaves Western liberalism at its present dilemma—
proclaiming a liberty but leaving mankind too devoid of moral
purpose to realise its potential. The consequence is on frequent

display in any Western society. The community is uneasy and dissatisfied with its spiritual lot. There are periodic appeals for politicians to show moral leadership, such appeals either being ignored, or taken up with unhappy results since the community cannot agree on the nature of the moral leadership it wants, or politicians rebuffing these demands relying upon the theory of separation between State and personal faith. (It should be noted, of course, that these dilemmas are the consequence of the success of liberalism from which we have all benefited.)

The second great idea implanted in Western liberalism and which has suffered a bad mauling is equality. Equality was a declaration not just of the rights of every man but, because it involved every man, it therefore became the basis for a new unity. It was because men were equal before the law and shared a common dignity that the opportunity arose to create a new society. This was a society which rejected previous distinctions between men based upon birth, property and wealth. It inaugurated a new age. The assumption was that because of the recognition of this natural right of equality that other distinctions within mankind based upon class, race, religion, ethnicity or gender were less important. It was because liberty and equality were the supreme rights that other differences between men would be consigned to the shadows.

But a peculiar fate befell the ideal of equality. Equality between men was translated—in Western liberal society without a theology—to mean equality between their beliefs. One man's idea was as good as another man's. Equality became taken for granted; it became a given. Once this happens to an idea then it loses its originating anchor and surrenders to reinvention. So equality was reinvented and became tolerance. The great value of liberal societies has become tolerance. Now there can be no doubt that tolerance is a great virtue, a necessary virtue after the intolerance of centuries. But tolerance has become almost the very definition of Western liberalism. One reason it has thrived, of course, is because of the great reluctance in Western liberalism today to identify truth. Truth is elusive. That popular conclusion is driven by both the decline of religious faith and the latter-day ethical crisis created by science which now involves questions such as 'what is life?' and 'under what conditions should life be created?', let alone 'who and under what conditions is allowed to terminate life?'.

The entire ethos of post-modernism rests on the premise that truth cannot be discerned. Because truth is elusive there is an acceptance that truth is relative. Relativism is the companion of tolerance. If values are mainly relative, not absolute, then tolerance is the essential requirement for the stability of society. Tolerance is the companion of relativism; these are the new bulwarks of Western liberalism.

This condition was observed at close quarters and vividly described by Alan Bloom, drawing upon his decades as a university teacher in Chicago in his book, *The Closing of the American Mind*:

> There is one thing a professor can be absolutely certain of: almost every student entering the university believes, or says he believes, that truth is relative . . . That anyone should regard the proposition as not self-evident astonishes them . . . Some are religious, some atheists, some to the left, some to the right, some intent to be scientists, some humanists or professionals or businessmen, some are poor, some rich. They are unified only in their relativism and in their allegiance to equality . . . That it is a moral issue for students is revealed by the character of their response when challenged: 'Are you an absolutist?' . . . The danger they have been taught to fear from absolutism is not error but intolerance.

The political manifestation of this process lies in the newfound attention accorded to minority rights. There is now an acceptance that such groups needed special executive and legislative measures to realise their true potential. Community groups— based on a definition of culture, race, sex preference or gender—receive special treatment to enable them to achieve equality or equal status with the rest of society. This is an admission, of course, that the traditional notion of equality before the law does not suffice; indeed, that it has failed them. So in this fashion equality has merged into tolerance. The question is whether the idea of equality is now being used to justify and entrench new distinctions in society when the original idea of equality was to unite society.

St James Centre Annual Lecture, 1996

PART II

THE COALITION IN POWER

THE PARADOX OF the 1990s is that John Howard has been a vulnerable yet dominant prime minister. He has never reached the commanding heights of either a truly popular leader or a leader who shaped his own era. Howard is regularly struggling, under assault from the media or a collection of interest groups, or battling to resolve the latest crisis—Hansonism, tax, Wik, the GST implementation or East Timor.

Yet Howard is dominant within his government and periodically ascendant within the country. The character of his government is indelibly stamped by his own beliefs, equivocation and priorities. Above all, Howard is his own government's voice. No prime minister has displayed such a penchant for talkback radio and few have been as transparent in the search for public justification.

John Winston Howard is an economic liberal and social conservative. His enduring legacy is likely to be that of a calculating economic reformer who helped Australia adapt to the global economy. For all this, the feature of Howard's prime ministership is the absence of a road map let alone a grand plan. Howard improvised as he went along, assisted by a booming economy, underestimated by his enemies and always the political professional seeking a populist pitch.

His 1996–98 first term was cast in shadow as many interest groups, suffering withdrawal symptoms from the long Labor era, questioned his legitimacy. Far more than most leaders Howard's prime ministership was a search for self-definition. He tried caution but when this tactic failed he resorted to

59

audacity on the waterfront and in taxation reform. In Howard's second term he displayed a far greater confidence and command though doubts about his leadership quality lingered.

By the end of 1999 Howard's imprint on Australian life was discernible in a prime ministership of some turbulence with Houdini-like episodes. It was characterised by a more dynamic, market-orientated and competitive economic structure and culture, a reduction in union influence, a philosophy of 'mutual obligation' at the edges of welfare, an overseas military commitment in East Timor amid a collapse of relations with Indonesia, a redefinition of the terms of our Asian engagement and a conservative bent on national identity issues typified by his monarchical faith.

Howard, loathed among the intellectual class, exploited and relied upon his 'common man' image. The turning points of his prime ministership were easy to identify—his 1998 re-election and the Howard–Meg Lees tax package deal which saved Howard's political neck and turned him into a negotiating prime minister.

But 1999 saw a changing of the guard. Howard's deputy prime minister and National Party leader, Tim Fischer, quit the ministry. Fischer had spent three full years in the political frontline. He had endured the most difficult job—pacifying the bush but staying mostly true to his principles of racial tolerance and trade liberation. He left a hero after a cameo ministerial career few had ever predicted.

The same year saw an elevation in the leadership ambitions of Liberal deputy and Treasurer, Peter Costello. He is tracking Howard. Costello, who prided himself on his economic management performance, is a younger man with the values of a younger generation. He used the republic to highlight his clean break with Howard. Costello is in waiting, the heir apparent.

Howard much negotiate two hurdles to retain the prime ministership at the next election—the implementation of his GST and showing that he has an agenda relevant to the early 2000s. A failure on either count would see his departure.

PETER COSTELLO,
A POLITICIAN IN WAITING

HE'S YOUNG, JUST 41, clever with a touch of flair, ebullient but cautious, infamous for his smirk, self-satisfied with his almost irresistible success, and he hopes to be the real winner of the 1998 election.

Peter Costello has a triple role. He's the Treasurer, the deputy leader of the Liberal Party and the future prime minister. The latter is his assumed destiny—assumed by friends, even enemies, most Liberals and, with little effort at concealment, by Costello himself. His eyes are on the Lodge.

But such destiny is not uncontested. Costello has serious opponents. Just ask that political hard-head with his own PM's baton, Peter Reith, or Costello's fiercest critic, Jeff Kennett or, in his private moments, John Howard, the incumbent. A formidable trio—unpersuaded or unreconciled to Costello's 'destiny'. John Howard won't endorse Costello as the successor. That's sensible, but pointed.

The public sees a lot of Peter Costello and yet, one suspects, it doesn't know him. The orthodoxies are that Costello's too arrogant, that he skates on thin ice because he's too relaxed, that he's a 'New Right' ideologue, that he's too narrow, unelectable and disliked by women. Like most orthodoxies, these have a grain of truth and a lot more myth. They obscure, rather than illuminate, Peter Costello.

The fault is his own. Costello is very secretive. He doesn't trust the media; he is a private person. One of the people who knows him best, says: 'Secrecy is a strong trait. The view is that

the less people know, the safer you are.' Affable but elusive—
that's the Costello trademark.

His friend Michael Kroger is correct in saying that family
and religion are the keys to his character. 'His Christian
upbringing helped shape his moral and political outlook,' says
Kroger. 'It was a conservative code, a view of the world where
a sense of decency, responsibility and frugality prevailed.'

He's very tall and rangy, 190 cm (6 ft 3 in), possessed of a
booming voice, a heat seeking eye-to-eye engagement, a defiant
habit of tilting his chin upwards, a purveyor of the lethal verbal
jab with a boyish penchant to refine the one-line gag. The attack
on Labor's Nick Sherry with the 'Oh possum, you're home'
punchline is now legend.

Costello is a formidable foe, a born actor but, as a performer, far better in Parliament than on television. He knows
he has a mission in this campaign—to wipe away the smirk.

He's trying so hard. That's the trouble. It's so spontaneous.
Why, that smirk just belongs to him. In the process Costello is
often seen to adopt the self-conscious grimace of the ever-so-
serious treasurer. The smirk avoidance technique.

Asked about Costello, social researcher Hugh Mackay says:
'His facial and body language often undercuts what he's saying.
Some people see him as more arrogant than Keating. The
boyish cheeky smirky look says to people he's not really serious.'

When asked about this and the more serious criticism that
he's too harsh, Costello offers a potential confirmation: 'I would
have thought for a politician that was half flattering. A tough
operator. Tough and fair. Let's face facts here, politicians are
not popular. Secondly, the guy responsible for raising the money
is always going to be much less popular than the guy spending
it. If you wanted popularity you wouldn't become a government
minister. You'd become a TV host. If that is the worst criticism—I mean, there could be worse criticisms, couldn't there?'

Obviously.

Costello admits he likes having fun but make no mistake,
he's serious. At one stage he gets philosophical, telling me,
'Paul, this is life, this isn't a dress rehearsal for something else.
This is the one shot and if you can't enjoy it and laugh at
yourself, well, you are missing a great side of human life.'

Quite.

The Liberals thrive on a golden-haired boy. It is a psychic

need and Costello is the latest manifestation. Born in 1957, son of a schoolteacher and Baptist lay preacher, educated at Melbourne's Carey Baptist Grammar, student leader at Monash University, lawyer, a barrister with spectacular success in attacking union power, a federal MP at 32, a candidate for deputy leader at 35, deputy leader and shadow treasurer at 36, treasurer at 38. This is his fourth election.

The rise and rise of Peter Costello has been the second biggest story in the Liberal Party in recent years, beaten only by the resurrection and agonies of John Howard. Give Costello his due. He handles the 'golden boy' mantle far better than others to whom it has fallen, notably Andrew Peacock a generation earlier and, more recently, Alexander Downer who enjoyed a brief interlude as leader in 1994. Costello hasn't stumbled. He's denied the critics their chance to indulge that great Australian pastime of pulling down tall poppies.

Indeed, Costello has handled each challenge with deceptive ease such that the shadow over his career is not any blunder but the suspicion that he's got it too easy; that he hasn't felt the blowtorch.

If Costello makes the Lodge he will represent an entirely new generational force. He will be our first post-Vietnam, post-sixties leader. Born in the baby-boom burnout, Costello was only eleven during that epic political year of 1968 and he was just entering university in 1975, the year of the Whitlam implosion and fall of Saigon. The consequence is manifest—Costello is largely devoid of any political romanticism from the sixties.

His political maturity occurred after the transforming fashions of that era—the battle over our Vietnam involvement, the faith in social democratic government as a problem-solver typified by the Whitlam 'It's Time' victory, and the permissive society as the means to personal freedom and self-realisation. Costello, in fact, had his first political battles at Monash University combating the dregs of the sixties revolution— the pro-collectivist, pro-communist, pro-Palestinian ugly but juvenile Left.

This rear-vision view of the sixties gave Costello a discerning advantage. He took as a 'given' the enduring principles from these battles—racial equality and ethnic justice—and rejected the political garbage.

As a student leader he fought the campus anti-Semitism of

the Left. This was the key racial campaign in which he was involved. But he did take another hero—Martin Luther King, playing tapes of King's famous speeches with his political mates.

Costello is a 'mission' politician. He's in Parliament to make a difference, not have a career. 'I am not going to retire in politics,' he declares. He's moved fast and he's impatient. Treasurer Costello depicts himself as a driving force for change within the government, which, apart from tax and waterfront, has been tempered by Howard's caution.

This election ushers in the Parliament of the millennium. The psychologists will have a field day. The millennium will exert a profound effect upon Australia's mood and, in generational dynamics, must give Costello leverage against Howard.

The Costello paradox is that many people think he'll be prime minister but few feel they have any fix on him. He's successful but not popular, smart but not creative, liberal not a radical. The keys to his character are universally ignored by the media—family, religion and political philosophy.

Costello is at ease within himself, the ease that derives from a conventional view of life. He's a well-adjusted human being who has moved from the family of his youth to the family of his adulthood. Costello jokes about the truth of his conventional existence—a proven foundation for the ambitious politician.

'Our place is a one wife, three kids, one husband house, where no orgies take place,' he boasts. 'We are very quiet and we get on well with the neighbours and mow the lawn on Saturday.' He booms into laughter.

His wife, Tanya, a lawyer, is the daughter of former NSW Liberal leader, intellectual and former *Quadrant* editor, Peter Coleman. They met at university in 1980. For Costello, Tanya represented political and intellectual connections beyond the realm of the Costello family.

Yes, he goes to church. 'I would go every week if I were free,' he says. So how often does he go? 'I would make it one in two.' And, these days, that's very good for a politician. Tanya is an Anglican and they attend the Anglican church, not Baptist. Tanya has sacrificed much for Peter but her influence is decisive.

'I am an orthodox Christian. I believe in the orthodox Christian faith,' Costello says. He doesn't present this as any key to his makeup, but merely part of the picture. He's also the Number One ticket-holder for Essendon—and this seems to excite him more than church. Did Costello purge a wilder side at university?

Shifting to self-mockery, he reflects: 'Yeah, I was a real long-hair. I was a bit of a long-hair rabblerouser. You know, grew my hair, go on the sort of backpackers circuit, go through the hippie phase. Nothing happened. [Pause for effect] I didn't inhale.'

He's pleased with his answer. Costello just can't help himself.

There are two Costello brothers, Tim and Peter; the Baptist minister with a commitment to politics and the politician with a commitment to religion. They're not opposites. In fact, they have much in common. 'Our father was a strong influence and seeing him in the pulpit exerted an influence,' says Tim, two years older than Peter.

'The Baptist church had a sense of the evil in the world. It was almost spiritual warfare. Where there is evil, checks and restraints are essential.'

Tim took the logical course and became a minister; Peter took the plunge into the 'fallen world' of politics. Yet Peter insists he deals with politics on his terms. 'I have always decided that, in my life, politics won't take its totality,' Peter says. 'I have a limited view of politics. There is an awful lot that politics can't fix. I think politicians have let themselves down by claiming to be able to do too much. People might be unhappy for a host of reasons: because their marriage has broken up; because they feel they have never got the recognition in life they deserve.

'You know this business is not religion. Within limited boundaries politics can make a difference but it's a limited science. Politics can't fill the vacuum of a family or religion or a community.'

Tim says: 'Our father had values from the Depression of responsibility and discipline. He believed you didn't get married until you were 30 with a deposit. Our home was middle-class Liberal and it was assumed that God had put Bob Menzies in the Lodge. Our father was a politics teacher and we grew up with a fascination for politics, almost a fear of it.'

The Baptists promoted the values of choice, with baptism given around the age of sixteen, after the individual had made a decision; independence, since the church historically was non-conformist, typified by John Bunyan's *The Pilgrim's Progress* and its assertion of worship according to conscience; autonomy and self-help—with each church reflecting the congregational ethic of adapting its own service.

So family and religion fused into Costello the notions of thrift, discipline, anti-collectivism, scepticism about government intervention and a disposition to small business virtues. In his eighties speech to the H.R. Nicholls Society, 'No ticket, no start—no more!' attacking the union closed shop, Costello recalled that the principle that an innocent man must be sacrificed for the collective good was 'the justification given for the death sentence imposed on Christ'.

He asserted that since 'the foundation of Christendom there has been a revulsion to that principle, a revulsion that has underpinned the British system of justice', which is why 'we should not tolerate the abuse of civil rights in the workplace in the all-so-brazen proclamation, no ticket, no start'. Here was as strong a declaration of the moral basis of individual liberty as any Australian politician has offered recently.

Given his academic ability and oratorical skill, Costello's entry into university politics was a natural extension. He campaigned against anti-Semitism, the pro-communist Left and against the monopolist stance of the Australian Union of Students (AUS) which, Costello says, 'I detested. I formed a very strong anti-compulsory union membership view.'

In fighting the AUS he operated closely with the ALP Right. So, the perennial question is: Did Labor ever have a chance of getting Costello at university?

Probably not, for three reasons. His family background, his Liberal wife and a distaste for the Victorian ALP, a body of unique self-destruct potential.

Costello was ripe for the intellectual climate of the eighties. He was a foundation member of the H.R. Nicholls Society, which sought an historic shift in the industrial system towards the market; a barrister supporting small business against union power; and a proponent of the economic liberalism he now pursues as treasurer.

In a memorable speech to the society, Costello invoked the British intellectual Paul Johnson, who resigned from British Labour because it had drifted to 'the ideology of collectivism'.

He quoted Johnson saying, 'I do not intend to travel even one miserable inch along that road' and then declared: 'Nor do I.' Costello's justification of an earlier decision, perhaps?

So where does Costello stand today? A critical question. The answer is complex but fairly transparent.

On the economy he's liberal. He backs a market-orientated economy—tight budget, low protection, deregulation and privatisation. His instincts have been reinforced by the Treasury, towards which he was initially suspicious. For Costello, 'the most important issue for Australia at the moment is whether it makes its economic destiny. We are either as a nation going to make our destiny or flee in fright. Making our destiny will mean attending to the big issues—tax reform, industrial relations reform, securing a budget position and securing foreign investment'.

On the Constitution he's now for a republic: 'I believe the head of State has to be appointed on the basis of merit rather than birth. I do not think the monarchy can continue to be an enduring symbol for Australia.'

After initially staying silent on Hanson he has emerged as a critic: 'I have always been a strong opponent of race discrimination. For twenty years. I am a strong opponent of the divisive politics of Hansonism on race and ethnicity. I am. I have spoken out very strongly on these sorts of issues. Spending on multiculturalism has got to be more accountable—but it seems that the further you get away from migrants the more threatened you become by them. And I would say there is no reason to be threatened.'

On the republic, Hanson and multiculturalism, he is a break from Howard; he's distinctly more progressive. But on Aboriginal policy he's much closer to his leader. He says an apology 'won't fix a thing', that the 'radical angry' Aboriginal leaders are counter-productive for their cause, that ATSIC 'must be held accountable' and that there's not much point in going over past mistakes.

He calls himself a conservative on moral issues—he rejects homosexual marriage, legalising drugs, argues a case for 'preventing extreme depictions of violence and sex' and compares this with support for gun laws by 'drawing some limits for the protection of society generally'.

The ritualistic criticism of Costello is that as Treasurer he's too narrow, too dry, too remote from people. Sound familiar? It was the standard line used against Paul Keating and couldn't have been more wrong. It's a bit like complaining that lion-tamers don't laugh enough. Being Treasurer is actually a serious business and unless you project a market-credible, low-inflation, pro-investment outlook, then a lot of damage will be done to your country, let alone your image.

Asked about his image, Costello gives a Keatingesque reply: 'I am not Treasurer of Australia because I'm looking for public gratification. If that were my motivation I would be in another occupation. If at the end of the day people said, "He was tough, he was honest, he was fair", that would be the kind of verdict you would be pleased with.'

Costello says he can be 'touchy-feely in my personal dealings but this is not a treasurer's job. When someone says to you, "Mr Treasurer, comment on the international trade in goods and services", a response along the lines of, "I just want to empathise with everybody who has had a bad hair day so that you will overcome it and find personal fulfilment by lunchtime", well, it doesn't work like that.'

The real criticism of him is different—that he's not as tough in Cabinet as he sounds outside and that, as Treasurer, he's a good lawyer: he knows the brief, but has little 'feel' for the economy.

Costello is far more conventional than Keating and less creative as a politician. But Howard, who endured five years as Treasurer to Malcolm Fraser, knows how to finesse a treasurer. This is the big difference. Howard won't let Costello run his government the way Keating tried to steer the Hawke government. No way.

In this 1998 campaign, Howard and Costello are colleagues and conscripts, bonded to each other as Prime Minister and Treasurer. Such intimacy promotes partnership but, when the chains are broken, fuels rivalry based upon deep psychological insight. The public grasps this well—they saw Hawke and Keating.

Howard and Costello will live or die together at this election. If they win, such winning only drives them apart. The compelling issue within the Liberal Party is whether a Howard victory can endure or merely set the scene for a Costello challenge.

Hugh Mackay says that among people there is a sense of inevitability of Costello as a future leader, but no enthusiasm for it. 'It's almost part of the folklore of the electorate that Howard will go next term. Howard is so personally unpopular and lacking gravitas that people say, "If they can't get Kennett, then it'll be Costello".'

Maybe. Costello entered this campaign super-sensitive about Howard. The worst mistake he can make is to fan the leadership issue. Asked if he and Howard will work together during the campaign, he replies in one word: 'Absolutely.' He must play the loyal treasurer. Costello jokes that he and Howard not only have 'a very close working relationship' but that they 'probably spend more time with each other than we spend with our wives or families'. Costello grins, 'Now my wife has certain attractions'.

Does he go to the Lodge for dinner? 'Sometimes several nights a week.'

So far Costello has played the leadership game superbly. Examine the record. After the 1993 loss, Costello stood for the deputy leadership and came second, 45 to 33, to Michael Wooldridge. Very respectable. This vote proved his future was backed by hard numbers.

As John Hewson's leadership faltered, Costello's nerve was firmer than that of his internal opponents. In May 1994, Jeff Kennett, fearful that Costello would emerge as leadership 'saviour', launched a fierce assault, declaring that 'this debacle—is being generated from Melbourne by the Costello camp—I have very strong reasons to be concerned about the integrity of that camp—it is not the time for Mr Costello'. Costello was enraged, but his public reply was measured. Yet Costello wasn't running.

The Melbourne push was for Downer: he and Costello were seen as generational rivals. On Friday 20 May at 4 p.m., Hewson announced he was calling a party meeting to test his leadership. At 4.15 p.m. Costello rang Downer and said: 'We have to put someone over the top. I am going to make you the offer of your life. I am going to put you one election away from the prime ministership. I am prepared to back you in and run as deputy.'

It was a brilliant call. Costello created a Downer–Costello

alliance, outsmarting Hewson. Nicknamed 'the dream team', they won. Costello became deputy and shadow Treasurer. But Downer faltered. He wasn't a leader. So Downer had to be sacrificed and Costello remained as deputy. The Melbourne powerbrokers, desperate to win, then made their most difficult decision—to support Howard's recall. Costello stood by Downer to the penultimate moment—and then, with Downer's support collapsing in February 1995, he told Downer to resign to allow a smooth transition to Howard. It worked. The Howard–Costello team won the 1996 election. It endured, successfully, a term in office.

Costello plans to cash this political capital; he has intervened twice, to assist Downer, then Howard, to become leader. 'On each occasion I put the interests of the party first,' he told me. 'I think the party realises I have deposited a lot of loyalty with the party in the bank. I am now the longest-serving deputy of the Liberal Party since Phil Lynch, which shows a great deal of patient hard work.'

The main disruption came in July this year when Costello, on Neil Mitchell's 3AW program, conceded that 'people' had raised the leadership with him. The story took off. It was the culmination of a period of tension between the Howard and Costello camps.

John Howard has two objectives in this 1998 election—to beat Kim Beazley and to consolidate against Peter Costello. Will Labor let him get away with it? The insight into Howard's thinking was his handling of tax reform.

The tax package was substantially reworked after the Queensland election and Howard had a major influence on its design. It is a joint Howard–Costello package, literally, but its Canberra launch on 13 August was a remarkable event. Inside the media lock-up, Howard and Costello held a joint press conference.

Howard took centre stage behind a podium, while Costello sat off to his left. Janette Howard was in the audience; no Tanya Costello. Howard spoke for twenty minutes and then took questions for 30 minutes. Finally, after 50 minutes, he handed over to Costello. If you're looking for a defining moment in the Liberal campaign, this was it—right at the start. Costello sat next to Howard, supportive, intent, serious and utterly patronised.

Howard declared the tax changes historic, branded them 'a new tax system for a new century', recalled that he (Howard) had announced the tax reform ambition in 1997, that he (Howard) had defined the five principles of tax reform, that each was now being 'faithfully honoured', that many of the decisions he had just announced were issues to which 'I have committed, in terms of policy change, more than half of my political life' but that 'you can never do these things alone' and it was all a team effort. So Howard thanked Costello for 'his fine work', along with several officials by name, most of whom worked for Howard.

This was a branding exercise. The tax reform is a team effort but Howard is head of the team. The public has little idea of the work involved in putting major tax reform together. This time, Costello estimates the full Cabinet 'had at least eight meetings, mostly 10-hour days'. At the end John Howard declared, 'This is good economy policy', with Costello immediately quipping, 'Don't prejudice it by saying that'.

Tax reform is the biggest challenge of Costello's career. He is savage on Beazley's ALP, saying what has changed our politics is not Hanson but Labor's 'embrace of populism'. Hanson and Beazley have 'more or less identical' economic policies and the transforming event has been Labor's 'lapse into irrationalism'.

Yet Costello still operates in Howard's shadow. That's because Howard has even more at stake than Costello. Tax will make or break his prime ministership and his government. If Howard wins, then Howard is vindicated and Costello gets his chance. The tension between them will intensify and the party will be forced into a decision about leadership and destiny.

Costello, like Keating, would unfold a new personality onto the PM's office because his real self is still contained in the treasurer's skin. But the smirk raises a deeper issue. Costello is young, but does he act younger than he is? Does he possess the maturity for the top job? That's the issue. It is an assessment the Liberal Party cannot avoid making.

The Australian Magazine, *26–27 September 1998*

IN SEARCH OF THE REAL
JOHN HOWARD

A YEAR OF GOVERNING CAUTIOUSLY

THE FIRST YEAR of the Howard government has raised the tantalising question about the Prime Minister—has John Howard, like Gough Whitlam, got to the Lodge too late?

At first sight the answer seems 'no', since Howard has achieved what the Labor Party of the past twenty years dismissed as impossible—he has become the dominant politician of his time.

Let's not fall for the trick that this was inevitable or likely. Howard, for years dismissed as 'little Johnny' by the ALP, has had the last laugh. Howard now discovers that marvellous wonder at the centre of government—the concept of prime ministerial authority. This is what the past year of politics is about.

Make no mistake; Howard, a politician whose entire career has been blighted by problems of authority, has established near complete authority. Howard's fascination with his metamorphosis is implicit in his prime ministership.

While Whitlam, Malcolm Fraser and Bob Hawke were all figures of authority or popularity before assuming the office, Howard wasn't. The office is what has transformed Howard and his life. How he must appreciate the ironies.

Consider the history. Having been humiliated by Fraser to the point of near resignation in the 1982 Budget Cabinet, Howard now dominates his own Cabinet; having been repeatedly traduced by Paul Keating in Parliament through the 1980s,

Howard is now firmly in control as he swivels his high-backed light green chair and stands at the dispatch box; finally, and most satisfying, having been mocked by Hawke for unpopularity and ridiculed as 'Mr 17 per cent', Howard enjoys the electorate's vindication of his judgment and persona.

These are the three instruments of his power—Cabinet, Parliament, electorate.

When I asked Howard to list the highlights of his first year, the top of the list was the Lindsay by-election in Sydney in October—classic 'battler' terrain. Few people, surely, would have guessed his choice. It's an insight into Howard's mind. Lindsay proved two things to Howard—that the Budget was right and that his government was 'on track'. It confirmed for Howard his judgment that the change of government in March 1996 reflected a tidal movement by the people that Labor had still not grasped.

Howard once blundered in 1986 by declaring that 'the times will suit me', referring to the pro-market economic liberalism of the 1980s. He paid a price for those remarks and his judgment was wrong. Although he would never repeat the slogan, Howard believes it is true today. He gives more attention to his relations with the electorate than any recent prime minister except Hawke. Like Hawke, Howard spends a lot of time travelling, campaigning and greeting. He will do even more this year. It's not that Howard thinks he is more popular than Hawke, but he does believe that his style and values have struck a chord with the people.

During the 1980s there was an orthodoxy about Howard—that he was the reforming spearhead of the Coalition, but weak on politics. Yet the orthodoxy today is more likely to be the reverse—that Howard is an adept politician with doubts about his ability to implement genuine change.

Many people think they know Howard. In the course of a 20-year career in Parliament he has had countless meetings, dealings and exchanges with thousands of people, often managing to convey an impression of a man who is diligent, credible and straight-up-and-down. But Howard is more complex. In truth, few people know him. He has always been a loner; reluctant to give too much of himself to his colleagues, leaving them to speculate on what he holds back and how much he has to give. He came to power as his own man, with virtually no debts to anybody. There are businessmen who saw him regularly who didn't know what he thought about relations with China, Aboriginal affairs or the environment. So today, in the boardrooms, the bourse and the bars, there is a constant discussion about the character of the Prime Minister.

It is still not understood how much of the government's character is shaped by Howard. Take, for example, John Herron's so-called paternalistic approach to Aborigines and the rift during 1996 between the government and blacks; or the crisis in relations with China last year partly provoked because of the new government's enthusiastic barracking for the United States and its alliance; or the savaging of Howard by the quality media over his handling of the Pauline Hanson affair; or the influence that Brian Harradine can occasionally exert on the government.

These things have not all happened by accident. They reflect the aspirations of Howard. They are symptoms of a cultural change contingent upon a change of government. For instance, Howard believes that Herron is one of his best ministers precisely because he has broken decisively from Labor's Aboriginal policy; he believes that the US alliance is deeply anchored within the psychology of the Australian people and his government was right to trumpet the alliance from the start, even given the unintended consequences; he believes that his handling of the Hanson affair was dead right, that it wasn't his task to personally repudiate her nor to deny the instincts she was articulating as distinct from rejecting her formal position; finally, Howard sees Harradine as a man with whom he can deal, whose values he can understand and whose role in the Senate means he should be appreciated.

Howard had a double success last year. He won office and he won power. They are, of course, not to be confused. He won office at the 1996 general election and he won power when Mal Colston defected from the ALP, giving Howard the Senate numbers to secure his two main election pledges, the partial sale of Telstra and industrial relations reform, as well as the bulk of the Budget.

By winning power via Colston, Howard ensured that his first term would not degenerate into a confrontation between the

House and Senate, and that he will enjoy a full three-year Parliament. While he has Colston he retains this power which is why Labor has Colston in its sights.

The key to Howard's government is to understand that he operates in the wake of two intellectual movements in the past fifteen years. The first, following the 1970s, was the conclusion that State power, regulation, high tax and high-spend policies didn't work with globalisation. This led to the deregulation and the economic liberalisation of the 1980s. The second, following the 1980s, is that market-orientated policies aren't enough to sustain democratic governments. This is the conclusion of the 1990s. This conclusion was imposed upon the Coalition at its 1993 election defeat. Now, it doesn't matter whether you talk to Bill Clinton, Tony Blair or Howard, they are all operating in this environment.

The task, and you see Howard putting it together, is to try to weave a new synthesis between economic reform and social reassurance. Keating tried to apply his own unique economic-social policy mix. But there is no ready mechanism. It's a process of adaptation, compromise, flexibility and the recourse to 'values' politics.

Howard's other lucky break, which he exploited effectively, was the guns debate. This not only projected his leadership but it offered a consensus for a major social policy initiative. Social issues will be vital, perhaps dominant, at the next election. Indeed, social policy may be the major difference between the government and the Opposition at that time. This is why Howard will keep a lot of focus on the family, law and order, rights and responsibilities, and national unity.

Yet there is a sense of disappointment about Howard's government, a mood of anti-climax. Is this all there is? Does the government have a program for the next two years or is it merely responding to events? Is it so against 'vision' that it succumbs to myopia?

The problem about the compromise nature of Howard's mandate is its transparency in decision-making. If the government does possess an overall frame of reference, then it's not clear. The impression is that policy is conducted on an ad hoc basis. This is reinforced by a series of brittle ministerial

performances, straight-out ministerial incompetence, considerable tension and misunderstanding between ministers and their
Public Service advisers, and growing signs that one of the
themes of 1997 will be deep conflict between the Howard
government and the non-Labor premiers.

A government's ability to have the people accept hard
reforms is greatest in its first term. The issue posed by Howard's
first year is whether he has misjudged this factor and erred on
the side of caution.

The Labor Party believes that Howard is merely riding the
honeymoon wave which still has a distance to go—but that,
ultimately, he will be revealed more as a Harold Holt than a
Bob Hawke.

If you asked Howard whether, as Prime Minister, he was
merely 'minding the shop' or changing the country, he'd be
insulted. But this is the exact question that is being asked. In
1986, Howard observed that 'governments on our side in the
past have been too timid about change'. Has his government
confirmed his critique or disproved it?

The resolution of the conundrum may come with next year's
election and whether Howard's political clout is such that he
wins a new mandate on his terms, not those being imposed by
his Labor opponents.

The Weekend Australian, *1–2 March 1997*

HOWARD'S BIG PICTURE AND BIG GAMBLE

THIS CAMPAIGN DOCUMENTS the paradox of John Howard. It
was inconceivable two years ago that Howard's re-election
campaign would see him trailing in the polls a fortnight out and
appealing to the battlers to accept a GST as patriots—for
Australia's sake rather than follow narrow self-interest.

Howard now projects as a crusader. A mission politician. A
great reformer. A man willing to sacrifice his entire career on
a vast tax reform when he only needed to hold an inquiry
anyway. When has the PM *chosen* to seek re-election on such a
huge and risky platform?

The John Howard on display in this election seems different
to the John Howard who has governed Australia for much of

the past two years. Or the Howard who won the 1996 election. The big difference between Howard and Keating in 1996 was leadership philosophy. Keating was an architect of leading from the front and of projecting his vision.

Not Howard. He said that leadership was more a matter of listening and responding to the people.

Is he listening and responding now? Or is he behaving in the classic 'crash through or crash' mode of a Whitlam? Is this the same cautious poll-driven John Howard, the leader who prided himself on stealing the battlers from Labor and keeping them?

The answer to all these questions is yes. It is the same John Howard. It is the John Howard often called the worst PM since Billy McMahon. It is a John Howard whose persona and whose party's dilemmas leading to this election are fairly transparent.

Howard, like the Liberal Party, still lives with the 'ghost' of the 1993 defeat, perhaps the most psychologically debilitating in the party's history. The Hewson defeat drove a wedge between Liberal belief and self-interest. The party had to ditch Fightback! and its plans for tax reform, a GST, smaller government, deregulation and privatisation. The voters had said 'no' and the voters must be right.

So pragmatism drove the Liberals back to the centre. They won in 1996 by denying Keating a target, by moving dramatically towards Labor, by pledging no GST, no wage cuts, no end to Medicare, even pretending to be greenies.

Howard, as Keating famously said, won 'a big majority on a small mandate'. He won almost on Keating's own agenda. It was a platform significantly at odds with Howard's own beliefs as revealed during his 'conviction' phase, the 1985–89 leadership era. This became a big problem.

It was manifested first in Howard's distinction between core and non-core promises to justify his savage Budget cuts in the name of fiscal responsibility. But the greater manifestation was the conflict in Howard between self-interest and ideology. It was the conflict between keeping his successful 1996 election technique of policy caution to hold mainstream voters as opposed to his ambition to 'strike out' and realise his deepest economic policy aspirations.

So Howard's prime ministership became a study in these competing forces. This was reinforced by a personal dilemma:

a confusion over when to stick and when to surrender, when to assert leadership and when to repose in unity, when to ignore Hanson and when to confront her, when not to sack ministers and when to sack ministers such as Warwick Parer, more guilty than those who had already lost their heads.

Howard buckled to the car companies over protection; refused to confront the Senate over his industrial reform bill; and cut immigration to play the populist card. He was clever, cautious, playing to the mainstream. But it didn't work and his problems deepened. He looked weak, visionless, with his government adrift.

So mid-term, with leadership rumbles underway, Howard resorted to faith and conviction. He decided the tough decisions to win a Budget surplus had been the best. So he embraced tax reform; he gambled to break the waterfront unions; and, finally, he presented a sweeping tax package including a goods and services tax. It was death or glory. The 1998 election will either purge the Liberals of their 1993 ghost or deliver them a second crippling psychological blow.

The issue at stake transcends Howard. It goes to the entire meaning and rationale of the Liberals and the Coalition. When he was stranded in 1997, Howard had to decide what his government and his prime ministership was all about. His answer was that the Coalition would stand for economic reform and those virtues of responsibility, incentive and fairness.

If Howard loses, the Liberal Party enters a new ideological twilight zone. The Nationals will be unpredictable in defeat, disillusioned with Howard's economic policies and vulnerable to Hanson-type social solutions. The Coalition could be finished.

Because Howard's social conservatism is so deep, a target of the opinion-making elite, contrary to the views of a sizeable lump of Australians and a source of division, he is always forced back to economic policy as his cardinal political weapon. This has been the story during both periods of his leadership. It is the story of the 1998 election.

But social issues affect economic issues via leadership. Howard lost much of his moral authority over Hanson when he failed to perceive the difference between social grievance and racial chauvinism, a tragic mistake.

In his policy speech, Howard talked repeatedly of love. His love for Australia. But Howard has failed to connect emotionally with the people. His political reform is an economic vision but Howard's problem is that he hasn't put this vision on a sustained basis as Prime Minister.

He's mucked about too much.

If he loses, the reason won't be the GST. It will be Howard's failure to sort out earlier what his prime ministership was about. If he wins, will he draw the lesson?

The Australian, *23 September 1998*

THE SWEETEST VICTORY

It is sweet political enjoyment of the most exotic kind.

—Prime Minister John Howard last night

The Democrats have won more in thirteen hours of talks with the Howard government than they did in thirteen years under the Labor government.

—Democrats leader Meg Lees

AFTER NINE EXHAUSTING days of negotiation, drama and reverses, the Howard government and the Democrats have done a deal on a new tax system for Australia.

The sense of triumph was manifest in John Howard last night. At a 6 p.m. press conference Howard announced that the deal was 'truly a historic moment in the economic modernisation of Australia'.

If the deal sticks, this package will bring to a culmination Australia's 20-year debate about a broader indirect tax base. For Howard it will be the greatest policy win of his 25-year career. He needed this—desperately. Howard's legitimacy and longevity as Prime Minister have been on the line for the last nine days. Now he has broken through.

A smiling Meg Lees met the media last night after the Howard–Costello press conference. She has been catapulted into prominence by outmanoeuvring the Labor Party and winning the most important concessions for the Democrats in their twenty years as a political party. This deal changes the nature of the Democrats and gives them a credibility never previously within their reach. It may be too much for some of them. Lees is happy to defend the new package and branded it a 'green and socially responsible GST'.

If legislated, this deal is a major debacle for the Labor Party. It means that Labor's decade-long campaign to stop the goods and services tax has been lost. It also means that Labor's tactic of total opposition has allowed a Coalition–Democrats deal and a tax package which, ultimately, will be more acceptable to the nation.

Howard claimed to have honoured the basic principles on which his tax package was based. He said he had kept 85–90 per cent of the original tax package on which he won the 1998 election. This is probably on the optimistic side, but Lees endorsed the 85 per cent estimate at her own press conference. Treasurer Peter Costello said it all: 'Eighty-five per cent sure beats zero.'

But the concessions made by Howard and Costello are significant—exclusion of basic food from the GST at a cost of $3.09 billion; a major concession on the diesel fuel rebate which enhances its environmental impact; reduced tax cuts for people earning above $50 000 a year and, in particular, above $60 000 which win back $1.1 billion in revenue; more generous compensation in relation to pensions, allowances and benefits worth an extra $730 million; further GST exemptions in health and education; a delay and deferment in the abolition of State taxes; and an extra $213 million for the Democrats' environment agenda.

Howard and Costello have made a bottom-line concession. In 2000–01 the surplus will lose $1.4 billion to finance these Democrats deals. That's about the same as Howard offered Brian Harradine a fortnight ago and it's worthwhile to carry the package.

Can the flaky Democrats stick by this deal all the way to the Senate vote? Will there be some defections? Howard and Lees were confident last night. The deal involves a Senate vote by 30 June.

Lees said all Democrats senators had signed off 'in principle' but everything depended upon the fine print of the amendments.

The pressure upon the Democrats to recant will be immense

but the long list of policy wins secured by Lees is enough to send her entire party on a drinking binge for a year.

This deal seals a victory for the unlikely Howard–Lees duo. They were all but strangers a fortnight ago. Now they are tied into an embrace of mutual interest. It is this type of political realism which makes so many Democrats so aghast.

As for Howard, he can comfortably live with this package. It is a compromise that will swim because most Australians wanted this anyway. In economic terms it is a third-best option for Howard. But it is a substantial reform and the changes have improved it politically.

Howard is hardly going to lose support for agreeing to remove fresh food from the GST. He has some hefty pluses— the 30 cents tax rate for 80 per cent of Australians; the compensation is stronger notably for pensioners; the better-off aren't winners to the same extent; the family benefits remain; the GST revenue still goes to the States; and most benefits for rural and regional Australia are preserved.

Lees said last night that this result—a GST without basic food—was what the people voted for at the 1998 election. The deal is a turning point for the Democrats. This is why it is so risky. Lees wants the Democrats to become a serious party; she wants them to leave behind their 'fairies at the bottom of the garden' identity; she wants them to negotiate with Howard and secure implementation of policy. For some Democrats that's just too hard.

Howard and Lees complimented each other and slammed the Labor Party. Howard called Lees 'forthright, honest and candid' while Lees said the negotiation with the PM had been 'a very pleasant and cooperative process'.

Lees ridiculed all the previous Democrat cooperation with Labor over thirteen years in an effort to highlight her own successes with Howard. It was so utterly unimaginable a fortnight ago. Former Democrats leader Cheryl Kernot won't be able to restrain herself. Just wait for her attack on Lees.

The political point is obvious—on tax the Democrats have occupied the middle ground, between Coalition and Labor. The ALP left the door wide open and Lees walked in. Make no mistake, cutting a deal with Howard will hurt Lees among her own Democrats membership. It will inject a poison between

Labor and Democrats for a while. But it will help Lees within the electorate.

Lees will wear some of the blame for the GST when it is implemented, notably the nightmare in demarcation over food.

But the public aren't mugs—they know the GST is a Howard–Costello creation. They know that the Lees contribution has been to remove basic food and win more compensation for pensioners.

A snap judgment last night was that Howard and Lees have given each other enough to emerge as mutual winners. There is another winner—the Senate. Howard and Costello won't like this. But the Coalition–Democrats package, if legislated, will validate the Senate as a house of review as distinct—and this is the key point—from being a house of veto.

But Howard won't mind too much. He has been fighting for tax reform for twenty years. He is now on the absolute brink of success—but he knows the sting with tax reform lies in the implementation.

The Weekend Australian, *29–30 May 1999*

A PROFILE OF TIM FISCHER

HE'S A BAFFLING paradox, Tim Fischer. He looks like a hillbilly, talks like a hick, is famous for his hat, hates standing still, loves travelling by train, won't forget your name and is a born grassroots politician. But Fischer is something more—the most misjudged politician in Australia.

He tortures the language so badly that people think he's a fool. Yes, let's get that claim in the open. Fischer knows what many people say. He still feels the media criticism in 1990 when he was the surprise winner in the National Party leadership ballot: 'I was immediately branded idiosyncratic, as under-whelming, as unable and not up to the job.'

To many he looked a third-rater, assuming the mantle of old 'Black Jack' McEwen and Doug Anthony. Well, the media got it wrong. Tim Fischer's not a fool. He's quirky and novel and not the nineties mass-produced TV lookalike politician. Fischer is an authentic; a strange blend of old and new, a scaremonger on native title and a critic of Pauline Hanson.

Fischer is trapped between his heart and his history. The result is a jarring paradox. Contrast, for example, his dedication to our national integration with Asia with his compulsive hard line on native title. Four months ago Fischer entertained Thailand's Deputy Prime Minister, Suwit Khunkitti, a personal friend with whom he has exchanged house visits, just one of many Thai friends Fischer developed from a conscious policy in the eighties of specialising in Thailand as a way of penetrating Asia. This is no tokenism; for Fischer it was integral to his way of life. How many federal MPs today are so focused on creating networks in

Asia? Answer—almost none. Fischer's personal commitment to an Asian path is remarkable within the Parliament.

Yet the same Tim Fischer, when he was in charge of the 'shop' during John Howard's November absence, raised the native title 'threat' to freehold to inflame opinion against Labor's amendments. It was a tactic which saw him denounced; it left freeholder owners more worried than before; it prompted the president of the Native Title Tribunal, Justice Robert French, to contradict the assertion; it outraged indigenous leaders; but it forced Labor to change its position. Howard was pleased. 'I do not make too much of it,' Fischer said. But he told the House that a couple west of Charleville, who believed they had title equivalent to freehold, had four separate Aboriginal claims of exclusive possession against them. This is Fischer performing a National Party ritual—the defence of farm interests. The politics of native title don't permit soft options for him. Fischer and Howard are locked into their 10-point Wik plan, the compact they reached with pastoralists during the stormy Longreach meeting last year.

Fischer's outstanding skill is the oldest in politics—meeting and greeting—and he has taught everyone a lesson by showing that it still works.

Maybe he looked silly wearing his Akubra hat to meet King Carlos of Spain last year. But Fischer says: 'With 50 people wheeling through the King of Spain's office in any one week, he'll remember me. We talked about his visit here, his daughter's honeymoon, so I extended an invitation for any further honeymoons from the Royal family and a lot of things flowed from that.'

This is Fischer doing business. The Pope—Fischer won a personal audience—blessed his hat and offered prayers for the El Niño effect. He's a shameless salesman, a media junkie whose techniques are bizarre but effective because they're authentic. Fischer operates as though the world is run like a corner store—it depends upon who you know. What a fool! He calculates that somehow, some way, it will work to our advantage. Like his first meeting with European Union trade boss, Sir Leon Brittan.

Fischer arrived in Brussels but didn't wait for the minister's meeting. He'd read that Brittan liked walking, so he rang and they had a crisp 45-minute early morning walk before the talks. It's been Leon and Tim ever since. China's economic tsar and likely future premier, Zhu Rongji, calls Fischer 'my friend'. It was the trust between Fischer and US trade representative Charlene Barshefsky that helped to deliver the international deal on information technology liberalisation. Barshefsky knows that Fischer's word is his bond.

Fischer as Trade Minister has travelled from Bhutan to Zimbabwe in the cause of exports. At home he's turned his hobbies like bushwalking into political events—witness his annual Tumbarumba trek. He's a man of curiosity and blessed with the stamina to pursue it.

'I'm curious, almost aggressively curious,' he says. 'I can't stand someone who's not interested in their surrounds, in not discovering a new city or new people. Aggressive curiosity annoys the hell out of some people. But I can't learn enough about a place when I arrive.'

Glance at Tim Fischer and you see an old-fashioned Australian. But appearances are deceptive. Fischer embodies in his life the transformation of Australia. He values loyalty, patriotism, decency and traditional morality—he's a living part of Anzac, a man of the land, a conservative nationalist and a Catholic opponent of euthanasia and political correctness. Perfect for a bush politician.

But just look at the other side—Fischer is a champion of a liberalised and competitive economy; a low tariff politician; an opponent of populists like talk-jockey Alan Jones who preach the phoney benefits of protection; he's an Asianist, an internationalist and he is locked in a death struggle with Pauline Hanson.

Fischer is a litany of paradoxes—he's a crafty politician but hates playing the man, insisting that his criticism of the High Court over its Wik judgment never went to individuals. It's a personal standard. He is a great survivor but has no real power base within the Nationals. His speech is convoluted, abrupt, and sometimes inarticulate—partly a legacy of an orthodontic problem as a child. But his judgment is good, apart from a joke about Boris Yeltsin on a 'vodka bender' and asking Yasser Arafat to visit. Fischer is more popular among rural people than he is among National Party members.

Make no mistake, Fischer plays politics the whole time because politics doesn't come harder than being National Party leader these days. He has led the Nationals through an exceptionally difficult period—a shrinking farm base, tensions between the NSW and Queensland branches and rows over the GST, racism, native title and guns. He has been abused, threatened and plotted against.

At the 1996 poll Paul Keating and Kim Beazley targeted Fischer as a 'nice' man out of his depth, a risk just a heartbeat from the PM's office. But Fischer is a man who keeps growing. Years ago, nobody would have taken him seriously as deputy prime minister. Today, Fischer has reconciled most people to that reality—on his terms.

Fischer is a baby-boomer, a country boy, a product of the Jesuits and a Vietnam veteran. Not a bad vintage. Each of these influences is decisive in his quirky but complex character. He was born of German/Dutch descent in May 1946 in the NSW town of Lockhart, to Ralph and Barbara Fischer, his father a stock agent and his mother a nurse. There were five children, one dying young, the rest (either through marriage or career) giving the Fischers a cosmopolitan gloss.

Fischer went to Boree Creek primary and then spent six years boarding at Xavier College as a loner, a battler burdened by a speech impediment, but finally, a success, securing a matriculation pass. This is the pattern of his life. Fischer soon found himself conscripted, courtesy of the Menzies/Holt government. It was the real turning point. Entering the army in 1966 he was selected for officer training school, graduated as a second lieutenant, then served in the First Battalion Royal Australian Regiment in Australia and Vietnam as a platoon commander and transport officer. 'I missed that year of just being a beach bum or backpacking around the world,' Fischer says.

The Vietnam experience left him with two legacies—a penchant for leadership and a fascination for Asia. 'Suddenly commanding 30 lives in an infantry battalion at the back-end of Asia, aged 21, you grow up real fast,' Fischer says. 'It taught me about discipline, man management, organisation and how to handle pressure.' Fischer is proud of his service but doesn't play the hero: 'I wasn't a perfect platoon commander.'

It also taught him about pain and shock. In a rocket attack on Firebase Coral which killed one of his colleagues, Fischer took some shrapnel in the upper body and was dosed on morphine when 'I had my first and last cigarette, it was so uplifting; but I then vowed I'd never smoke again unless I was legally high on morphine again. That word is l-e-g-a-l-l-y, in case you miss it. So I've never smoked again.'

Between the fighting, the boy from Boree Creek was overwhelmed by Asia. It was R&R in Taipei, Singapore and Bangkok, a world for Fischer filled with 'vibrancy, colour, this whole get up and go mentality'. He returned to farming to 'get my breath and recover from malaria but I felt I was just parking myself'. Fischer didn't want to spend the rest of his life as a wheat grower.

What was driving him? Fischer's explanation is the key to his politics: 'I wanted to reach out and advance agendas I could see developing in Asia. But it was also selfish—it was a bread ticket out of the way of life I could have had as a farmer'—a mixture of opportunity and self-interest, the hallmarks of Fischer's career.

So he joined the Young Nationals and then the seniors. Located amid the NSW State seat of Sturt, Fischer was sounded out along the lines of 'why not run this time to get known and in fifteen years time you'll be ready to win'. Fischer's reply was typical: 'I'm aged 24. I've fought for my country. I've got a good education. I'll run to win or not at all.'

So he became a professional politician at 24, elected in 1970 to the NSW Legislative Assembly's bear-pit, travelling by slow train between Boree Creek and Sydney, chatting during the late hours, talking but listening, trying to keep warm, changing from the south-west mail to the Narrandera train on Junee's icy platform, having a bangers and mash breakfast during the freezing winters, getting to know the guards, the drivers, the ticket collectors, working through the ranks to becoming Whip and then even a shadow minister, changing State seats because of a redistribution and then, when a federal redistribution extended the seat of Farrer from Mt Kosciuszko to the South Australian border, making it into a bizarre, elongated seat taking in half of Fischer's State seat, and after Wal Fife and Noel Hicks said they didn't want it, then Tim Fischer decided this seat was for him. So he went to Canberra.

'You're mad, you'll be a State minister within four years,' Nick Greiner told him. But Fischer, poor fool, replied, 'Them are the breaks and the risks', and left. He was elected to federal Parliament at the 1984 poll, in a campaign which saw commentary about his sexuality. What price him becoming deputy prime minister? You couldn't have written longer odds.

But Fischer never really thought like that. Asked if he contemplated the federal leadership back in 1984, he says: 'Oh no, you do carry a general's baton in your kitbag. I thought it was unlikely to be a chance but I would do the party the best.' A typical convoluted reply. The tone means 'yes' even if the words imply 'no'.

Fischer's relations with flashy Ian Sinclair have never been good. He voted against Sinclair at the 1989 coup when youthful Charles Blunt was installed as leader for the Peacock–Blunt 1990 Coalition campaign. It didn't work. Fischer himself was the main beneficiary of the Peacock–Blunt 1990 failure when, as an unknown, unmarried Catholic (at least he was a farmer!) he surprised everyone (including many Nationals) by winning the leadership ballot, defeating another youthful contender, John Sharp. This time Fischer added cunning to discipline. The party room went for safety and Fischer read its mood. He occupied a leadership vacuum.

The media was agog at his victory press conferences when Fischer declared that he was 'a strong supporter of a super-freighter interstate concept of two-kilometre long freight trains, triple stacked motor cars, double stacked containers operating as unit trains from Parkes to Perth'. Yes, the man said it. 'Two Minute Tim' was short on leadership aura. The media lapsed into caricature. Sinclair told Fischer to get a wife. And Fischer had his first fight with John Hewson. The omens were not promising.

Yet Fischer displayed a political stamina to match his bush-walking. He became a survivor, a character and a loyalist. Fischer accommodated Hewson and his Fightback! He grasped the basics—the Nationals needed the coalition with the Liberals, desperately, but the party's craving for a separate identity had to be nourished and Tim was the man. He learnt from Blunt's failure that 'you can't be bland as a leader of a third party'. Hence the hat, the trains, the trips. But two events transformed his life—he found a wife and touched death on a country road.

Judy Brewer must be the best decision Fischer made. She's bright (qualifications in cattle management, computing, taxation and a lecturer in business administration at Charles Sturt University); she's political (former president of the Young Nationals, former member of the party's federal executive, former endorsed candidate and often mentioned as future federal MP); she has a Catholic background and still has her own farm near Wodonga; she's had the lion's share of raising their two boys, Harrison and Dominic; and, by the way, she's nice. The talk at dinner is all politics, domestic and then Asia, Britain and the Middle East. Judy might not try to influence Tim but have no doubt—she does.

When I asked Judy how many nights he had been home for a family dinner in the past month she replied 'two'. Judy, like everyone else, is amazed at Fischer's capacity for work and travel. Since becoming a minister he's made twenty overseas trips and visited 48 nations, many several times. The truth, though, is that he's being stretched thin. Tim can't keep going the way he is now.

He slows visibly when talking about the fatal crash: 'I took a full month off, for the first time. That was a bad mistake. It should have been three but politics, you know, it was just before John Hewson got knocked off . . .'

The two occupants of the other car were killed. They pulled in front of Fischer. The crash has left its mark. 'It was the first time, physically, that I started to feel limits to my stamina,' Fischer says. 'The functions I do today will be fine, but tomorrow I won't be as quick as I used to be. Mentally, you want to make every day count but balance priorities, get back to the family a bit more.'

His marriage and the car crash have combined to mellow and deepen Tim Fischer. Beneath the frenetic exterior he's more philosophical. Married relatively late, at 46 years, when he was already leader, Fischer reflects on the suicide attempt of Labor's Nick Sherry. 'Anybody in a single phase of their life has no-one to turn to for shared confidences,' he says. 'In politics there are no friends, only shifting alliances.' You realise, suddenly, that 'Two Minute Tim' has been lonely for much of his life. The family has 'added a great depth to my personal life' but, ever the professional, Tim gives the career assessment that the family is an 'added comfort zone' for him.

I spent a recent Saturday with Fischer. After putting down the phone to John Howard at 11.15 the previous evening, Fischer rose at 5.45 a.m., listened to the news and early 'AM'. At 6.15 he rang the local police, having heard about a tragic single engine plane crash in his electorate, with three killed. At 7 a.m. he arrived at Wagga airport by light plane after a 20-minute flight from his Boree Creek property.

We headed by car for Junee with Fischer cramming into my hand a document listing trade successes under his ministry. He's into exports from the start; it's a Fischer obsession. Then the countryside, it's a good season, and then, as we cross the train line, into rail transport, another obsession.

'A steel wheel on a steel rail has about a seventh of the friction of a rubber tyre wheel on a bitumen surface,' Fischer begins in the front seat as though he's addressing a mass audience. 'Therein lies the core advantage of rail for heavy duty freight task work and dense passenger movement, because it's so efficient.'

It's 7.15 a.m. Fischer summarises the national rail condition: 'Suburban—that's fine, freight—we're getting there. Where we are way off the pace is high speed passenger.' A Sydney-Canberra-Melbourne VFT is 'important in the medium-term'. They should sell tickets to the Cabinet discussion.

Fischer attends a Junee breakfast, next to the fire station. I'm struck immediately that he listens as well as talks. He knows many of the people by name. His speech is folksy, personal, sympathetic and about the hard economic decisions. He admits the government's in a 'rough patch' and that being National Party leader 'isn't easy' but 'we hang in there'. And everything is changing—there was once a time when State governments owned butchers' shops; now, farmers use computers to get into niche markets. Australia sends carriages to Malaysia, plastic keyrings to Iceland, whips to America, Jacob's Creek wine to the United Kingdom, which proves that 'distance neutral exports' can work from Junee. Get it? Fischer sounds disconnected—but the people always get the message. Always. Tim makes the connection.

We inspect the fire station, then we join the start of the Junee parade, but Fischer disappears and I find him at the Loco Hotel shouting a beer for some old mates. As we leave the pub the Sydney freight train is slowing passing through and Fischer calls over 40 metres to the driver in a friendly exchange that reveals both the train's weight and that Fischer can strike a dialogue with anyone, anywhere. It's 10.20 a.m.

We repair to the Junee Roundhouse, now a museum which, with its 100 foot turntable, has serviced every class of locomotive over five decades. It's the fiftieth anniversary celebration so Fischer tells the audience: 'Turn to the person on your left or right and give them a kiss or handshake, as may be appropriate.' It's a hoot. He holds up a train ticket to announce he's soon leaving on the 'XPT, 1.52 p.m., platform one, to visit another part of regional Australia'. Lunch is with the Country Women's Association, followed by a meeting with the Junee Council, and as we walk onto the platform Fischer has the mobile hard to his ear talking to John Howard. Yes, it's the Ministry reshuffle. As the XPT pulls in Fischer turns off the phone. He's happy. He's kept three Nationals in the Cabinet.

We hop aboard and I realise that Fischer doesn't walk down an aisle, he greets down the aisle. It's 50 minutes to Culcairn, into the car and another Fischer commentary: 'This is Remembrance Drive. About two kilometres along there's a tannery on the right and an abattoir on the left. The leather goes to Melbourne, it's prepared for car seats, then it's sent to Johannesburg where it's fabricated into a BMW car seat and then sent to Germany.' I'm feeling weary.

We finish our interview sitting on a rock at Morgan's Lookout (named after bushranger Dan Morgan) overlooking a magnificent vista. Fischer, under attack all year for his stance on Wik, says he 'has a spiritual feeling for the land' and that 'I never doubted the Aborigines had a deep-seated spiritual connection with the land'. Then, we're off again. It finishes as a twelve-hour day by air, car, train and foot. A Saturday.

Tim Fischer knows his worst moment since the Coalition's victory. It was that day in September last year at Gympie when

Fischer, with violent threats against him and his effigy hanging from a bloody noose, faced down an angry rally with firearms owners' boss, Ian McNiven, who had previously strutted his Adolf Hitler stuff. 'It was awful, just awful,' Fischer says, 'one of my most awful days in politics. We won but so what . . .'

Fischer's rough ride since the Coalition's 1996 victory has been caused by three breakaways—guns, Hanson and Wik. None could have been predicted, but they have threatened Fischer's leadership. Howard became a hero over the gun laws, but Fischer bore the backlash. He was rolled in Cabinet on a softer line and taunted in the bush for having 'no clout'. Stories appeared that his leadership was in trouble.

That's why Fischer had to win by keeping the $1.4 billion diesel fuel rebate and why he insisted from the start on a hard line after the Wik decision. It was a core constituency issue. Yet on Wik, Fischer had faced a fierce backlash by endorsing Howard's 10-point plan and abandoning the demands of many Nationals for blanket extinguishment of native title. Again, he was on the edge.

Fischer's dilemma is that there aren't easy solutions for rural Australia. The age of high tariffs and excessive price support schemes are gone. Howard's populism extends into regional Australia, which both helps and hinders Fischer. Yet loyalty is his watchword; he won't say a word against Howard though Howard is often insensitive to Fischer's problems with his own constituency. Fischer suffers from the delusions of the Queensland Nats, a party within a party. The debt the Liberals owe Fischer is profound—he has delivered a stable coalition amid an unstable National Party. There is a written coalition agreement, negotiated after each election between the leaders, dealing with Cabinet and Ministry representation. Fischer knows the Nationals are a very junior coalition partner; he says 'I'm not interested in false threats' to the Coalition, unlike others.

Fischer, unlike Howard, repeatedly attacks Hanson who, in turn, wants to destroy his leadership. He brands her policies as 'morally repugnant, just human indecency of an agenda which is racist' and 'equally importantly it is just tearing up our bread ticket'. Fischer dismisses as 'nonsense' any claim that Asia has to trade with us; the truth is that 'Asia can turn to other places'. As usual, Fischer appeals to self-interest against Hanson. But this is a fight for rural Australia's heart. What happens to Fischer if the Queensland Nats give Hanson their preferences?

It's obvious that Fischer is more liberal than National Party leaders are supposed to be. Once again, he's being stretched thin. Last year he floated support for a republic, but had to retreat in the teeth of party pressure. On the environment he warns that 'large areas of the northern hemisphere may face production restrictions' and that Australia is 'brilliantly situated'. His preferred legacy in public life is to create a nation 'engaged with the world and not insularised or a fortress Australia which would be absolutely the wrong way to go'. He sounds like Keating!

Fischer says he has five jobs—federal MP for Farrer, Minister for Trade, leader of the National Party, deputy prime minister and acting prime minister when Howard's abroad. That's how he plans his life. As our interview on the rock ends I ask Fischer how long he can keep going with his incredible schedule, his different jobs, his family responsibilities.

'I took off five days in winter,' he says. 'I took off about five, no I didn't as a matter of fact, I got squeezed out last summer. But, good question, haven't thought about it, just thinking quarter at a time, one quarter ahead.' This is how Fischer has always lived. Far from being a fool, he has learnt from the experiences of life. His achievements have been against the odds and this reveals his mettle. Fischer is a man of very ordinary ability and extraordinary stamina, courage and will to self-improvement.

The Weekend Australian, *10–11 January 1998*

PAUL HASLUCK ON AN
EARLIER LIBERAL AGE

Paul Hasluck's career has been remarkable, probably unique, by Australian standards. Hasluck was not only a journalist, historian, public servant, politician and governor-general but also a man who left a distinct contribution in each of these capacities.

He was of the old school. When Hasluck first came to Canberra, he rode a horse to work adjacent to a series of billabongs, now Lake Burley Griffin. Hasluck's values and style are reminiscent of an earlier age when life was slower, judgment was more measured and proper behaviour had a clear meaning.

Hasluck would have been dismayed by the subversion of the contemporary political process, by the media-induced circus of the daily five-second television sound bite, symptomatic of how technology and polls are debasing democracy.

Hasluck wrote throughout his life and *The Chance of Politics*, edited by his son, Nicholas, is a series of pieces Hasluck lodged with the National Library in his retirement, supplemented by further articles extracted by Nicholas from his father's writings. This book is an easy read that deepens the insight, a rare combination. It represents a genre that is virtually nonexistent in Australia—not a diary, neither a history nor a post-career memoir, it is rather a series of synchronous political portraits that are destined to become classics. These portraits have a freshness and power because of the advantages enjoyed by Hasluck—he was a professional writer with a grasp of the art of politics, evaluating his colleagues as an insider and writing at the time, not for publication but for the indefinite future. The result is riveting.

Hasluck describes these portraits as the result of his penchant to 'scribble' a few notes 'now and again when I had nothing better to do' and that he had 'no purpose in mind' but 'my own amusement'. Such modesty contrasts with the self-importance of today's literary lions who prowl but rarely strike. Yet Hasluck's modesty should not be mistaken for lack of care. He adds that, while the sketches 'are not to be taken as my final considered judgment' on each of the characters, in copying them to make the collection, 'I have not found occasion to make any alterations'.

Hasluck writes with a purpose. These sketches are robust, often harsh. The men of power whom Hasluck evaluates are drawn with their human frailties and usually found wanting. This book will carry weight when future histories are penned because of its ring of authenticity. The most powerful image is that of a post-Menzies Liberal Party bereft of talent, run by mediocrities, devoid of principle or direction, and consumed by petty jealousies and corrupting ambitions. Such a view of this period is not new; but it is something again to have it not merely confirmed but reinforced with such candour by Hasluck, the participant, who saw it all at close range and wrote his impressions.

The author engages in self-criticism, a welcome discipline and protection against the inevitable accusation that his sketches are influenced by personal resentments. Hasluck judges himself by the same standards he applies to others. For example, this is Hasluck's description of his own and of the Liberal Party's seminal reconciliation to Harold Holt as successor to Robert Menzies:

> There was still a considerable lack of confidence in him [Holt]
> in the party, however, and about 1960, when party members
> started to speculate about the successor to Menzies—and partic-
> ularly after the election of 1961—I was frequently sounded out
> by various persons usually along the lines: 'Harold just can't
> make it' (for this reason or that reason, but nearly always a
> different reason) 'and some of us were thinking about you'
> etc., etc. I discouraged these approaches, some of which had
> the signs of becoming very serious. There were several reasons

why I did so. Perhaps the strongest one was that I did not want to be prime minister . . .

I also made a political judgment with, I hope, full objectivity, that Harold Holt, though my inferior in intellectual grasp, understanding, knowledge and powers of analysis, was a far better parliamentarian than I could ever be, had an ardour for politics and political discussion that I did not have, had greater adaptability than I had and a cheerful sort of resilience that would help him to wear far better in the circumstances following a succession to leadership after Menzies than I would ever wear . . . In good conscience, I could not see anyone in the Liberal Party, not even myself, whom I could prefer to Holt. After a while, when Harold showed some wariness towards me, I told him plainly that I was not a rival and would support him.

There is an honesty in the high-minded Hasluck's sketches that gives weight to their credibility.

When *The Australian* obtained the serialisation rights to the book it was on the condition specified by the book's editor, Nicholas Hasluck, that the chapter on Sir William McMahon not be serialised. It is a searing, withering condemnation, perhaps the most damning portrait of a senior Australian politician ever penned by a colleague. Hasluck says:

I confess to a dislike of McMahon. The longer one is associated with him the deeper the contempt for him grows and I find it hard to allow him any merit. Disloyal, devious, dishonest, untrustworthy, petty, cowardly—all these adjectives have been weighed by me and I could not in truth modify or reduce any one of them in its application to McMahon. I find him a contemptible creature and this contempt and the adjectives I have chosen to apply to him sum up defects that, in my estimation of other people, cannot be balanced by better qualities . . . Contempt is a hard feeling towards another person. I suppose it may mean a failure in understanding. It certainly means a failure in balanced appreciation. It more widely removes one person from another than does scorn or hatred or even physical repugnance. McMahon is the only person with whom I have had close association over a number of years whom I have found contemptible . . .

He was disloyal and he could not be trusted and he worked for his own advancement by trying to destroy the

reputation of his rivals. He gave away Cabinet secrets, sometimes out of vanity and sometimes corruptly in order to buy
favours for himself from the press or to injure his colleagues.
He was [a] habitual liar and also a man who lied by calculation
about other people and about himself. He worked against
Menzies, against Holt, against [Sir John] McEwen and against
[John] Gorton.

Three years after Hasluck wrote these words, McMahon became
Prime Minister of Australia. This was the man chosen by fellow
Liberals in a party-room ballot and backed by a powerful media
cabal. What does this tell us about our democracy? Yes,
Hasluck's is just one man's view of a rival, an insider who had
nineteen years of experience of McMahon on which to draw. I
suggest that among Canberra veterans few would dispute
Hasluck's assessment. McMahon was unfit ever to become prime
minister and the party that elected him was similarly unfit to
govern. The law of politics, however, like that of physics, is that
vacuums must be filled.

McMahon, in fact, was the third prime minister in that
depressing post-Menzian troika during the 1966–72 period that
was the prelude to Gough Whitlam. Hasluck surrendered the
Menzian succession to Holt; after Holt drowned he ran and was
defeated by Gorton in the ballot for the prime ministership; at
the third stage when the Liberals, desperate over Gorton, finally
lurched to McMahon, Hasluck was ensconced at Yarralumla,
where his duty was to swear in the leader he had described as
'this puny little fellow with his platform soles and padded
shoulders'.

Hasluck also offers a searching critique of Holt as a politician lacking 'any wide range of thought or depth of
understanding or even occasional wisdom'. He rejects the orthodoxy that Menzies 'had consciously groomed Holt to be his
successor', arguing instead that Menzies had doubts about Holt
and thought no more than 'that Holt was the best available'.
Drawing upon his experience in foreign policy, Hasluck laments
that Holt could not see beyond his close relationship with
United States president Lyndon Johnson to the issue of Australian national interests, that he overvalued absurdly being able
to start a letter with 'Dear Lyndon' and that 'all the way with

LBJ' was 'one of the most harmful slogans we had to counteract in our Asian diplomacy'.

It just gets worse. Hasluck depicts the cheerful Holt as naive, shallow and flashy. He concludes that Holt should be judged only as 'a politician and a superficial man' and that Holt and his wife, Zara, were 'both vulgar people' who inflicted the 'ghastly' taste of their 'ill-formed personalities' upon the Lodge.

There is a deeper implication here, although it is not drawn by Hasluck: this is a prime minister devoid of any sense of Australian cultural self-confidence, with everything that means—a second-rate society unable to assume responsibility for itself. And McMahon was waiting in the wings!

In a second sketch written three months after Holt's death, Hasluck makes the hard call: death came when Holt could still be counted a success, while a year later he would probably have been seen as a failure. He depicts a prime minister on the verge of being overwhelmed by problems, growing tired and uninterested, the give-away being when 'a cheerful man becomes thoughtful'.

Hasluck's critique has consequences that extend far beyond Holt. His judgment implies that Menzies, the creator of the Liberal edifice, concealed by his own dominance the immaturity, dearth of talent and lack of political principle that bedevilled its ranks and was exposed by its subsequent history.

In his account of the crisis following Holt's death, Hasluck reveals he not only concluded that McEwen was justified in his refusal to work with McMahon as prime minister, but told the Country Party leader that 'I myself would find it impossible to work with McMahon'. With this account Hasluck confirms the report 30 years ago by journalist Alan Reid that Hasluck, like McEwen, vetoed a McMahon leadership at that time.

It is inevitable perhaps that Hasluck's opinion of Gorton deteriorated almost from the day that Gorton defeated him in the party ballot to replace Holt as prime minister. A fortnight after Gorton was sworn in, Hasluck declares that 'I have been living in a state of political innocence'—a conclusion prompted by his discovery that Gorton was scheming against Holt even before his death. Hasluck is puzzled by Gorton, who is more intelligent than Holt but mentally undisciplined. Gorton possessed instant charm, but could be embarrassingly rude; he was filled with great self-confidence, but had little self-knowledge;

most of his political ideas were rationalisations of what he already intended to do. His work habits were untidy and irregular, typified by uncertainty over when he would arrive at work or whether he would keep appointments, and he had a staff that acted like 'undisciplined pet dogs'.

In his 1970 sketch written from Yarralumla, Hasluck blames Geelong Grammar for not doing a better job on Gorton and concludes: 'I do not think he can be a great prime minister for, apart from the shortcomings I have mentioned, he seems to be lacking a clear purpose.' What was Gorton's purpose except to have power and stop the other fellow (that is, himself), Hasluck asked, and then answered his own question: 'I have not been able to see it.'

There are many other notable sketches. Hasluck, who was close to McEwen, provides a wonderful portrait of 'Black Jack', confirming his standing as superior to all politicians of his time except Menzies. McEwen saw politics 'as a contest for advantage, not a matter of doctrines or principles' and was 'a very selfish man' who 'expended himself beyond all reason in order to gain his own ends'.

The reputation of Richard Casey takes a further knock, with Hasluck branding him a man who found it 'congenial to be on parade', with an 'officer and gentleman' mentality. Hasluck debunks Casey, whose priority was to impress people rather than to master issues (the precise opposite of Hasluck), and reveals that Casey was a failure at the Cabinet table.

There are fascinating support pieces. Hasluck is baffled at Menzies' affection and regard for Defence Minister Athol Townley; he displays a chronic inability to read Whitlam, correctly fluctuating from distaste to admiration to disappointment; he makes an exaggerated assessment that Shane Paltridge had the makings of a good prime minister; he gives short shrift to Sir Garfield Barwick ('as well as being a batsman he wanted to be the best bowler too'); and he revives the credentials of World War I Defence Minister George Pearce (who Menzies once called 'the best allrounder' in politics).

There are two omissions from this book, one understandable, one not. No writer worth his salt discusses the court and ignores the king. The more one reads this book, the more one regrets that Hasluck did not sketch Menzies. The great writer needs to be tested against the great subject. Why did

Hasluck shirk the test? Nicholas Hasluck is acutely aware of this omission and spends a lot of the introduction referring to mentions of Menzies in the other portraits. The omission, however, leaves a vacuum at the heart of this book since it overlooks the colossus of this period; not just our longest serving prime minister but a leader about whom personal and historical judgments differ wildly and on which Hasluck could have exerted an influence. The excusable omission is the absence of a self-portrait. But it is really unnecessary. The reader will know the author by the book's end and, I suspect, the politician too.

Let me offer this description of Hasluck:

> [He] had fine integrity, high intelligence, strength, dedication and a sensitivity that had prevented him from fitting comfortably into the harsh political environment in which he had been thrust by the Liberal-Country Party victory of 1949. Rather withdrawn and with a larger sense of mission than of humour, he lacked the redeeming quality that so many democratic politicians have of being able to laugh at themselves and their pretensions . . . He believed that merit should bring its own reward and did not recognise that men like McEwen and McMahon and Gorton . . . genuinely assumed that their merit was superior and were prepared to work at the task of persuading their colleagues into acceptance of this assessment . . . Hasluck would have preferred voting for party office to be guided by some mystic spontaneous force rather than by lobbying, energy and organisation on the part of the candidate. Hasluck was moralistic, believed that ambition should be paraded, not in honest nakedness but modestly clothed . . .

The author was Alan Reid writing in 1968 in *The Power Struggle*. I am presumptuous enough to suggest that, had Reid the chance to review Hasluck's book, he would not have changed a single word of his portrait of Hasluck.

The Australian's Review of Books, *9 April 1997*

TIME TO RECONSIDER THE MANY FACES OF MENZIES

Leadership is persuasion . . . If I were to rate one postwar leader even above the others, it would not be one of the legendary European or American figures. It would be Robert Menzies.

—Former US president Richard Nixon

HE IS JOHN Howard's hero, the slayer of Labor's dreams, the hate figure for our intellectuals, a caricature as the Queen's man, an utter spellbinder as a performer and our most successful politician.

The huge inescapable figure of R.G. Menzies dominates our past but baffles our comprehension. There is little agreement about Menzies 105 years after his birth, 60 years after he first became prime minister and 33 years since his departure. Is Menzies a national embarrassment or a supreme political artist of the century?

His career of promise, success, rejection, reappraisal, defeat and then sustained victory offers conflicting interpretations. Menzies won seven elections, a Bradmanesque record never likely to be equalled. Labor had only one resort: to de-legitimise the man and his legacy. Paul Keating continued this campaign into the 1990s knowing that destroying Menzies' reputation is the key to discrediting the Coalition tradition.

The second volume of Allan Martin's biography of Menzies completes the most authoritative account of our most dominant

101

prime minister. Martin has now written more than 1000 pages on the Menzies story in a fifteen-year effort.

The book highlights the obstacles to debate about Menzies. There is the impression that his election wins owed much to luck—more the result of the Labor Party split than Menzies' own political skill. Next is the paradoxical assertion of critics that while life in Australia improved greatly during Menzies' 1949–66 rule, such gains, somehow, amazingly, had absolutely nothing to do with him.

Finally, the sheer length of his rule means there are many Menzies—the failed war leader, the free enterprise champion, the anti-communist crusader, the full employment specialist and the Vietnam commitment instigator. It is easier to embrace a stereotype than to incorporate the many parts into a leader of complexity.

Menzies has been loathed by the intellectual class. Humphrey McQueen said that 'he switched from British sycophant to American lick-spittle and back again . . . he undoubtedly could have found the resources within himself to lead a Vichy-style regime for the Japanese'. Donald Horne said Menzies' 'great talent was to preside over events and look as if he knew what they were all about'.

Martin's book should provoke a deeper and wiser debate about the multifaceted Menzies. His work leaves us with three impressions—that Menzies' success, far from being inevitable, was a close-run thing; that in his strengths and failures Menzies was a man of his times; and that Menzies succeeded not because of some national aberration but because he appealed to deep instincts and needs within our political culture.

This volume opens in 1944 with Menzies, having returned to the Opposition leadership, taking charge of a rump of twelve MPs, facing a successful wartime Labor government. Menzies had to create the Liberal Party, rehabilitate his image, counter the slogan 'you can't win with Menzies' and absorb a crushing 1946 election loss to Ben Chifley which was a personal rejection of himself. In January 1947, Menzies confided his deepest fear to his mentor Owen Dixon, that 'he knew that he was the subject of dislike and hostility throughout the community and thought perhaps his party could not win under his leadership'.

Chifley's effort to introduce socialism via bank nationalisation gave Menzies the kiss of life. His free enterprise crusade became the unifying theme at the watershed 1949 election, when defeat would have cast Menzies as our greatest political failure.

That Menzies' victory opened the way for 23 years of Coalition rule is totally a judgment in hindsight. The 1949–54 period was high-risk consolidation. It meant a double dissolution in 1951, surviving the early-fifties inflation boom and crunch, and defying expectations of a Labor win to prevail at the 1954 election. It was at this point that Menzies broke Labor's spirit.

Menzies was a man of his time. After beating Chifley in 1949 he retained Chifley's advisers, his immigration program, his development ethos, his Keynesian economics and his public enterprises. While backing free enterprise, Menzies expanded the role of the Commonwealth government, grew Canberra and underwrote the transformation of Australia in the great university expansion. Martin notes that in 1957 there weren't many votes in being pro-university.

Menzies' total lack of interest in meeting Aborigines, along with an absence of encouraging women to break from the home, can be branded as reactionary today. Yet such attitudes merely typified his times, despite some honourable exceptions. His exploitation of the communist issue has passed into Labor folklore, yet Martin argues that Menzies was also genuine—he feared another war, possibly a world war, against communism.

It is true that by the sixties Australia was changing beyond Menzies. Sometimes he adapted adroitly, such as his State aid policy for the 1963 election. But other examples display a frozen rigidity, notably his refusal to change the White Australia Policy.

Menzies lived in a different age—no fax, no talkback. His standards in public life would be a beacon today. Yet he never saw government as being dominated by the task of reform. Menzies was a great political artist and his judgment of the people was acute. If you like to fantasise, think of Menzies being interviewed by today's talkback sultans, Alan Jones and John Laws, how he would engage them and then dispatch them.

The Australian, *17 November 1999*

PART III

THE MOOD OF THE 1990s

EACH DECADE IS given its own character by the media and the entertainment industry. The 1990s will surely become the decade when technology empowered individual liberty. The final decade of the twentieth century saw the decline of many of the institutions which had guided the State and society for so long and, in their place, rose a new potential for individual accomplishment. But the microchip and the Internet do not create a successful or stable society.

The 1990s saw a shift back towards individual responsibility, thereby reversing the century-long rise of government authority. The truth is that globalisation and market forces have reduced both national sovereignty and State power. Governments have only a limited ability to solve social problems and promote individual happiness. Globalisation demands a new strategic role for governments—a more limited role such that governments focus on what they do best. That means sanctioning the operation of the market but deciding the rules by which it should be policed.

The paradox is that while governments have less power political leaders are more important than ever. The industries of politics, entertainment and religion are merging. The millennium leader is expected to be a politician, a manager, and a therapist for the nation. The ruthlessness of market forces has renewed the debate about society. The first requirement of political leadership is to support the philosophy of an inclusive society since the pressures for fragmentation are so great.

The upshot in Australia is a debate along two lines—the need to manage a successful open economy and to run social policies which give the individual and family an ownership in the new economy.

THE CULTURE OF THE 1990s

THE *AUSTRALIAN* RECENTLY published a special section to commemorate the 1000-day presidency of John Kennedy on 22 November—the 30th anniversary of his assassination. It seemed a natural publishing initiative, and our circulation, I am pleased to report, rose appreciably that day. But in many ways it was unusual; going to such lengths to commemorate the leader of another country who died 30 years ago and who had little real contact with Australia.

I am sure that most people would recall the factors which made the Kennedy presidency memorable in his time and still vivid in our time. I don't want to discuss Kennedy's merits as a president, but I would highlight several aspects of Kennedy's political ethos which dramatise for us today just how different political leadership is in the 1990s.

First, people believed in the early 1960s that governments could solve the economic and social problems of the age; there was a faith in government and in government's ability to produce solutions. This reached its zenith in America in the Kennedy/Johnson years and in Australia during the early Whitlam era.

Second, in the 1960s, people were prepared to believe in and follow a strong and communicative leader—charismatic was the word—and this belief, perhaps even this trust, reflected the hope and optimism of people.

Third, Kennedy was a war president. The Cold War, of course. The ethos of the time was pervaded by the war-like confrontation between democracy and communism. Leadership was a daunting task then. But Cold War leaders had some advantages that today's leaders don't have—they had the focus of a permanently external enemy, a mystique of leadership that had not been penetrated by the media's obsession with private lives, the kudos from being seen to have out-nerved or out-smarted the communists and the appeal to unity and the common interest necessitated by an external threat to the essence of democracy.

Fourth, the Kennedy period, although it was not recognised at the time, was the final high tide of American hegemony. Those leaders governed from a position of strength and this was recognised by the people.

Fifth, Keynesian stabilisation policies still continued to be successful and this post-World War II era was a time of steady growth, job creation and price containment.

By contrast, what do we have today?

We have an international environment where uncertainties, confusion and new issues abound. It is a period when the magnitude of the problems seems to far outweigh the capacity of leaders to imagine, let alone execute, solutions.

Where people previously believed in government, they are now sceptical of government—yet they have no alternative faith. Where people previously believed in at least some political leaders, today there is cynicism, mistrust or disgust with leaders and the political system itself. Where people previously responded to the challenge of the Cold War, they are confused and dismayed by the uncertain peace in its wake. Finally, where people were comforted by the dominance of the West in both military and cultural terms, we are now seeing the East rise again—Asia is an economic miracle, a new political dynamic and a growing military force. Where people had the confidence of prosperity, they now have the recent experience of the worst recession in 60 years and the relative economic decline of many Western countries.

These five fundamental changes, which I believe can be shown dramatically in the contrast between the Kennedy era and the Clinton era—and are reflected in Australia as well—provide the international framework for the politics of the 1990s.

I want to discuss what might be the culture of 1990s politics.

My starting point is that the 1990s are different, and will become even more different. They won't be a repeat of the

1980s. Anyone who fails to grasp this will be left behind. Who would have predicted two or three years ago that Clinton, not Bush, would win the White House, or that Keating, not Hewson, would win the Lodge, or that Mabo would dominate domestic politics in 1993, or that the Soviet Union would no longer exist, or that Europe would be plunged into its worst war since 1945, or that the LDP would lose office in Japan?

Success will come to those who pick the trends. I don't pretend to know what these trends are, but I have some speculations for the 1990s road map.

I want to begin by sketching, at the broadest level, the two great forces that are now coming into conflict, not just in Australia, but in most of the industrialised democracies.

The first force is the continued power of free market ideas, underwritten by economic and financial globalisation. I argue that, despite the severity and length of the 1990s recession, no alternative policy paradigm has been found to reverse the direction of the 1980s. I'm not saying there won't be policy changes; of course there will be changes. Many people want to see the 1980s market-oriented policies reversed completely. What I am asserting is that the intellectual case for a new model has not really been put, let alone won.

This is quite extraordinary. Let me illustrate the point with reference to Australia.

Despite 11 per cent unemployment and a prolonged downturn, the financial system has not been re-regulated; the protection cuts have not been cancelled; the declared stance of government remains that of cutting the federal deficit to the equivalent of 1 per cent of GDP—that is, an ongoing budget deficit is not seen as any solution to our problems; there is strong official and political support for maintaining low inflation; it is the orthodoxy that we must run an open competitive economy integrated into the Asia–Pacific. I am not aware that the recession itself has produced any new or revived role for government in solving our problems. However, we are yet to see how Mr Keating responds to the Green Paper on unemployment. Even if we see a greater degree of government intervention to address long-term structural unemployment, it is doubtful whether this will be at the cost of fiscal policy.

Even in those areas where the Keating government is failing, it still professes to believe in the 1980s philosophy. For example,

Laurie Brereton's new industrial law is presented as a flying wedge for new enterprise agreements, although it is nothing of the sort. The Keating government still formally supports more microeconomic reform, greater structural change and privatisation despite the lack of recent progress in some of these areas.

Contrary to what many people would like and what many others would assert, the recession hasn't smashed the 1980s policy mould. There is no new design to replace the 1980s system. To grasp this fully, one needs to observe events, not just in Western Europe and the United States, but in China, Indonesia, India, Mexico and Eastern Europe. In these countries deregulation, privatisation, microeconomic reform, new investment and structural change proceed apace. What this means for Australia is that there is no going back from the new direction we charted in the 1980s. The world simply won't permit us this luxury.

In my book *The End of Certainty* published in November 1992, I identified the forces driving our national adjustment. These forces will offer us no respite. My argument was that in five areas, Australia is undergoing decisive transitions, although they are occurring at different speeds. They are:

- the replacement of White Australia with multicultural Australia;
- the shift from protection to a relatively open economy;
- the move from centralised wage fixation towards a new enterprise-based culture;
- the decline of reliance upon government to solve problems and its replacement by a greater sense of individual responsibility; and, finally,
- the collapse of imperial benevolence, which means an acceptance of national maturity in our recognition that a great power will no longer bale Australia out.

In summary, the recession has slowed the pace of some of these changes, but they still continue. The forces propelling Australia's transition are powerful and international. They are implicit in the operation of global markets for finance and products; in the collapse of the Cold War security system; in the rise of the economic power of the Asia–Pacific; in the new world of instant communication technology. The 1990s will see policies being adapted and altered but, so far, they have not produced a new philosophical framework to replace the 1980s paradigm.

There is, however, another great force which has emerged—the people are in revolt. There is a new assertion of democratic power coming from the grassroots. More precisely, the middle class is sceptical and hostile. Paul Keating and Bill Clinton both won their last elections through exploiting this middle-class sentiment. The middle-class revolt is against the 1980s, against the policies and consequences of the 1980s. You remember the 1980s—they promised a nirvana and ended in recession.

The middle class thinks the 1980s tax cuts favoured the rich. It thinks the sharemarket was largely manipulated by corporate crooks. It believes that easy bank lending led to the crash; that deregulation was too often a licence for greed. The middle class is shrinking. A small element at the top has broken off to become rich, but a much larger chunk has fallen off the bottom to join the underprivileged. The middle class feels under threat at home and at work. It is worried about employment security, income maintenance, the upheaval in the family, changing social and sexual norms, and it is fearful about the rising incidence of crime. People are worried that they can't control their lives any more.

Hugh Mackay has captured this mood superbly. In his research he has mapped the psyche of 1990s Australia and has called this the age of discontinuity and of redefinition. Mackay says: 'The story of Australia between the early 1970s and the early 1990s is the story of a society which has been trying to cope with too much change too quickly and on too many fronts.' I can't think of a clearer warning for all those economists who believe that the national malaise demands faster economic change for the rest of this decade.

The people are shell-shocked. Paul Keating won the last election on a campaign against the GST. But this succeeded because the voters wanted security and feared radical change. The public wants economic progress but it also wants social security. People won't gamble on economic change for its own sake. The dominant middle-class sentiment is to distrust economists and to look sceptically on politicians. The middle class is suspicious about market forces and is hostile to the slogan of economic rationalism. In the election, John Hewson was the radical and Paul Keating depicted himself as the mainstream politician. Keating won despite the recession because, ultimately this middle-class sentiment broke his way.

Listen to Hugh Mackay again: 'The common cry now being heard around Australia is, "why does everything have to change so fast?", the common complaint is that individual Australians feel as if they have lost control of their own lives and their own destiny . . . growing numbers of Australians feel as if their personal identities are under threat as well. "Who are we?" soon leads to the question "Who am I?".'

Of course, this is tied to the loss of faith in institutions and the decline of traditional values. The dwindling support for our mainstream institutions is manifest—Church, Parliament, marriage, trade unions, political party. There is great anxiety now over gender roles, the strength of the family, financial security, moral values and cultural and race relations.

I now want to put together the two trends I have identified. On the one hand there is globalisation which demands greater competitiveness and more economic reform. On the other hand there is the demand from the people for more stability and security. The upshot is a profound tension in our political system as these two forces collide. The economic market demands one solution but the political market is demanding another.

The tension is clear in most Western countries, but it is particularly strong in Australia and New Zealand. The result is the current unsettled period of relative inactivity in economic reform, of political compromise, trade-offs, the search for diversions by some leaders and a series of lost opportunities.

Political leaders are searching for a way through this gulf between the demands the economic market places on them and the contradictory pressures from the political market. We can put two interpretations on the current situation in Australia, both of which have some validity. The first is that we have lost our way as a nation; that we are stranded halfway or thereabouts on the path to a new political culture; that we have broken decisively from the past, but have lost our directional compass and our courage to keep pressing forward. The other view, more optimistic, is that human nature being what it is, it is therefore sensible for governments to soft pedal reform after the recession; that it is desirable to wind back the pace of change, reassure the voters and stabilise the system. A further ration-

THE CULTURE OF THE 1990s   115

alisation here is that it was also time for corporate Australia to get its balance sheets in order—to reduce debt, cut costs, streamline procedures and change its strategic outlook.

It is true that during 1993 both the rhetoric and the policy momentum for ongoing economic reform has been conspicuously weak. Where is the real champion of economic reform today in federal politics? In truth, there isn't one. I would make the point that you can't expect people to support ongoing and faster economic reform when the case is not being argued on a sustained basis by political leaders. Don't expect the people to support a cause if the cause isn't being championed.

Paul Keating's challenge is to overcome the essentially status quo platform on which he won the 1993 federal election. The interesting and basic questions for Keating's prime ministership is whether he will advance the cause of those economic changes which he advocated as Treasurer. It would be a singular irony if Keating as Prime Minister were retarding the next stage of the very reforms he initiated as Treasurer.

One danger for Australia is that the Labor government may think it can rely on the gradual upswing in the world economy and the business cycle to deliver it the next election. The problem here is that Australia may get caught short on the structural reforms needed to underwrite any sustained recovery.

As for the federal Coalition, it remains crippled by its 1993 election defeat. The Liberals put the case for economic change, but in a lopsided, GST-biased and ultimately unconvincing fashion. Their defeat was a setback for reform. Now the Liberals are bitter at their loss, sceptical about putting their cards on the table, unsure of their beliefs and, to the extent they still back economic reform, are yet to fathom how to present the case to the voters.

At another level, Paul Keating has two choices in appealing to voters, both of which represent alternative re-election strategies. The first is the 'true believers' strategy; he can try to resurrect the Whitlam constituency of sectional interests—unions, artists, women, migrants, Aborigines, Australian nationalists and public sector employees. I don't believe such a strategy would suffice. The 'true believers' approach can briefly invigorate the Labor Party, but it can't win an election. At a deeper level such rhetoric only conceals the basic political issue which will confront the Labor Party in the future—how does the ALP, whose formation and success as a party has been closely associated with the old Australian Settlement, reinvent itself for the Australia of the twenty-first century which has left the Australian Settlement ideas far behind.

Keating's alternative election strategy is to construct a new coalition for growth in the 1990s. I believe this is the preferable approach. The strategy would be to fashion a coalition that supported vigorous growth politics within a framework of social justice. This is the position I outlined on the last pages of *The End of Certainty* when I said Labor's challenge was to 'attempt a new synthesis between the ALP ethos and the Hawke–Keating legacy of market economics'. I went on to say that the challenge for our political leaders was to internationalise the economy within a framework of traditional Australian values of justice and equity.

Economic reformers must change the political ethos in which they operate. If they don't then they will fail in the 1990s. We need a new ethos for economic growth in Australia, and this both begins and ends with the persuasive argument that economic growth and social compassion are closely linked. Too often in the past, growth and structural change have been sold the wrong way. The emphasis has been on the means, not the ends—cutting programs, cutting wages, cutting off people from their lives to which they have grown accustomed. In short, growth has almost taken on an 'anti-people' overtone. All such rhetoric and thinking must now be cast aside.

People will make sacrifices and they will respond to real leadership. The people know Australia has deep-seated problems. They don't expect overnight solutions, but they do want an agenda of solutions because they care about the future of their children. They are profoundly disenchanted with the existing leaders and existing parties. They want honesty and they want politicians who can speak clearly and directly. The political leader who does this will be able to mobilise community opinion.

Economic reformers will get nowhere in the 1990s if they only rekindle in the public's mind the fear of another bout of social Darwinism. People aren't interested in society as a survival of the fittest. The Australian people want social justice, and economic reformers need to talk and address the issues of equity and access, not just growth. Any attack on the welfare state ethos will be disastrous—yet people will support governments denying welfare to those who don't need it, or taking action to wind back the open-ended nature of unemployment benefits.

The people are weary of the divisive nature of established politics. They want leadership which tries to establish a basis for social cooperation. People don't want their society divided and they don't want an economic underclass.

Economic reformers should be aware of the stakes involved in the coming debate about how to address levels of high unemployment. There will be a political battle in which some people will want to cancel the gains of the 1980s. So economic reformers must win this political fight. The truth is that Australia can't turn around and march backwards, deny competitive pressures and try to resurrect barriers to markets. The community will respond if politicians speak with more honesty, demonstrate political skills and get the right balance in rhetoric and policy between growth and compassion. The leader who charts a fair way forward for Australia will prevail in the 1990s.

Speech to the Institute of Public Affairs, Melbourne, February 1994

THE MYTH OF AUSTRALIA
AS A TORN NATION

AUSTRALIA IS DEPICTED as a 'torn country' engaged in a futile and misguided effort to redefine itself as an Asian society, according to an influential book recently released in the United States.

The analysis that catapults Australia's identity debate into the international arena of ideas is provided by Professor Samuel P. Huntington, whose article 'The Clash of Civilisations', published in *Foreign Affairs* journal in 1993, sought to establish a new paradigm for the post-Cold War world.

Huntington's article did not mention Australia. But the book *The Clash of Civilisations and the Remaking of World Order*, which elaborates the original thesis, argues that Australia, along with Turkey, Mexico and Russia, is engaged in a doomed endeavour to remake its culture.

Huntington's argument constitutes a powerful critique of the national direction charted by Paul Keating. His book suggests that Australia's identity debate will attract greater international attention and that the cultural issue, implicit in the anti-Asian cry of Pauline Hanson, must be addressed at a deeper level.

Huntington's thesis can be summarised in four propositions: that in the post-Cold War world, civilisations, not ideology, will shape power rivalries; that the balance of power among civilisations is shifting against the West; that efforts to shift nations from one civilisation to another are unsuccessful; and that the survival of the West depends upon a reaffirmation by

Western nations of their civilisation as unique and abandoning its universalist pretensions.

'A torn country', according to Huntington, 'has a single predominant culture which places it in one civilisation but its leaders want it to shift to another civilisation'. Torn countries are often identifiable by their leaders referring to them as a bridge between two cultures.

Mustafa Kemal Ataturk (who led the Turkish forces against the Anzacs at Gallipoli) made Turkey a torn country by rejecting its Islamic past and launching a massive effort of Westernisation.

During the 1980s, the primary aim of Turkey's Western-oriented elite became to join the European Union—an ambition so far denied because Europe feels that Turkey, with its 60 million Muslims, does not fit culturally within the EU. The upshot is that Turkey is stranded between Mecca and Brussels, a torn nation.

Huntington argues that Mexico became a torn country with President Carlos Salinas de Gortari pursuing economic liberalism and taking Mexico into the North American Free Trade Agreement—his objective being to shift from a Latin American to a North American identity.

Australia, by contrast with Turkey and Mexico, has been a Western society from its inception—but is now trying to defect.

Huntington asserts: 'In the early 1990s, Australia's political leaders decided, in effect, that Australia should defect from the West, redefine itself as an Asian society and cultivate close ties with its geographical neighbours. Australia, the Prime Minister Paul Keating declared, must cease being a "branch office of empire", become a republic and aim for "enmeshment" in Asia. The case for redefining Australia as an Asian country was grounded on the assumption that economics overrides culture in shaping the destiny of nations.'

Australia's Asian ploy, according to Huntington, cannot succeed for three reasons. First, there is no consensus from Australia's elites for the switch, with the Liberal Party being ambivalent or opposed. Second, public opinion is also ambivalent. Third, and most important, 'the elites of Asian countries have been even less receptive to Australia's advances than European elites have been to Turkey's. They have made it clear that if Australia wants to be part of Asia it must become truly

Asian, which they think unlikely if not impossible . . . Asians see a gap between Australia's Asian rhetoric and its perversely Western reality.'

Huntington quotes Malaysia's Prime Minister, Dr Mahathir, saying that 'culturally Australia is still European' and hence should not be a member of the East Asian Economic Caucus.

Huntington's conclusion is that Asians are determined to exclude Australia from their club for the same reason that Europeans do Turkey—'they are different from us'.

He argues that Keating's ambitions for Australia had a global import: 'Australia could be the first of possibly many Western countries to attempt to defect from the West.' This choice may be seen, ultimately, as a 'major marker in the decline of the West'.

Australia, according to Huntington, should seek deeper alignments with the US and a Pacific community whose values, 'accord far more with Australian values than do those of any Asian country'. By pledging to Asia, our leaders will induce a cultural schizophrenia.

Huntington's argument about Australia will attract much attention—but is he right?

Sadly, it seems the Harvard guru has misunderstood the intentions of both Keating and our 'Asian enmeshment' advocacy.

The best outline of Keating's position came in his Singapore lecture last January when he said: 'I've never believed that Australians should describe themselves as Asians or that Australia is or can become part of Asia . . . I have said more than once before we can't be Asian any more than we can be European or North American or African. We can only be Australian and can only relate to our neighbours as Australians.'

This involves a repudiation not just of Huntington's view of Australia but of his theory of civilisations.

John Howard, of course, insists that Australia is not Asian, that it is not trying to switch cultures. Howard wants a closer relationship with the US, but says that our links with Asia and the US are not mutually exclusive—that we can have both.

Huntington's thesis on Australia is provocative, but wrong.

Enmeshment with Asia does not mean that Australia becomes an Asian society or tries to switch civilisations. It means, in fact, we become a more pluralistic, multicultural society, more influenced by Asia and, in turn, influencing Asia.

But the Huntington thesis can serve a purpose—it can help our leaders to define their vision with more precision at a time when this is a domestic necessity.

The Australian, *27 November 1996*

VALUES AND THE CONSTITUTION

DEMOCRACY HAS JUST achieved its greatest triumph—the victory over totalitarianism—but there is a paradox within this triumph. It is the cynicism, apathy and distrust that characterises the public's attitude towards the system of democratic government in many of the world's democracies, including Australia.

A pointer to the malaise is that at the recent United States election the turnout fell to 49 per cent—a gradual deterioration from nearly 63 per cent at the Kennedy–Nixon 1960 election. It is the worst turnout since the 1924 election.

It is easy to understand the cynicism at the process of demand and promise which is now an agonising ritual. The politicians compete with election promises; the media discharges its responsibility by demanding maximum detail; the voters cast their ballots; the winner adjudicates on which promises to honour and which to abandon; the public's cynicism is confirmed and the media cries 'foul'.

The lessons to be drawn from this ritual are reasonably simple.

First, the people expect too much from government and ask too little of themselves. Second, the politicians promise more than they can deliver, a condition that arises not from miscalculation but from ambition. Third, it is better for unsustainable promises to be abandoned than implemented. Fourth, the danger of demanding that politicians provide details of their election promises is that it only encourages those whom it fails to shame. Fifth, the community no longer expects the promises to be honoured, which raises questions as to their value in the first place.

Democracy was not intended to be like this. The more scientific our politics becomes, the less successful is our political system. Market research is so precise that leaders know what the people feel and how they express those feelings. Accordingly, in their campaign pitch the leaders promise voters what they want in the very language that the voters have used in survey groups. The paradox is why the voters so distrust the leaders who articulate so closely their own moods.

There are many responses required to address the condition of our democracy, but one of them must surely relate to values.

As a nation we have made a virtue of making fairly minimal changes to our system of governance and a typical remark today is that 'our system works well, so why change it?'

But our system doesn't work too well if there is such scepticism towards our governance. Another point that is often underestimated in Australia is that democracy needs to be renewed. As part of this process our community should have a more rigorous debate about values with the aim being to enshrine the core values in our Constitution.

Critics will say this is creating division for mere symbolism; the answer to them is that divisions are being created now that could be reduced in the future by this endeavour. There is an ideal time for this move—the 2001 centenary of Federation. That event should be the occasion for celebration, recognition of our achievements but, also, an affirmation of our beliefs. The exercise must be bipartisan across the main parties and this should be possible.

One option is to include such value statements in a new preamble to the Constitution; another would be to include the preamble in the Constitution. The outline, if not the detail, of the core values is reasonably clear.

The first should be a recognition of the Aborigines and Torres Strait Islanders as the original inhabitants of the land. There will be no satisfaction in Australia until such constitutional recognition is afforded. It is a moral imperative given the historical record; it is an opportunity to redress, on the Centenary of the Commonwealth, the racial bias in the original document.

The existing Constitution makes no mention of the indigenous people. That should now be corrected given the High Court's decision in the Mabo case and its rejection of the doctrine of terra nullius. There should perhaps be a further recognition that the Aborigines and Torres Strait Islanders seek to live in a reconciled and peaceful State under the law with their fellow citizens.

Second, there should be an explicit constitutional commitment to racial non-discrimination as a cornerstone of our society. This is particularly important for Australia given our history. It is racial values where Australia's ethics have changed most over the past hundred years. The White Australia Policy that was tied to the Australian identity has passed into history; the age that produced that philosophy has gone.

Australia has moved decisively to become a multiracial and multicultural society united in the one nation. This principle of racial non-discrimination is fundamental to our new sense of identity. It should be recognised in our Constitution. In this fashion it will be a constant reminder for Australians of their core belief and, just as potent, it will remind the international community of what sort of ideals exist in this land. With such a constitutional provision the nation would have been far better equipped to handle the recent debate triggered by Pauline Hanson.

The bipartisan resolution of federal Parliament was necessary precisely because there was no overarching statement of the nation's values on this issue. The resolution reaffirmed the commitment of the Parliament 'to the rights of all Australians to enjoy equal rights and be treated with equal respect regardless of race, colour, creed or origin'. It reaffirmed the commitment 'to maintaining an immigration policy wholly non-discriminatory on grounds of race, colour, creed or origin'.

The Prime Minister told the Parliament that the resolution contained commitments 'to the kind of Australian society that I believe in and have always believed in'. He said it contained a commitment 'to some common Australian values which are held by Australians' irrespective of where their ancestors came from.

There will be many tribulations ahead for Australia as it continues its remarkable transition from an inward-looking white Anglo-Celtic fortress to a multicultural nation integrated into the Asia–Pacific.

It is because there will be unpredictable debates and storms in the future that the core values should be given constitutional sanction.

The responsibility for producing a new constitutional preamble could be assigned by the federal Parliament to the Coalition's promised constitutional convention.

The exercise should deal only with the core values—liberty, equality, voting rights in our representative democracy, racial non-discrimination and recognition of the indigenous inhabitants. It is appropriate that such rights be complemented by a commitment to the unity of the nation and a responsibility to Australia.

There will be an immense pride in our national achievement as the centenary of Federation approaches. It is hard to believe there will not also be a willingness to respond to a sensible ratification of core values in a move sponsored across the major parties.

Democracy needs renewal. Any notion that democracy exists in a deep freezer for preservation is misconceived.

The Australian, *11 December 1996*

TARIFFS, A FALSE MOVE

DURING A DISCUSSION fifteen years ago about Asia's economic success, Prime Minister Lee Kuan Yew told me that he intended to move offshore most of Singapore's footwear, clothing and textile industry.

The reason? Lee explained that he wanted Singapore to develop as a high wage, high education, high export, high value-added society. His vision was clear and he was true to his word. Per capita income in Singapore today ($42 600) far exceeds Australia's ($28 770)—although it was far behind during this discussion on Malcolm Fraser's plane as we left a conference in India.

Singapore now is close to a free trade nation, with more than 96 per cent of its import value being duty free. It is a classic study in the nexus between open trade and national prosperity.

Lee didn't have to worry about democratic delicacies. And exact parallels between Singapore and Australia are false. But the story has a message for Australians today as the Howard Cabinet decides on the Productivity Commission's final report calling for a further tariff cut in textiles, clothing and footwear.

The TCF industry rejects the commission's recommendation that from 2001 tariffs be cut from 15 per cent and 25 per cent to only 5 per cent by 2008. This would maintain the current steady cuts in protection. The industry demands, instead, a pause in tariff cuts from 2000 to 2005. This mirrors the Cabinet's decision on cars.

The executive director of the Council of Textile and Fashion industries, Peter Kreitals, says the aim is to see the industry 'start to grow again' during the tariff pause. He predicts that if the Productivity Commission report is accepted and a tariff pause rejected, then the industry will lose jobs on a massive scale.

At a meeting ten days ago, the TCF industry and unions felt they got a good hearing from the Prime Minister. In a decisive signal, John Howard publicly said that job security would be 'absolutely paramount' in the decision and attacked Labor as the tariff-cutting party. All the signs last night were that the Prime Minister favoured a five-year pause.

This decision is the real test of the post-pneumonia, 'new look', reforming Howard, who since his return from sickness has championed tax reform and the Wallis financial reforms, and evidently wants to tackle waterfront reform, too.

But TCF is the litmus test. It will tell us whether the 'new look' Howard is fair dinkum or just a phoney tough.

It's the litmus test because it is a hard reform that takes skill, since it will hurt some people. It's the litmus test because many senior ministers—Peter Costello, Tim Fischer and John Anderson (you can add Alexander Downer)—have signalled their support for more TCF trade liberalisation, which means that Howard either backs them or denies them. It's the litmus test because it will determine whether the government's support for trade liberalisation as outlined in its recent White Paper is to be taken seriously or dismissed here and overseas as rhetoric.

Finally, it's the litmus test because it requires a compelling vision (yes, vision) of Australia's future as an outward looking, highly educated, value-added, strong job creation economy with a government ready to implement that vision.

The government's obligation to the industry is to assess what sort of viable TCF sector Australia can sustain in a 2010 climate of free trade. Industry Minister John Moore understands this well. Its obligation to the 97 000 TCF workers is to improve the productivity and wages of those who remain in the industry and make strenuous efforts to retrain and re-employ those who leave—and nobody thinks that will be easy.

Howard's worst mistake would be to succumb to mob opinion fanned by many radio talkback hosts, those agents of Australian decline who typically push two myths.

First, that tariffs save jobs. They don't beyond the short term. The entire TCF history disproves this theory. If the Cabinet does nothing, parts of the industry will still disappear. Effective protection to the clothing and footwear industry increased greatly in the decade from 1974 and employment was cut by 20 per cent in this time. Treasurer Costello told the truth when he said 'the only thing that will give long-term secure business prospects in a competitive world is a competitive business'.

The labour-intensive TCF sectors are migrating to low-wage nations—and tariffs can't stop this. Nor should we try. The average hourly rate in the clothing industry in 1995 was $11.95 per hour, compared with $16.18 for the economy as a whole. Australia doesn't want to compete at this level against low-wage labour-intensive countries.

The second myth is that protection is a viable position for Australia because our neighbours won't cut tariffs. The leading nations are moving towards free trade. The White Paper explained that China and our neighbours in the Association of South East Asian Nations have cut their tariffs significantly during the past decade. The reason trade liberalisation has continued since the late 1940s—the greatest prosperity phase in history—is because of its benefits. In TCF, most Asian nations have higher protection than Australia, but our exports have preferential access to many developed markets. The real point is that lower protection will assist growth and jobs in our economy overall—more skilled, higher paid jobs.

During the past decade, TCF employment fell by 18 per cent while employment in the economy overall grew 25 per cent. But protection cuts have seen some parts of the industry move into exports; others have moved their operations offshore.

Yet the industry still needs urgent reform. The commission said: 'In general, TCF manufacturing workers tend to be lower paid . . . older, female and born in non-English-speaking countries.'

The TCF industry is a classic study in how the industrial system inhibits productivity. The federal awards covering the sector are 'long and complex'. Some restrict casual and part-time employment; the clothing award requires union approval (barring unusual circumstances) for Sunday work.

If the Cabinet endorses a tariff pause it will hurt the economy overall, delay the inevitable adjustments in the TCF industry and perpetuate the myth that it can save jobs that can't be saved.

The Australian, *10 September 1999*

CAN DEMOCRACY SURVIVE?

AUSTRALIANS THRIVE ON democracy but deplore their politicians, a sentiment echoed around the world. Yet distrust of politicians has turned into a deeper issue: a crisis in the democratic method of government.

The universal gripe is against the system, not just the practitioners. Nobody wants to admit the obvious: that democracy itself is in trouble. Of course, democracy's always been in strife. An old Greek idea given a post-Enlightenment kick, democracy has been easy prey to tyranny, apathy, intolerance and most other evils. It is elusively robust and, as Churchill famously warned, it's riddled with defects but still better than any other game in town.

Yet democracy won't be immune from future shock. The twenty-first century, unlikely to put a premium on past success, will seek a governing system that fits with high-tech, customer choice and fast response yet underwrites a core stability. Democracy will have to adapt, in Australia and elsewhere, and the main question in any essay upon democracy is whether the next 100 years will witness its resilience or its demise.

It is a millennium paradox that as the century ends democracy is triumphant with more than three billion people living in democracies, a majority of the earth. Yet amid the older great democracies (including Australia) there are signs of an arthritic malaise. Right now democracy is winning the numbers, but not necessarily the hearts and minds. The twentieth century is the perfect window onto democracy's deceptive power and its hidden flaws, the key to its future. The battlefield of ideas is now littered with its defeated enemies. Hitler, Stalin and Mao shaped the century but lost the future. It's true that in the thirties democracy had a brush with oblivion courtesy of fascism, communism, depression and a culture of appeasement. During the dark days of the forties there were only about a dozen democracies left. Democracy seemed too weak an instrument to harness State power for scientific progress.

Yet the Berlin Wall is now gone, along with the Iron Curtain and the Soviet Union. China will become the world's biggest market economy. Russia has become a democracy; what odds would you have got on this fifteen years ago? Philosopher Francis Fukuyama was moved to ebulliently proclaim *The End of History* (the title of his book), meaning that liberal capitalist democracy was 'the end point of mankind's ideological evolution' and the final form of human government. That's a big call, too presumptuous of the next century.

The wellsprings of democracy lie in capitalism, science and the rights of man. A formidable trio. This is why skin deep democracies are phoney; real democracies don't arise overnight, but are founded upon a weight of social evolution. They are sustained not by brute power but by complex bonds. Arthur Schlesinger Jr, writing for the 75th anniversary issue of the journal *Foreign Affairs*, argues 'democracy requires capitalism but capitalism does not require democracy, at least in the short run'.

Democracy cannot exist without private ownership since it is private capital and property secured by law which is the power basis for the individual to challenge the State. On the other hand, great capitalists such as Lee Kuan Yew and General Pinochet didn't need to be Western-style democrats. Science created a new form of progress in the industrial revolution and technology, Schlesinger says, produced the clock, the printing press, the compass, the steam engine, the power loom and other inventions. Such innovations, in turn, created not just capitalism but the revolutionary belief that the national income from progress should be shared across all society. Aristotle got it right: 'Oligarchy is to the advantage of the rich, democracy to the advantage of the poor.' The third factor in democracy's evolution was belief in the rights of man, the theme which unites the very different American and French revolutions and which attained its pinnacle in Thomas Jefferson's 'inalienable rights' of mankind.

Yet full democracy is strictly a twentieth century practice. Only four countries—Australia, New Zealand, Norway and Finland—had given women the vote prior to World War I. The interwar years saw democracy in retreat. It was only in the generation after World War II, a short 50 years ago, that full democracy prevailed in the industrialised West; even then Portugal, Spain and others took another generation. The past ten years have seen an explosion in democracy through Asia, Africa and Latin America.

Democracy has become the fashion but it is being reinterpreted. Fareed Zakaria in last November's *Foreign Affairs* probes a new phenomenon. 'Popular leaders like Russia's Boris Yeltsin and Argentina's Carlos Menem bypass their parliaments and rule by presidential decree. The Iranian parliament—elected more freely than most in the Middle East—imposes harsh restrictions on speech, assembly and even dress. Ethiopia's elected government turns its security forces on journalists and political opponents. Illiberal democracy is a growth industry.'

Many countries are settling into a form of government that combines degrees of democracy and illiberalism. It is a reminder that traditional democracy draws its strength from another source: constitutional liberalism. Democracy is a virtue, not the only public virtue, not the greatest public virtue. Democracy comes from two Greek words; *demos* (people) and *kratos* (rule). There are many mechanisms to effect the rule of the people. The most important is representative democracy, the election of governments and parliaments to rule on behalf of the people but implanted within a constitutional framework. This denies mob rule, the tyranny of the majority and enshrines rule of law to protect individual liberty.

There are two certainties for democracy in the twenty-first century; its fate will be turbulent and these forces—capitalism, science and the claim of inalienable rights—will force democracy's adaption or its demise. Such forces, paradoxically, are both democracy's saviour and its enemy.

Technology will make the twenty-first century an age of individual empowerment that poses a threat to representative democracy. The movement is stirring. Politicians, parliaments, governments and parties are the targets. The public wants to exercise a direct control, just as it wants to elect our future president. It is contemptuous of the methods and techniques evolved over time to make representative democracy work. They are seen as anti-people. The authority of Parliament, though not its law-making function, has been ceded to the self-appointed judges of the mass entertainment industry.

This process has just begun and has a long way to run. Parliament is an institution born of another epoch. It is a fading magnificence where bells ring, people call each other 'honourable', obscure rules govern process and politicians struggle to reconcile their calling with the public's irritable disillusion. The new log of claims will soon hit the table; direct democracy, regular plebiscites, voting by the people through computer technology on a vast array of issues. This interactive politics will be called pure democracy. It will set the people against the Parliament. What is the need of a politician if you can vote on a measure though a switch pointed at your television without having to put down your beer?

George Orwell's *1984* probed the equation but got a mostly wrong answer; technology, despite its capacity to promote uniformity, will liberate the individual, accentuate decentralisation and fragment the power centres. The issue of the twenty-first century is whether representative democracy is obsolete. For those who grew up with the twentieth century institutions of governance (and still like them) it's impossible to believe the answer can be 'yes'.

However, within representative democracy the twenty-first century chemistry of global capital and high technology will be explosive. Just extrapolate three of the great trends: the decline in State power; the rise of the corporation; and the scientific method of winning elections.

Globalisation means that the ability of governments to solve problems is in retreat. The high tide of State power was the post-World War II Keynesian age in the West and the centrally planned command economies in the East. That age is gone. Faith in government was the hallmark of the Whitlam era, the Kennedy/Johnson period in the US and Harold Wilson's Labour government in the UK.

But government can't deliver any more because it doesn't

have the power. Power, like sovereignty, has been exported. In Bob Woodward's book *The Agenda* he describes the defining moment of the Clinton presidency; how Clinton reacted with anger when told that financial markets would determine the success of his presidency. But Clinton learnt and acted. Governments in the twenty-first century will retreat from enterprise involvement and focus more on getting the framework right. The power of the central government will flow outwards to the global system and downwards to the town and community.

For democracy it's a threat and an opportunity. The rise of the twenty-first century corporation and its ties to the information explosion will offer society a bizarre range of options from *Blade Runner* to Silicon Valley. Access to information will be the new determinant of class. Walled cities, private security, segregation by knowledge power, vast regional inequalities created by rapid structural changes and the tyranny of a manipulated popular culture will give democracy a battering. Robert Kaplan in his *Atlantic Monthly* essay 'Was Democracy Just A Moment?' predicts a society so hooked on mass entertainment it succumbs to servility. Kaplan puts the crunch case for democracy's end-game: 'Precisely because this technological future in North America will provide so much market and individual freedom, this productive anarchy will require the supervision of tyrannies—or else there will be no justice for anyone.'

Aside from the apocalyptic, there is a more mundane challenge. Democracy must keep muddling along; it must work, at least tolerably. Yet frightened practitioners are debasing democracy daily. Never before have politicians had such access to the feelings and sentiments of voters on any issue at any time as they possess today. It's the triumph of market research and survey groups; the scientific approach to politics. The result is a conundrum. The leaders regurgitate what the people say and the people's contempt for their leaders only grows.

So what is happening here? The people, surprise, want the politicians to add value, not to refine self-abasement by bowing before every passing electoral breeze. In his *Atlantic Monthly* (August 1996) essay Jonathan Schell insists: 'A whole new framework for political life is needed. It requires looking less at focus groups and exit polls and more at the nation's and world's problems. Above all, it requires that individuals, political parties and public institutions develop the fortitude to hold fast to new convictions, even in the face of initial unpopularity and rejection. If no serious proposals are put forward, the voters' choices lose their meaning and public opinion turns to mush.'

It is a classic twenty-first century choice: does democracy have a future as a means of solving problems or will it sink in the mush?

The Australian Magazine, *30–31 May 1998*

AUSTRALIA AND KYOTO

THE KYOTO PROTOCOL is a 'win–win' for Australia. Our efficient energy industries and jobs are saved—for a while. Land clearing on this continent will slow. And Australia now has time to restructure its greenhouse intensive fossil-fuel sector.

Kyoto is a landmark in international environmental cooperation—but only if the hard lessons about the honesty, realism and fairness are learnt. The messages in this decision to cut global emissions by 5 per cent by 2012 in relation to 1990 levels are that Europe's grandstanding didn't succeed; that the deal won't be carried by the US Congress until the gulf between Congress and administration is bridged; and that the chasm remains between the developed and developing world with China and India defying the US.

The result that allows an emissions increase of 8 per cent for Australia is a victory for the federal government. The ideas that Australia pushed—different targets according to national costs, modest targets to launch a mandatory regime and a market-based system of emissions trading—all made great progress.

The lesson from Kyoto is that the greenhouse debate over the past six months has been fantasy and propaganda, replete with good guys and bad guys (Australia being a bad guy). The greens, having preached that Australia was a pariah nation without influence, now peddle the line that somehow we conned the world at Kyoto!

This was a de facto trade negotiation, driven by self-interest, conducted in the language of international environmental concerns and sanctioned by a bizarre combination of science and morality.

From the start, Australia was frank and pragmatic. It saw that two issues were involved—how the international community could best establish an emission reduction regime and how Australia's economy could best be maintained in the process.

Australia fought with guts and persistence, although not without tactical blunders and inadequate public relations. John Howard, Tim Fischer, Alexander Downer and Environment Minister Robert Hill, who had the final carriage, displayed a tenacity against the odds.

But Australia always faced the prospect of being seriously disadvantaged, an outcome it has avoided. This is because our economy is fossil-fuel intensive. We produce coal cheaply, which produces cheap electricity which, in turn, powers mineral processing that is integral to our prosperity. Australia is an energy exporter, unlike other industrial nations which import energy. Howard's stance was driven by these realities. It is inconceivable that an Australian government would not seek to protect the national financial interest.

Two other factors contribute to Australia's emissions. The first factor is our high population growth, expected to increase by 30 per cent over the 1990–2010 period, compared with 3 per cent for Europe.

The second factor is that a fifth of Australia's 1990 emissions derive from excessive land clearing. For Australia, land policy has been a net source of emissions—while for Europe it absorbs emissions. So Australia wanted land policy included as a measure both for accuracy and as an incentive to slow our land clearing as a means of cutting emissions. To their shame, this was opposed by the greens at Kyoto.

Before Kyoto, Howard warned that Australia could not accept the EU's uniform target, which 'would impose a cost on all Australians that other countries would not accept'. Precisely.

Because the EU pledged a tough line on emissions—a 15 per cent cut on 1990 levels—its position became the internationally 'green' sanctioned benchmark. But Europe's position was a clever deception.

Why? First, the target was achievable only because of the incorporation of the emission-intensive former East Germany and Britain's 1980s decision to scale down its coal industry for economic reasons. Accidental pluses.

Second, the EU was hypocritical since it allowed differentiation among its members but insisted upon uniform targets for non-EU nations. So the EU said Portugal could increase emissions by 40 per cent but Australia must cut by 15 per cent. So much for fairness! In addition, in a system of emission trading, Europe, by moving its credits about, could gain a huge competitive advantage over the US and Japan.

The story of the Kyoto protocol is that of the world calling Europe's bluff. It happened after US Vice-President Al Gore's appeal for negotiating flexibility when the US and Japan, facing European intransigence, began to organise a new trading umbrella group of Asia–Pacific nations including Australia, Canada and Russia to cut their own deal. It was more leverage than reality, but it was a reminder that too many nations were being squeezed by the EU.

The conference saw a shift towards Australia's principle of differentiation—as opposed to uniform targets—because it combines the fairness and realism needed in a successful protocol. It also offers a future path for involving the high-emission developing nations.

The overall outcome of a 5 per cent reduction is much less than sought by the EU. It is significant, however, that the US, which went to Kyoto with a position of stabilisation, finished with a pledge to cut by 7 per cent, a concession that gives Bill Clinton green credentials but makes implementation a hard call.

So what does the outcome mean for Australia? It means our energy sector is given time to restructure. After the federal government's 20 November greenhouse measures affecting building, transport and industry Australia's emissions were projected to grow 18 per cent. The new Kyoto target is 8 per cent, but we will be greatly assisted by inclusion of land use with emissions from this source continuing to fall.

At Kyoto, Hill spoke to Howard by telephone each day, with the PM giving the final 'yes'. Australia played a game of brinkmanship, saying it wouldn't sign an unfair deal. But the world wanted Australia 'in' and our sustained campaign saw many nations recognise the force of our argument.

Yet the media spent the year ridiculing Australia's position morally and politically, refusing to confront the reality of our economy and accepting uncritically the critique made by foreign governments of our position. Why?

The Australian, *17 December 1997*

RECONCILIATION, SO CLOSE YET SO FAR

RECONCILIATION ALMOST TOOK a leap forward yesterday. Almost. John Howard offered a qualified personal apology to the indigenous people for past injustices.

His speech, opening a highly charged Australian Reconciliation Convention, was unsympathetic in tone, lecturing in content and it failed to inspire trust. But there was an expression of sorrow—for the first time. Pat Dodson, Chair of the Reconciliation Council, grateful for small mercies, said Mr Howard's remarks were 'a start'.

South Africa's Deputy Chair of its Truth and Reconciliation Commission, Alex Boraine, after watching Howard's address on Wik and the stolen generation to a critical audience, said: 'Your Prime Minister's got balls but he hasn't got a hell of a lot of heart.'

Reconciliation is still alive but it is a very different process under the philosophy John Howard outlined yesterday. The opening ceremony exposed the depth of the dangerous divisions now afflicting Australian society—but it did not extinguish hope.

Howard was not alone. ALP leader Kim Beazley avoided any apology but called for a 'positive' response on stolen children and signalled Labor's support for Parliament to 'pass an expression of profound regret for the injustices and dehumanising treatment' of indigenous people since 1788.

The basis surely exists for some collective statement of regret or apology by the national Parliament, given the juxtaposition of the stolen generation report which outlines a clear-cut historical injustice, and this week's 30th anniversary of the 1967 referendum creating a Commonwealth Aboriginal Affairs power.

It is critical to harness as much goodwill as possible immediately since the federal government and Aboriginal Australia remain on a collision course over Howard's 10-point Wik program.

The opening ceremony yesterday revealed John Howard's essential difficulty in dealing with the indigenous people—it is a problem of the heart not the head. Mr Howard was on the verge of a great breakthrough yesterday. But his spirit couldn't reach out.

His is a failure to relate and that failure, felt at the level of human contact, breeds distrust. It is this distrust which is the vital ingredient now threatening reconciliation.

This was a moving, troubling and important opening ceremony. Cheryl Kernot stole the audience with her apology for past injustice, her appeal that 'it's not so hard to say you're sorry, isn't that what we teach our children' and her warning that Australia today faces a 'stark and nation-defining choice'.

Howard's message was significant, although its tenor was flawed. His address before 2000 delegates was almost tragic as some insulted him by standing and turning their backs, only to turn back in hope when he apologised and then turn away again when he began to lecture on Wik.

The Prime Minister declared his faith in reconciliation and defined the process in three ways: a shared commitment to raise the living standards of indigenous Australians; a realistic acknowledgment of interrelated histories; and a mutual acceptance of the need to work together.

Howard's views contained much truth. He said reconciliation had to come from the hearts and minds of people; that it would not work if symbolic gestures become more important than practical needs; that it would not work if dominated by guilt and shame; that it must not lead to different systems of accountability and law on the basis of race.

The conundrum is that Howard wants indigenous Australians to accept his view of reconciliation and not that of the Keating government.

He must know as a practical politician that he needs to give something—and what is easier or fairer than a national apology? You can't put the past behind until you confront its truth.

The Australian, *27 May 1997*

HANSON, A SYMPTOM OF A DEEPER PROBLEM

Pauline Hanson is an authentic Australian creature and a manifestation of forces deep within our political culture. Yet the rise of Hansonism was not inevitable and many such forces find political expression short of the formation of a new parliamentary party. Hanson is a traumatic event in Australian democracy and casts a shadow over our community, society and prosperity.

Her One Nation party is a protest movement with populist targets—Asians, Aborigines, banks, international capital, immigrants, multiculturalism, native title, the judiciary, Canberra, the ALP and Coalition parties, political correctness, crime, market-orientated economics, the media and the urban culture of the information age. Hansonism makes three core claims—the political system isn't working; the elites have betrayed the country and its values; and Australia has been on the wrong track for the past 25 years. Almost everybody will agree with some of these sentiments and this is her appeal.

In its isolation and xenophobia, One Nation resembles the fringe movements that have emerged in other democracies. Hanson's power lies in her certainty, her plausible but phoney vision, her manipulation of grievance and exploitation of rural resentments, funny money quackery and racism. Many such protest movements flicker across the landscape and then extinguish; others gain momentum and claim a minority position in parliaments. When Hanson emerged after the 1996 federal election it was typically expected that she would fade after a brief performance—a view held by the Prime Minister, John

142

Howard. Such assessments proved to be wrong. The nation's response to Hansonism is a study of institutional and leadership failure. Hanson has been assisted towards a critical mass by a variety of friends and enemies in what constitutes a failure of judgement by the Coalition, the ALP and the media, among others. One Nation's success at the June 1998 Queensland State election gave Hanson the chance to convert her movement into a parliamentary party with potentially great influence at the federal level. Integral to this process was a broadening of One Nation's policies to embrace an economic populism that matched its initial anti-immigration and racial exclusivism. The 1998 federal election assumes a dual significance—it is not just a contest between Coalition and Labor but a test of whether One Nation can poll sufficiently to derail Australia's economic and social modernisation and entrench a bitter domestic clash over national direction.

Pauline Hanson's speeches and One Nation's policies have assumed a unity based upon an assembly of grievances. One Nation is a throwback. It wants zero net immigration, arguing that the rationale no longer exists for the post-World War II immigration program; an end to multiculturalism and a revival of Australia's Anglo-Celtic cultural tradition which it believes has been devalued; an abolition of native title and the Aboriginal and Torres Strait Islander Commission (ATSIC); an end to special Aboriginal funding programs; opposition to Aboriginal reconciliation on the grounds that it creates two nations and a questioning of the 1967 constitutional referendum which gave the Commonwealth power to legislate nationally for Aborigines.

On the economy, One Nation seeks to reverse the internationalisation of our economic processes by supporting protection and trade retaliation, imposing tougher restrictions on foreign capital and winding back of overseas capital flows. Hanson said there must be an end to 'kowtowing to financial markets, international organisations, world bankers, investment companies and big business people'—a call to revert to Fortress Australia in response to globalisation. One Nation opposes privatisations, notably Telstra, rejects competition policy, deregulation and measures to achieve an internationally competitive economy involving tax reform with a GST. Hanson is critical of our integration into Asia, shows no inclination to accept Asian nations as friends—let alone as economic, political and security partners—insists that our Asian neighbours are anti-white, wants to review our UN membership, seeks to repudiate our allegiance to United Nations treaties, cut foreign aid and ban foreigners from land ownership. She rejects the idea that Australia's integration into the Asia–Pacific means the ongoing creation on this continent of a more diverse society, insisting instead that the real purpose is the 'Asianisation of Australia'.

Finally, One Nation's policies display a grasp of Australia's pork-barrel technique, typified by her pledge of a new people's bank to offer farmers loans at a fixed 2 per cent with small business and manufacturing industry also eligible for this easy money. It's the oldest trick in politics. Such cheap loans can only be offered by using taxpayers' funds or by lifting interest rates for other borrowers as a source of subsidy. It is a rort, pure and simple. Hanson, contrary to her claims, doesn't believe in equality but would exploit the financial system to direct money to supporters and target groups.

What is the 'bottom line' from Hanson's overall philosophy? There is one message—the policies won't work for most Australians or for their society. It is unlikely a majority would ever accept the moral basis that Hanson espouses. But the risk is that political support for market-based economic reform is collapsing with Hanson's solutions only likely to damage ordinary Australians.

In a global age, the economics are a prescription for a low growth, high unemployment economy, fewer trade deals and a weakening in exports replete with injustice and the social problems bred by economic decline. The social policies guarantee a new division in Australia by resort to absolutist solutions of repudiating immigration, Aboriginal reconciliation and the worth of ethnic diversity. Finally, the strategic implications are that Australia would be left without friends, influence or partners in Asia, the Pacific and America. (Hanson's hostility towards multiculturalism brings her into direct conflict with the US whose philosophy is to accept the peoples of the world and make them Americans.) Within Asia, Hansonism is interpreted as a reversion to the White Australia Policy, and this is the final calculation in reaching Hanson's 'bottom line'—making Australia into a pariah nation. Our neighbours would treat us as an outcast. Our security would be compromised; our isolationism would be entrenched; and the future of our children would be compromised.

It is precisely because One Nation has achieved such success that the consequences of its policies should be evaluated remorselessly. The failure in the response to Hanson has been emotion devoid of intellect when the reply should have been intellect without emotion. Hanson's policies can be demolished by argument but they are emotionally flammable. Cool reason geared to self-interest is the best response but, until recently, it has rarely been deployed.

During 1997 and 1998, the Hanson 'genie' escaped from the bottle and it is uncertain how long it will take to put back. Why was Australia so incapable of managing Hanson? There are three reasons and they document the complex place of Hansonism in the 1990s Australia. They relate, in order, to our history, our national transition and our democracy.

Hanson represents a flawed mirror image of our history and of ourselves, distorted yet authentic. That is deeply disgusting for many Australians yet also a source of secret support among others. Hanson shakes the cage into which Australia has consigned its history. She is an echo of our Anglo-Celtic origins; the claims of the once mighty bush to define the Australian legend; a descendant of the romanticism and racism of Henry Lawson whose hold on national identity was once so comprehensive; a reminder that our politics have always revolved around helping the individual by making claims upon the State; the latest manifestation of our reflex to distrust authority, abuse our elites and damn our leaders in a psychological displacement for our own worst failings; a symptom of how in this country it is possible, even easy, to steal community legitimacy by genuflection before the ethic of egalitarianism while simultaneously mocking its very idea; and above all, Hanson is a nightmare that survived the dawn by bringing to life the ghost Australia had consigned to its past—that our nationhood, our pride, our federation, lay in the fusion of racism and nationalism which is why for so long we treated the Aborigines with injustice and our Asian locale with such apprehension.

Hanson is a challenge from within; a battle for the heart, values and destiny of the nation. Hanson herself insists upon this. It is manifest in the blunt clarity of her own vision for

Australia which is the clearest vision put forward since Paul Keating quit politics.

This cultural backdrop is the key to the reaction which Hanson inspired. John Howard, a critic of the 'black armband' view of Australian history, a social conservative, a passionate defender of Australian achievement and a leader profoundly uncomfortable with the modern requirement to manage and market community diversity and inclusion, was less alarmed about Hanson's emergence because he was more attuned to her message. Howard believed that his 1996 election victory should be interpreted as a rejection of Keating's national vision—that Keating had gone beyond public tolerance in championing an emerging multicultural republic tied into Asia and atoning for its sins against the indigenous people. Howard sought to redraw the political boundaries on these issues, not as far as Hanson later proposed, but in that direction; he saw Hanson's win in the former ALP-held seat of Oxley as an offshoot of the senti- ment which delivered him the election; he interpreted Hanson within the paradigm his director, Andrew Robb, advanced to explain the 1996 election victory—that Keating Labor was stranded between the Whitlam generation of an upwardly mobile, better educated urban elite and its forgotten working- class base with the latter defecting en masse to the Coalition and immortalised as 'Howard's battlers'.

So Howard reacted according to inclination and calculation. He was reluctant to challenge Hanson on principle because he was less persuaded that great principle was at stake; he saw Hanson as more Labor's legacy than the Coalition's nemesis; and his experience told him that Hanson would not long endure when faced with political tribulation and his own tenacity. Howard was wrong on each count.

But Howard made a more serious blunder. He failed to take a sustained stand against the introduction of racial chauvinism into our politics. Howard did not draw a proper distinction between deeply felt social grievances and resort to racial chau- vinism. His failure on this point disappointed many Australians and is the key to the reaction against him.

His worst tactical mistake was not just a failure to define a preference tactic for the Coalition but an implicit approval of the decision by the Liberal Party at the June 1998 Queensland election to give preferences to One Nation ahead of Labor. This supported the decision by the senior partner, the National Party. The result was a triple blow for Howard as well as a humiliation for the Coalition government led by National Party premier, Rob Borbidge. First, the Coalition still lost the election to Labor. Second, the preference decision meant One Nation dominated the entire election with its vote more than doubling during the campaign. It won eleven out of 89 seats, eight of them solely because of Coalition preferences, thereby gaining greater momentum across the nation. Third, the result confirmed what many Liberals had refused to admit, that One Nation did far more damage to the Coalition than Labor. The Coalition parties were promoting their own self-destruction. The Queensland result destabilised the National Party and the federal Coalition; weakened federal National Party leader, Tim Fischer; catapulted the Kim Beazley-led ALP Opposition into its strongest position since the 1996 poll; deepened internal resistance to Howard's policies of selling Telstra, a GST-led tax reform package and promoting a competitive economy; and raised more doubts about his leadership.

It cannot be asserted that a different appreciation and response from the Prime Minister would have destroyed Hanson. But it would have changed the atmospherics and it would have strengthened rather than weakened Howard's own leadership. But Howard misjudged on another factor—the response of the media, another victim of history and culture.

At some future point, the media must assess its own role and motivation and the consequences flowing from its coverage of Pauline Hanson from the time of her maiden speech to the launch of the Queensland campaign. It is the media that made Hanson a national figure and kept her a national figure. The upshot is that Hanson had, by 1998, become the best known and most reported Australian public figure in the international media from Europe through Asia. This was a distortion of her importance and news value. In the process, Australia became typecast abroad by Hanson. It is inconceivable that any other nation would have responded with such obsession about an extreme right-wing populist occupying just one seat in its national parliament. Yet the foreign coverage merely reflected the tenor of the local coverage.

There are two observations to be made about this coverage by the quality media. First, it began not with the coverage of

Hanson's maiden speech but with Howard's reaction to that speech. The media story was always a Hanson–Howard story; that story was always Howard's failure to address, condemn or counter Hansonism. The psychology was transparent: here was a progressive media whose outrage at Hanson was matched only by its outrage at Howard's refusal to crusade against Hanson. The undefined connection was also transparent: that Howard had a responsibility for Hanson and her racist message. This sentiment reflected the quality media's difficulty in accepting the legitimacy of Howard's social views because he would not champion racial tolerance. The quality media's long-held and well-grounded belief was that Howard's outlook was faulty on racial grounds. This originated with his inept 1988 comments warning that Asian immigration levels might need to be reduced, and was reinforced by his handling of Aboriginal policy as Prime Minister. From the start, quality media coverage of Hanson was deeply influenced by its view of Howard. Second, the media's coverage of Hanson was far greater than her considerable news value as a sole independent justified. Hanson received an exaggerated coverage because the media, profoundly hostile to her views, felt that exposure was the prelude to extinguishment. The unintended consequence was different. Hanson's support and importance rose to reflect the coverage she had received. A cruel irony and a miscalculation by the quality media.

The second underlying factor in the national response to Hanson is the transformation occurring in the Australian polity which involves the dismantling of the post-Federation Australian Settlement. Australia, in effect, is undergoing a political revolution. It is making the adjustment to a global economy but also far-reaching social adjustments such as Aboriginal reconciliation, a strong ongoing Asian component in immigration, and the adoption by successive governments of multiculturalism as a social objective.

The reason these policies overall constitute a political revolution is because they involve a remaking of the Australian political tradition. In each case, a struggle is underway to substitute the original post-Federation belief with a replacement credo. The scope of this project in the 1990s is even broader than it was in the 1980s. It includes the replacement of white Australia with multicultural Australia, trade protection with trade liberalisation, wage arbitration with a more market-orientated wages system, reliance upon government with a greater acceptance of individual responsibility and private capital, a recognition that a new compact must be struck with the indigenous people, and finally, the maturity to manage our own interests in the world because the global empire on which we once depended no longer exists.

The single most important feature of 1990s politics is the launch of the counter-revolution against these changes. This counter-revolution is fragmented but pervasive. It is best represented by the ideological assault upon the artificial construct of 'economic rationalism' which is depicted by a heartless, immoral doctrine, and the fear that Australia is being converted into a 'nation of tribes'. These beliefs are widely held but are rarely mutually held. Such sentiments run, in part, through the media elites, the political parties (ALP, Liberal, National, Australian Democrats and the Greens), opinion-making centres from trade unions and churches to universities, a populist-tabloid brand of talkback radio, and, most critically, they are fuelled by a grassroots voter backlash. This should surprise nobody, given the scope of the transformation. The rise of Hanson is best grasped within this context. One Nation is merely an extreme form of this counter-revolution. Its distinctive features are its campaign to roll the tide back 'all the way' and its opposition to virtually all aspects of the transformation—social, economic, strategic.

The conclusion is obvious—Hanson is a problem but her rise is symptomatic of a deeper problem. Australia is in danger of losing its way in the late 1990s. It is fair to say that in 1998, the only two political leaders who are plausible champions of ongoing economic and social reform are the Victorian premier, Jeff Kennett, and Liberal deputy leader, Peter Costello. There is an absence of intellectual leadership and a failure to put a sustained case for what should be the majority position—an open competitive economy and inclusive social policies. This is the position of Bill Clinton and Tony Blair but, paradoxically, it is in severe retreat in Australia.

The Howard government and the Beazley Opposition have struggled to balance the trade-off between voter anger and prudent policy. Howard deserves credit for pushing the cause of economic reform, notably fiscal consolidation, a more flexible industrial system, privatisation and taxation reform. But his tactical ineptitude and contradictory 'stop-start' signals have weakened public support for economic reform. On the social policy front, the government has been ineffective despite important reforms to immigration and eventual passage of the Wik legislation. The chief defect is that Howard has forfeited trust on racial issues and made some unwarranted spending cuts. On the other hand, Kim Beazley's aim has been to distance the ALP from the failure of the Keating government and reconstitute its base vote after the 1996 debacle. This has involved a repudiation of much of the Hawke–Keating economic principles (such reforms integral to four successive election victories from 1983 to 1990). Support for market-orientated growth policies has all but collapsed within the ALP and this will post a severe test for the party's capacity to govern successfully. But Labor, unlike the Coalition, has been firm on the need for inclusive social policies.

The risk here is that of throwing out the baby with the bath water. No political revolution is bloodless, painless or mistake free. The economic reforms of the 1980s have left losers as well as winners, and a legacy of far greater income inequality. The social reforms have placed too much emphasis on ethnic rights and too little on obligations to Australia. Policy towards the indigenous people has fallen hostage to the disastrous impression of racial atonement. These defects need to be addressed.

The response to Hanson must be based in policy as well as presentation. Mass panic—the National Party reaction—won't work. It seems evident that economic and tax policies must give more weight to equity; that multiculturalism as a definition symbol is probably finished and needs to be replaced with a message that stresses 'diversity within unity'; and that the language and tenor of the debate about Aboriginal rights needs to be recast along with a better policy emphasis on responsibilities to match rights. In a democracy there must be an accounting and that is now underway, driven by the voters. The risk for Australia is that the counter-revolution will run too far, that it will be dictated by opinion polls not intelligent leadership, and that the sound policy directions established over the last fifteen to twenty years will be sunk, not just modified.

Integral to these fears is the rise of a new form of political dishonesty. It takes many guises—that Australia can prosper by resorting to protection; that job security can be guaranteed in a workplace changing faster than ever; that cutting immigration will reduce unemployment; that the nation will be better off by slowing the rate of economic change and accepting permanent high unemployment; that unity and social diversity are incompatible; that Australia can live off Asian economies while closing its mind and borders to Asian people.

Hanson espouses each proposition. But she is not unique. The political ground was made fertile for One Nation long before Hanson arrived. Hanson merely follows the left-wing in her campaign against market economics and immigration, and tracks the right-wing in her attacks on Aboriginal policy and multiculturalism. The power of Hanson is that she represents a synthesis between economic protection and monoculturalism; she bends the spectrum so that the Left and Right are combined against the Centre. Hanson embraces the principal slogans of the counter-revolution—the evil of economic rationalism and the championing of an ethnically pure nation—which are the 1990s version of the mindless 'threat from the north' mantra that was deployed by conservative politicians so successfully during the 1960s. It is alarming that Hanson is able to paint a more vivid image of her Australia than either Howard or Beazley. She will be exposed by her own flaws and contradictions, but One Nation has the potential to thrive in the mood of public pessimism and policy confusion of the late 1990s.

The third factor linked to the rise of Hanson is the condition of Australian democracy in the late 1990s. Australians thrive on democracy but deplore their politicians. Yet distrust of politicians has turned into a deeper issue—distrust of the system.

Hanson is a major beneficiary because she has been seen, to this stage, as a non-politician. Indeed, she is seen as falling almost outside the system. In this fantasy land, she is a pure commodity as opposed to dirty politicians; she tells the truth when politicians lie; she is courageous, a female David, against an evil system. Finally, being a woman is an asset. Politics is filled with grey suits. Australian society is being feminised and the image of a strong but sincere woman is the perfect positioning.

Hanson is advantaged because she is a vehicle for the disenchanted and alienated; she doesn't have to worry about solutions that work because she is never likely to hold office; and she has a celebrity status unlike, for example, Graeme

Campbell who champions many of her policies but whose impact is marginal. Finally, if One Nation polls strongly in the Senate there is a chance it could hold the balance of power in the Upper House, thereby winning an influence out of proportion to its vote.

Such advantages arise from deep changes underway in Australia's political system.

First, globalisation weakens national sovereignty and government's authority as a problem solver. Public expectations of government now outstrip the ability of government to deliver. This is the chasm in which Hanson operates. It fuels voter resentment which will endure until such unrealistic expectations are purged. Governments can't deliver on benefits beyond the limits of the economy or revenue system; they can't ensure voter happiness; they can't fill the void left by family and personal tribulation. The politicians are trapped between the limits to government and their delivery ability. They still make too many promises and are forced to back down as both Paul Keating and John Howard had to back down, thus incurring further voter hostility. Democratic government has a long distance to travel to adjust to the reality of globalisation.

Second, technology is dictating a convergence between the media, entertainment and political industries. Technology now shapes the pace and often the content of politics. This is the age of the permanent campaign—every hour, every day, on radio, television or by print. The politicians exploit the media for their campaign message. But the media also exploits the politicians. It is a self-corrupting embrace with the public alert to its nature. The media treats politics as a product to lift its ratings and win revenue—witness the Bronwyn Bishop, Cheryl Kernot and Pauline Hanson phenomena. The media brings its values of celebrity, novelty, confrontation and entertainment to the task. It reports politics through this prism. Hanson was made a celebrity; she was a fresh commodity; and she drew confrontation like a missile searching for a target.

This is the context for the rise of the populist talkback jockeys who are the champions of Hansonism. They are rightwing; they read the market research; and they saw another opportunity to advance their own credibility by undermining the credibility of the established politicians. The populist talkback industry (which reaches a mainstream audience in its breakfast programs) thrives by discrediting the system. It abuses and de-legitimises the political system on a sustained basis. It seeks to win listener loyalty by offering a bizarre therapy based upon a blame culture. The culprits, typically, are the banks, the bureaucrats and the politicians; in short, the elites. This is credible because it's often true but it has now assumed the status of epic myth. The talkback culture has helped to convert Australia's healthy scepticism about politics into a loathing alienation from the system. There is no doubt that powerful elements in the talkback media along with many voters were attracted to Hanson as a form of 'terrorism' against the system.

Third, the nature of campaigning is changing because of a deeply cynical electorate. Cynicism makes a negative campaign more powerful and a positive campaign more difficult. Market research shows that a negative campaign line is credible while a positive line will be met with voter derision. This pushes the politicians into negatives and away from positives. But the ultimate negative campaign is Hanson's because it's mounted against the system itself. It is a campaign whose credibility suggests that democratic government could be in trouble.

Fourth, the scientific approach to politics, guided by market research, is now becoming a threat to democracy. In his *Atlantic Monthly* (August 1996) article, Jonathan Schell raises the questions—would the response to Hanson have been more effective if parties weren't influenced by market research but reacted on the basis of merit and principle?

The rise of globalisation and the decline of party loyalty and government authority puts greater demands upon political leadership. The task of leadership has grown both more simple and more complex. The leader is expected to propagate a vision, create a sense of confidence and trust, and have the ability to sway opinion in defence of principle. The argument against Hansonism is based upon national self-interest and moral principle. That is a very powerful nexus. Yet the case has not been put on a sustained basis, let alone won. This fault lies essentially, though not solely, with John Howard. He failed to grasp the principles at stake for Australia and the Liberal Party, and he misjudged the politics.

From Two Nations, *Bookman Press, Melbourne, 1998*

HOWARD'S MANDATE

*The mandate of 1972 was the most positive and precise ever
sought and ever received by an elected government in Australian
history.*

—Gough Whitlam

AUSTRALIA IS HEADING into an old debate, with the first
48 hours of John Howard's re-election littered with efforts to
de-legitimise his victory typified by the misuse of the mandate
theory.

Governments have mandates that are created by virtue of
their election. Oppositions don't have mandates; neither do
minor Senate parties. Mandates, under the classical theory,
relate to governments. The mandate is the link, the trust, the
bond between the ruler and the people. It originated in Chinese
philosophy, where the 'Will of Heaven' or 'Mandate of Heaven'
reflected the principle that the rulers were but stewards for the
people.

The notion was passed through the Greeks into Western
democratic philosophy and was given its most forceful Australian expression by Gough Whitlam, whose biographer Graham
Freudenberg documented at length the centrality of the mandate to Whitlam's political life.

Whitlam claimed a mandate for his 1972 policy speech, for
his 1972–75 legislative program and for the executive decisions
made by the Whitlam–Barnard duumvirate.

The first act of the Whitlam government—the release of seven
men imprisoned for refusing to be conscripted—was advised by

Whitlam to the Governor-General solely in terms of the mandate. Whitlam argued that, since 'it was part of my party's election program', the new government 'has a mandate to take these steps'. He invoked his mandate to establish diplomatic relations with China, terminate sporting ties with South Africa and re-open the equal-pay case before the Arbitration Commission.

The mandate is a polemical device. Whitlam deployed it with limited success as a weapon to combat a hostile Senate because the Constitution empowers the Senate to reject any or every Bill proposed by the Lower House. The Constitution, as law, can render Australia ungovernable or endanger our governance. That's why we need other conventions, rules or theories to make our democracy work.

Howard's election win means Australia will have a goods and services tax because a majority of both the new House of Representatives and Senate favour a GST. But the Coalition and Democrats differ widely on the type of GST, and the final tax will be a negotiated compromise—perhaps with food exempted—reflecting numbers and power.

At one level, the row about mandates is really the start of this negotiation, which will last well into 1999. But, at another level, the mandate debate is a symptom of the malaise afflicting our politics.

Howard won the election last week, barring a surprise in the late counting. But our politicians haven't behaved as we teach our children—with any trace of generosity towards the winner. There has been instead an avalanche of 'slide rule' politics—a campaign against his claim of a mandate.

It's familiar. Howard's majority is too small—just as Whitlam's nine-seat 1972 majority and five-seat 1974 majority were deemed too small—or it's that the swing was anti-government, or the primary vote low, or the Senate controlled by an anti-government majority, or the two-party preferred vote was less than 50 per cent, or all of these.

The purpose is manifest: to undermine the legitimacy of the re-elected government.

The entire Senate wasn't even elected last Saturday. The Senate can't claim a mandate on a GST because this was a half-Senate poll. The arrogance for the people held by some senators who claim mandates when half their numbers didn't even face the voters is as breathtaking as it is contemptuous.

The mandate—the trust between the elected government and the people—can't apply to the Senate because the Senate doesn't determine the government and the Senate as a whole didn't go to the election.

It is true that the politicians, assisted by the media, have trashed the mandate theory. Every Senate independent or minor party claims a mandate. But our system can't function with equal and competing mandates given the Senate's powers. The system can work only if the Senate discharges its house of review functions recognising the legitimacy of the government's program.

If the Democrats have a mandate, then One Nation has a mandate—a mandate to halt immigration and terminate Aboriginal reconciliation. This is the crazy logic we have created for ourselves.

If the mandate is killed, then you kill the central means of keeping governments honest. The government has a right to implement its policies; but it has a responsibility to honour its promises. A government that breaks its promises is abusing its mandate. An Opposition that denies a government a mandate denies any expectation that its promises will be kept.

Journalists were right to attack the first-term Howard government for breaking its promises. But a government expected to keep its promises must be given support to implement its promises. Otherwise our politics becomes a farce and our media reduced to hypocrites.

In his 1975 Chifley Lecture, Whitlam attacked the Coalition for its interpretation of the mandate in its 'weakest sense', merely as a 'mandate to govern'—Kim Beazley's exact words after the election. Whitlam said he interpreted the mandate as including 'a specific mandate to implement the undertakings we made'.

Howard, like Whitlam, claims a mandate for every aspect of his tax package. But mandates can't be absolute and it's an ambit claim. Ultimately, a deal will be cut and Howard, being a realist, will take the best deal that's available.

In the interim, it is in the interests of workable government and political trust to uphold the principle of the mandate, not discredit it.

The Australian, 7 *October 1998*

LABOR AND THE
NEW AGENDA

LINDSAY TANNER'S BOOK *Open Australia* should be the clinching argument for the Labor Party that it needs a new framework for politics and that neither a loved leader nor an impressive 1998 election clawback can deflect this imperative. Tanner has called an end to the big bluff in which Labor has engaged since the 1996 Keating defeat. He argues that the ALP 'must do two things in order to achieve government: reform itself and build a new agenda'. It is a manifesto for sure trouble. It means a painful, dangerous and probably protracted reappraisal.

Within the ALP, there will be much resistance to this message and lots of token lip-service to it. But Tanner's core argument is convincing. It is time the ALP admitted the need for a new path between pro-market economics and old-fashioned interventionism. If Labor persists with its juvenile claim that Tony Blair's 'third way' is a mirage, then it should solve this problem by using another term and proceed apace to define its own new path.

Tanner is tenacious in his assertion that a successful future for Australia depends upon a national choice to be an open society. His message is that Australia must accept the reality of globalisation and construct policies to make it work—not join the populist anti-market crusade.

In taking this stance, Tanner identifies the absolute issue for Australia today. He says: 'The facile notion that the Australian economy is a static entity in the process of being subjected to various economic rationalist policies should be dispensed with. The policies described as economic rationalism are essentially a response to these changes, not their cause. They are occurring in various forms throughout the world and, in part, are unavoidable.'

Let's hope that Labor MPs, starting with Cheryl Kernot, can belatedly grasp the argument. That Tanner comes from the left-wing and the union movement marks this book as a pivotal point. So does its launch by Paul Keating, whose historical role was to turn Labor towards the open marketplace. Tanner says globalisation means that traditional economic regulation is crumbling and that 'a new role for government is beginning to emerge'. But defining this new role is hard. Tanner calls it 'government as facilitator'—a mechanistic and uninspiring label.

Tanner's second over-arching theme is that a new Australia must be open in both economic and social dimensions. So he is a champion of more immigration, multiculturalism, Aboriginal reconciliation and the republic (Keating's social agenda), seeing a fusion between an open economy and a redefined Australian identity.

With his polemic, Tanner has probably put the final nail in hopes that Labor could linger in a policy 'comfort zone'. Tanner, like Mark Latham, knows this won't work. Though their ideas often differ, Latham and Tanner share the strategic belief that globalisation is an historic event for nations and demands a new approach. They are striving to lift Australia's debate from the provincial mediocrity into which it has recently slumped.

There are three chief strengths in Tanner's work: his analysis of the new economy; his argument for a new approach to education and communications; and his warning that Labor is in a state of internal decay, an admission that is surely an embarrassment for the entire media, which has missed this for the past two years.

Tanner recalls that when he became active in the clerks union, it had almost 700 workers at Tattersalls, but by the time he became secretary there were only 40 left. He documents the destructive impact of the new economy, but his focus falls upon the immense opportunities it generates.

Along the way, he slams two myths—the exaggerated claim that cheap labour nations are undermining Australia's living standards and that jobs in the services sector aren't real jobs because you don't use a shovel. He draws a mixture of lessons from the new economy: that it puts a premium on skill; that it has a vast job-creation potential in new industries based on technology, information, services and entertainment; that governments should focus on creating new jobs, not saving disappearing jobs; that intervention is essential to check the income inequality driven by markets; that the bonds between the individual and society need to be rebuilt; that industry policy must enhance the foundations of competitiveness rather than offering an easy tax break; that the Productivity Commission be saved to guarantee transparency over funds to assist industry; and that foreign investment policy be liberalised beyond John Howard's regime, but that 'hot' speculative money be limited.

There is a conflict between Tanner's analysis and his remedy. The former is sweeping; the latter is vague or timid. This discontinuity is stark—just as it was in Latham's book. Of course, such criticism applies to all analysts who address these issues today because the answers are still evolving. And that is a real problem for a politician.

The 'new path' policies are far short of being defined. Tanner makes it clear the old Left is finished with its obsolete mix of personal libertarianism and collective action. But he still clings to strong industrial regulation, hesitates about privatisation, advocates changes to world trade and finance beyond our power, flirts with taxing the super funds to generate regional investment, opposes a goods and services tax, rejects boosting jobs by wage restraint and advocates a new regulatory approach to the financial system.

Overall, Tanner's agenda is too open; it needs priorities. It needs, more urgently, much more work on the policies. The paradox of his book is its persuasion that a new path is essential while exposing the depth of the policy challenge this involves.

The Australian, *10 February 1999*

PAUL KEATING

THE ERA OF economic liberalisation which so dominated the English-speaking democracies during the past fifteen years was driven by a range of remarkable political leaders from Margaret Thatcher to Sir Roger Douglas.

In the story of this international era, Australia warrants a fascinating chapter in its own right with its reforms spearheaded by a Labor government which won five successive elections before losing office last year.

John Edward's biography of Paul Keating is the most detailed and illuminating of one of the achievers of this period, that larger-than-life instinctive politician from Sydney's working-class west, Paul Keating, who was a remarkable and, to many, a baffling concoction of overpowering charm, policy architecture and lethal intimidation.

Keating is the most interesting Australian politician of the past generation and John Edwards captures his personal growth from a skinny impatient fifteen-year-old school leaver to the snappy Zegna-clad Treasurer gliding between the European central banks and the antique shops of Paris, moving gears between analysing capital flows to searching out First Empire prizes.

Keating's story offers a political parable; a life of a Labor politician confronting and, in the process, being transformed by the issues and frustrations of his age; a man who grasped that politics is performance driven but who realised that the politician who performs constantly risks losing his real self.

The story ends, eventually, after 500 pages, in defeat, another leader unable to hold together the demands arising from

the national economy, prime ministerial popularity, and social
fragmentation implicit in the 1990s condition.

Keating's achievements, by any measure, are substantial.
They involve, first, a long eight years as Australian Treasurer
during which he was the spearhead of the internationalisation
and historic opening up of the economy; second, forming with
his prime minister, Bob Hawke, a partnership based upon
Hawke's popularity and Keating's firepower, that became the
most successful in the history of Australian federal Labor and
won four successive elections; third, driven by his long ambition
and provoked by Hawke's breach of a pact to retire, Keating
mounted a challenge and eventually prevailed, thereby deposit-
ing Labor's most successful leader; finally, Keating won an
election in his own right, giving Labor a fifth term during which
he reinvented his political persona by championing a vision of
Australia's destiny based upon a republic, reconciliation with the
indigenous people and engagement with the Asia–Pacific as the
path of the future, all of which culminated in a humiliating
election rejection last year and his exit from politics aged 52.
Quite a career.

The flickering image of Keating abroad conveyed a distortion—the anti-British bias of his republicanism, his touching of
the Queen when guiding her at a reception, and his penchant
for abuse of opponents as an almost endless collection of scum-
bags, stupid foul-mouthed grubs, pieces of criminal garbage,
gutless spivs, gigolos, dimwits, blackguards, sleezebags, toffs and
friends of the tax avoidance industry. Nothing was heard of his
memorable one-liners, such as, when taunting Andrew Peacock
about a comeback, he mocked 'Can a souffle rise twice?'

It must also be said that serious analysis on Australia is
prejudiced by a breed of expatriate typified by John Pilger whose
bent for polemics usually offers a lopsided or ludicrous view of
Australia or a combination of both.

John Edwards, the author, like Keating, hails from Sydney's
west and has worked as a union research officer, journalist,
ministerial adviser and economist. The book has its own history.
Edwards approached Keating in 1990 for an interview for a
book. What happened from this point was quintessential Keating: he rang Edwards at his hotel room at 12.40 a.m. saying he
was happy to give an interview, but what was the point? 'How
much,' recalls Edwards, 'in the time available, could he really

tell me about the last eight years?' If Edwards was serious, then he should work for Keating. So Edwards came, as adviser and in-house historian with access to the confidential documents.

The upshot is not just a biography but an insight into how Labor governed and how Australia was run. The unifying thread of the book, as it was for the history of the time, is the personality of Keating—mercurial, confronting, ambitious, funny, obsessive and self-deluding. It is because Keating let people know how he felt that the nation was forced to interpret itself through Keating's own moods and preoccupations.

This is a self-made career by a man who educated himself on the run. Born into a Catholic and Labor family, by the age of eleven Keating was handing out how-to-vote cards, as a 20-year-old he organised to take control of the Labor Youth Council, as a 24-year-old he won a bitter pre-selection contest and at 25 took his seat in 1969 as the youngest member of Australia's House of Representatives.

This book falls comfortably into three parts, each possessing its own character. The first is the story of the young Paul Keating, a wonderful account of a Sydney political family and the humdrum workings of branch politics overlaid by the Cold War and the battles over communist influence.

The second and longest section, where the author makes his greatest effort, documents Australia's economic policy, culminating with a forensic study of the monetary policy mis-calculations by Keating and the 'official family', the Treasury and central bank, as Australia, overbalanced by the 1980s boom, slid into recession. Finally, Edwards deals in a rather brief and anecdotal fashion with the four-year Keating prime ministership.

Keating began his career as a political operative, narrow, focused, factionalised. He knew where power was located from the ground up. Keating was the best and fastest numbers man in the Labor caucus; he was a champion of the NSW right-wing, his factional springboard; he cultivated the media—journalists, then editors, finally proprietors; he expanded rapidly his range of contacts beyond Labor, to businessmen, then to financiers at the 'big end of town'. Keating often told me that in policies 'you don't have a moment to lose' and this reflected his approach. He refused to wait in line.

From the start Keating had a genius for harnessing tradition but never succumbing to the dead weight of the past; he was both a Labor believer yet searching to adapt and bend the party's thinking towards the future.

Above all, Keating's style was hot; part-hustler, part-apostle, he simply overwhelmed his audience. During the current account deficit crisis of 1986 Keating had a blackboard established in his office and would scribble graphs and jottings for his journalistic guests such that one of my colleagues sadly confided, 'I don't want to go into that room again because I know he'll convince me'. Nobody was exempt, certainly not US President George Bush who arrived in Sydney just days after Keating became Prime Minister. Sensing Bush's weariness, Keating launched into an exposition of how US engagement with Asia was the key to its national revival, while his guests were largely rendered mute. Edwards notes that it was almost impossible for Keating to conduct a serious conversation that was 'not directed at enlightening, improving, persuading and inspiring his interlocutor'.

Keating was a lateral thinker. Unburdened by the discipline of tertiary training, he thought not in logical progression but through random insights which would be reconfigured into a 'big picture'.

His colleague, former finance minister, Peter Walsh, said that Keating was the best salesman he ever saw, the problem being that Keating's first convert was always himself. When Keating discovered a new idea he seized it with the conviction of a man unaware of its history or its pitfalls.

Keating's strength as Treasurer derived from his clout in Cabinet, the quality of his official advisers, his courage and political skills and also because he lived in an era that lent itself to sweeping redesign. His historic achievement in this portfolio was to terminate the Australian economic tradition of introspection and protection. The old ideas were designed to sustain a British democracy with a commodity-driven economy located in Asia, a part of the world alien to its culture.

As Edwards explains, Hawke and Keating were pragmatists, politicians trying to run a growth economy and win elections. Keating made policy as he went, responding to events. Their initial framework was to utilise their accord with the trade union movement and wind back the budget deficit.

The major economic achievements were: the float of the Australian dollar and the abolition of exchange controls, thereby introducing a new discipline into economic management; the application of the accord to restrain wages and promote strong growth; reform of the direct tax base after Keating's defeat in a solo campaign to introduce a broadly based indirect tax; a program of tariff reduction designed to change Australia from being a relatively closed to a relatively open economy; a budget surplus by the late 1980s which finished as a large deficit in the 1990s; and all the time trying to combat a current account deficit which reflected Australia's poor competitiveness and inability to save.

Keating throughout was resolute in public but searching in private; trying to fit together the pieces of the jigsaw, to master how the economy, how the world, really worked. His advisers, like their colleagues in Britain and America, struggled to understand how monetary policy operated in a deregulated economy where a failure of precision could cause unemployment for hundreds of thousands of people. Keating felt his judgment was better than theirs; he complained that economists thought their work was science, but it wasn't, it was really about art, about discretion.

It was a conclusion he reached during countless talks through the afternoon light and the evenings about when to tighten, when to ease, whether to wait another month or three, about how the lags worked. Then when the crunch hit and Keating branded it 'the recession we had to have' his career seemed finished.

With a mighty flourish Keating resurrected himself. As Prime Minister he rode the business cycle up and looked to fresh visions, provoking his curiosity to rekindle his passion. Keating fought against a sense of disappointment that he'd got the top job too late. As a young PM he charmed Indonesia's President Suharto and as a contemporary he lunched with Bill Clinton explaining that Australia's greatest task was to find its sense of self and its identity in the region.

So Keating indulged his artist's instinct for 'the big picture'. His mistake was to think he could govern on his terms, not those of the electorate. He became obsessed by his own vision and forgot that many Australians rejected that vision and that others wanted a slower pace of cultural change. But Keating's definition of leadership was to lead—and he pressed ahead with Aboriginal reconciliation, an Australian republic and engagement with Asia—only to lose to the Liberal leader, John Howard, who pledged to be responsive to the community and make the people relaxed and comfortable, which sounded like a line from a Keating joke.

The strength of this indispensable book on Australia is its grand treatment of economic policy and its capture of the complex Keating personality. By contrast, its coverage of the prime ministerial period is too much a diary account.

As for Keating himself, the magnitude of his defeat leaves open the question of how much of his vision will be undone, and prompts the conclusion that as a political artist he overlooked the need for on-site engineering to better sustain his work.

Unedited review of Keating: The Inside Story, *by John Edwards in* The Times Literary Supplement, *11 April 1997*

PART IV

THE INTERNATIONAL SCENE

FOR AUSTRALIA THE key trends in international politics in the late 1990s were the great success of the Anglo-Saxon economies, the East Asian financial collapse and the crisis over Indonesia and East Timor.

They posed many questions and few answers. Would the twenty-first century also be an American century? Was the age of the Asian economic miracle now consigned to history? Can Australia successfully maintain its ties with both America and Asia? How will Australia handle the decline of its relations with Indonesia? How will Australia integrate its support for an independent East Timor with its ongoing engagement with Asia?

There was a celebratory tone among the pundits. It was suggested that liberal capitalism had triumphed in an 'end of history' finality; that more democracies meant fewer wars because democracies never fought each other; and that capitalism had moved to a new phase beyond its old cycles of boom and bust. Yet reality kept undermining theory.

The US was a flawed superpower. Its capacity for economic renewals was striking, even assuming a Wall Street correction. But America was becoming more introspective and domestic support for its international leadership role was fast evaporating. There was a bigger question posed by US success in the 1990s—whether America as a society was best equipped to handle the coming age of globalisation. Those seeking to predict the future looked to the US where innovation, technology and entrepreneurship were most advanced but where democracy was in strife.

169

The decade finished with shadows over Asia—Japan struggling after its long recession, China stranded with the most daunting modernisation task in history and handicapped by its communist legacy, South East Asia in confusion and retreat and Indonesia in a systemic crisis. Cyclical trends will dictate an Asian recovery of some magnitude. The real issue is the region's ability to address the need for fundamental economic and political change.

Australia learnt from these triumphs and tragedies. Its mixture of British heritage, US connections and Asian experience means that Australia is well positioned to adapt to international shocks. But the test of this theory has come with East Timor and Indonesia. This is Australia's most challenging foreign policy issue for a generation. The outcome will be decisive for our engagement with Asia.

THE AMERICAN MIRACLE

THE UNITED STATES is undergoing a great leap forward as it
prepares to become the first true society of the age of
globalisation, a remaking on a scale that is seemingly out of
control.

Australia is in danger of losing touch with the US, whose
progress stretches beyond our imagination. Spend a fortnight
in the US and the impression, hopefully glib, is that Australia
is being marginalised. You arrive in the US thinking America's
the joke with its Monica Lewinsky obsession. That's fair
enough, too. By the time you arrive home, you realise the joke's
on Australia with its policy debate trapped in a time warp.

Let's have some snapshots from the future. The most
common surname for new home buyers in Los Angeles is
'Garcia' followed by 'Lee'. It took Jeff Bezos, who runs the
on-line bookseller Amazon.com, six weeks to make his second
billion and he still lives in a small, rented flat. The drug
authority has just approved Thalidomide, once infamous for
causing deformity, to help cure leprosy after a research breakthrough. The average American woman will soon have as many
husbands as she has children. President Bill Clinton has intervened to help save Russia, once the evil superpower, from
financial ruin. And the jobless level for American blacks, long
the most depressed section of US society, is 8.2 per cent—about
Australia's national average in our seventh year of recovery.

The mistake Australians make about the US is observation
by category. They study the share boom, the jobs boom, the
technology boom—and conclude that an overdue correction

171

bringing the US 'back to the pack' is imminent. This is partly true—but it misses the bigger picture.

The US is heading into another zone. The economic cycle— and an inevitable downturn—will check its progress but the transforming forces are deep and structural. The split in national character has rarely been so vivid. The US is in optimistic overdrive while Australia, with an economy still likely to grow near 3 per cent, is riddled with pessimism that isn't just Hanson-induced.

The US is not all good news. Where has it failed? Don't look beyond guns and health. If you're going to get sick, don't pick the US. Kerry Packer can afford it but bankruptcy can't be ruled out.

Handguns exist in 40 per cent of US households. Taking your kids to a friend's house means a responsible parent asks: 'Do you have guns?' Incredibly, many are too embarrassed to ask. After the horrific story of 11-year-old Christopher Murphy, of Staten Island, New York, who went to a friend's house to play Nintendo and was dead 30 minutes later in a gun accident, New York has acted: it now insists upon guns having safety catches!

So after the snapshots, what are the big trends? A decline of politics as a focus of national life; the rise and rise of finance reflected in share ownership and new business start-ups; a faith in immigration to improve the US; the looming twenty-first century disintegration of Anglo racial dominance in city after city; the greatest creation of high-income, high-technology jobs in history; the greatest shift from welfare to low-paid jobs ever engineered by a democracy; a new economic paradigm of low prices and labour shortages which sees inflation still dormant and unemployment down to 4.5 per cent; a mass entertainment culture that dulls the brain but promotes cultural homogeneity; lack of concern about the rest of the world; and signs of that old triumphalism.

The sense of American ascendancy is pervasive. The US is making an old claim in a new guise—to be the successful society of the early twenty-first century.

This has a strategic dimension. Remember that the US, Canada and Mexico are tied into a free-trade zone. Consider the geography. New York and the East Coast have long been an Atlantic community tied to Europe; Miami is a 'capital' of Latin

America; the Vancouver-San Francisco-Los Angeles belt links the US to East Asia; while across the southern border is a Hispanic America of poverty, cheap labour, legal and illegal migration. Clinton has just told Americans that they have 'the lowest unemployment in 28 years, the lowest crime rate in 25 years, the lowest welfare rolls in 29 years, the first balanced budget and surplus in 29 years and the highest home ownership in history'.

The key to US success is a set of self-reinforcing policies and ideas. The economy is remarkably open, competitive and flexible—for capital and labour. Since 1980, 44 million jobs have been lost in downsizing and re-structuring while 73 million jobs have been created in the private sector, a net gain of 29 million. In recent years, the new jobs have been in mid-to-high incomes in a 2:1 ratio compared with low-paying jobs. By contrast, Australia's priority is protecting old jobs rather than creating new ones.

America's low-wage economy fuels a huge job expansion in the services and sales sectors. This has helped the great shift from welfare to work with the welfare rolls under Clinton falling from fourteen million to nine million.

The fashion in US shares is the overpriced technology stocks. The Internet is an extension of American culture: about 90 per cent of Web sites are American. New business fables are being spun: Yahoo Inc., the World Wide Web directory, is now worth more than the New York Times Co. Its projected profits of only $23 million mean a price-to-earnings ratio of a fantastic 445 compared with the average p/e ratio of 28 for the top 500 companies. On-line bookseller Amazon.com Inc. is capitalised to the value of America's two biggest book retailers combined.

There are two responses to this: yes, it's crazy—or is it? The irony about Amazon is that it makes e-commerce successful by selling books, the medium the Internet was supposed to destroy. Moral: you can't predict the impact of technology.

In California alone, 70 new high-tech companies are launched a week—by future billionaires and bankrupts. Clinton long ago declared US ownership of the digital revolution, tying its spirit to the original American Revolution. The US is dominating the computer and information industries of the future through the age-old techniques of training and big investment. Electronic commerce will be a $US300 billion industry by 2002.

But traditional industries, services, retail, transport, are being upgraded via high technology.

Meanwhile, at the Pentagon during a briefing oozing with goodwill for Australia, concern is expressed at future defence links because Australians can't stay abreast of US weapons technology.

In his latest *Altantic Monthly* excursion, writer Robert D. Kaplan identifies the contradictory sides of Tucson, Arizona, as a metaphor for the US. Here is a city booming in a desert, where small towns die and urbanisation is dominant, with a Mexican underclass, a medium income of $US22 000 compared with $US26 000 in 1970, where a fifth of all households arrived in the previous year and whose only future lies in relocation of high-tech firms. A city coordinator says 'my neighbours are Pakistani doctors, Silicon Valley types, ingenious entrepreneurs, wealthy Lebanese and Chinese'.

Out on the streets, Clinton envisages a greater America despite its present population of 260 million. In an important recent speech, he declared: 'The driving force behind our increasing diversity is a new large wave of immigration. Each year nearly a million people come legally to America . . . because of immigration there is no majority race in Hawaii or Houston or New York City. Within five years, there will be no majority race in our largest State, California. In a little more than 50 years, there will be no majority race in the United States.'

Yes, there are risks. But the US is prepared to back itself against risks, be they stocks, welfare reform or immigration. America, where talk of fragmentation has been a fashion since the 1960s, seems to be more 'together' than usual.

Contrast Clinton's unflinching belief in diversity with Australia's present ambiguity: 'Let me state my view unequivocally. I believe new immigrants are good for America. They are revitalising our cities. They are building our new economy. They are strengthening our ties to the global economy.'

At one extreme is the idea that the US will dominate the next century, a triumphalism put by the Editor-in-Chief of US *News and World Report*, Mortimer B. Zukerman, in a recent issue of *Foreign Affairs*: 'The American economy is in the eighth year of sustained growth that transcends the "German miracle" and the "Japanese miracle" of earlier decades. Everything that should be up is up—GDP, capital spending, incomes, the stock market, employment, exports, consumer spending, business confidence. Everything that should be down is down—unemployment, inflation, interest rates. The stock exchanges have added over $US4 trillion in value in the last four years alone . . . This is no fluke.' It was 'the unique American brand of entrepreneurial bottom-up capitalism' which would 'provide the basis for extending America's comparative advantage over time'.

The US's most famous economist, Paul Krugman, punctures such euphoria: 'The current sense that the US is on top of the world is based on a huge exaggeration of the implications of a few good years here and a few bad years elsewhere.'

It's morning again in the US. The issue is not how long it will last. It can't. It's whether the US has got the best blueprint for the long term.

The Weekend Australian, *25–26 July 1998*

THE EAST TIMOR LEGACY

THE SOONER THE federal government releases all documents relating to the 1975 incorporation of East Timor by Indonesia the better. Nevertheless, some judgments are possible based upon already extensive disclosures.

The first point to make about Gough Whitlam's 1975 East Timor policy is that it failed. It is the worst foreign policy failure of the Whitlam period. This is the outstanding conclusion, yet it is hardly mentioned.

The seeds of this failure were sown at the outset. This was at Whitlam's meeting with President Suharto on 6 September 1974, at Wonosobo, near Yogyakarta, six months after a new government came to power in Lisbon and pledged to start decolonisation. East Timor was one of Portugal's smallest possessions.

This Whitlam–Suharto exchange was decisive. It defined an Australian position that would endure, indeed, that would be difficult to change. Whitlam told Suharto 'Portuguese Timor should become part of Indonesia' and that 'this should happen in accordance with the properly expressed wishes of the people'. That is, incorporation by consent.

It was unqualified. A firm, almost dogmatic Whitlam position. It left no exits, no flexibility.

The outstanding theme running through advice to the Whitlam government is that incorporation by consent was the best result. If East Timor voted to join Indonesia then life would be easier for everyone. Whitlam was certainly convinced of this.

But long before mid-1975 it was clear this policy was

unachievable. From the start, it was highly optimistic although understandable; its impossibility became obvious as 1975 advanced.

The position Whitlam gave Suharto at Wonosobo was a personal view which became Australian policy. From first to last, Whitlam made Timor policy.

Whitlam made two other points to Suharto at this meeting. He rejected independence saying East Timor was 'economically unviable' but his real motive was political since he said 'independence would be unwelcome to Indonesia, to Australia and to other countries in the region'.

Second, Whitlam cautioned that Suharto should be aware 'of the effects on public opinion in Australia of incorporation of the province into Indonesia against the wishes of the people'—a bid to persuade Suharto against force.

Suharto told Whitlam there were only two options for Portuguese Timor: independence or incorporation with another country. He dwelt on the problems of independence. A weak Timor would look to outside powers such as China or the Soviet Union and become 'a thorn in the eye of Australia and a thorn in Indonesia's back'.

This would become a constant refrain from Jakarta. It was part-belief, part-propaganda. Suharto's outlook was no surprise since he came to power as survivor of a pro-leftist coup that saw his fellow generals murdered.

Suharto identified the contradiction in Whitlam's position, saying an act of self-determination which supported independence 'would certainly give rise to problems' for Indonesia.

The meeting would only have encouraged Suharto to a policy of incorporation, if he had not already decided on this. Evidence from a number of Indonesian sources is that Suharto decided on incorporation during 1974, at an early stage of the process. The record of this Whitlam–Suharto meeting implies this but is not explicit.

The final interpretation of this meeting comes from Whitlam himself. In a subsequent letter to Suharto, he said of their Yogyakarta exchange: 'We *agreed* that the solution which we preferred was that the territory should become part of Indonesia' via self-determination.

Australian journalist Hamish McDonald reported in his 1980 book on Indonesia that Suharto 'felt he had reached an intuitive understanding with Whitlam' symbolised by his taking Whitlam alone into a cave believed to be the dwelling of the clown god Semar.

Yet this was a fateful decision. Given incorporation was Indonesia's policy if, ultimately, it could not be achieved by free choice, then force would be needed. If Australia was ever going to support or tolerate Timor's independence then it had to signal this from the start. Whitlam, in effect, closed the option.

His most penetrating critic was regional veteran, journalist Peter Hastings, who in late 1974 wrote: 'Why in the name of all that is cautious, the unseemly public haste to hand Portuguese Timor to Indonesia?'

Hastings advocated Australia and Indonesia support a continued Portuguese presence in Timor to allow time to sort out political options. By late 1974 he was opposing integration as premature and undemocratic. He wrote that Whitlam 'practically gave East Timor to Indonesia'.

In December 1974 at a Colombo Plan meeting in Singapore, Australia's Foreign Minister, Don Willesee, contradicted his Indonesian counterpart Adam Malik, who asserted that independence was not a practical option. Willesee, according to his then aide Nancy Viviani, took a different view to Whitlam.

After the Portuguese coup, three parties emerged in East Timor: Apodeti which sought integration; Fretilin which wanted independence and was depicted as pro-communist by Jakarta; and UDT which favoured an ongoing Portuguese role but which later merged with Fretilin. The forces favouring independence were increasingly ascendant.

By early 1975, Australia's dilemma was apparent. The chances of incorporation by consent were fading but Australia could not change Whitlam's line without courting severe Indonesian displeasure and finding itself isolated.

Meanwhile, Suharto had given responsibility for East Timor to his confidant Ali Murtopo and his 'special operations' outfit. Murtopo was to 'manage' the desired result in Timor and Lisbon drawing on his West Irian experience.

Hamish McDonald said of Suharto that 'a purely military solution had been ruled out . . .' It was a point that would occur often in the 1975 cable traffic: Suharto was a dove resisting the hawks led by General Benny Murdani who wanted a military takeover.

However, in February 1975 there were Indonesian troop movements reported by Hastings and alarm in Australia that Indonesia might resort to military action. This prompted Whitlam's 28 February letter to Suharto at the time Dick Woolcott became the new ambassador to Indonesia. This letter is the high tide of Whitlam's efforts to dissuade Suharto from military action.

Whitlam argued there was 'no evidence' of the external dangers to Timor about which Suharto had been so worried; he referred to the 'great sensitivity of Australian parliamentary and public opinion to any suggestion' of unilateral Indonesian action; he stressed his government's support 'for the close and mutually advantageous relationship between our two countries which has been and will remain so important to succeeding governments in this country'. Finally, he was optimistic that the East Timorese and Portuguese would agree on a program for the transfer of power and that independence was not an imminent issue.

Just six weeks later, Whitlam met Suharto at length in Townsville over 3–5 April 1975.

Whitlam began this meeting by noting Portugal was moving further to the left and that Fretilin and UDT were 'demanding immediate independence'. The record reveals Whitlam's fears about the domestic opinion in Australia. He told Suharto there was both 'an extreme right' and 'the left, including people in his own party' who would try to undermine the Indonesian relationship.

The language of the record is revealing. Whitlam said 'he still hoped that Portuguese Timor would be associated with or integrated into Indonesia; but that this result should be achieved in a way which would not upset the Australian people'. He floats the idea of United Nations action.

Whitlam, overall, is more defensive, prepared to fleetingly contemplate a looser association between Indonesia and Timor. He appeals, in effect, to Suharto not to ruin the domestic basis for pro-Indonesian policy in Australia.

His references to the principle of self-determination, by contrast, are passing and weak. In an exposition on the Portuguese Timorese, Whitlam ends with the feeble remark that 'in time they would come to recognise their ethnic kinship with their Indonesian neighbours'.

Yet Whitlam is adamant that Australia is not a party principal, that the issue is 'essentially the responsibility of the people of Portuguese Timor, Portugal and Indonesia'.

He told Suharto: 'The question of Portuguese Timor was simply not the responsibility of Australia.' This reflects Whitlam's powerful anti-colonialism (Papua New Guinea was about to gain its independence). It is a signal that Suharto must solve the issue; yet Whitlam wants the solution not to prejudice Australian opinion.

Suharto took his cue. On the invasion question, he told Whitlam that 'as a country which endorsed the principles of freedom and democracy Indonesia would never contemplate such a course of action'.

Suharto gave his word: no invasion. Whitlam must have felt reassured. But Suharto said, 'Indonesia had concluded that integration with Indonesia was the best solution'. This was unqualified.

Suharto said Portugal believed integration the best result provided the people consented. He seemed optimistic that Indonesia and Portugal could devise a decolonisation process that got Jakarta the result it wanted.

In August 1975, the East Timor situation fell apart. The parties started fighting and UDT staged a coup. Fretilin responded, got access to Portuguese weapons and established its dominance. The Portuguese administration fled. Indonesia was alarmed: it faced the independence party, Fretilin, in near control.

It was a decisive turning point, clearly unforeseen by Suharto when he gave his 'no-force' pledge to Whitlam.

On 17 August Woolcott opposed a suggestion from Canberra that Whitlam send another message to Suharto. 'We are dealing with a settled Indonesian policy to incorporate Timor,' Woolcott cabled. 'Indonesia is simply not prepared to accept the risks they see to them in an independent Timor and I do not believe that we will be able to change their minds on this. We have in fact tried to do so.'

Woolcott told Canberra that what Indonesia needed from Australia was 'understanding'. He said Australia had already made 'more representations . . . than any other country'.

He saw force as an option for Suharto, advising that from here 'our policies should be based on disengaging ourselves as far as possible from the Timor question; getting Australians presently there out of Timor; leave events to take their course; and if and when Indonesia does intervene, act in a way which would be designed to minimise the public impact in Australia and show privately understanding to Indonesia'.

Woolcott reported a conversation with the US ambassador: US Secretary of State Henry Kissinger had instructed the ambassador to disengage from Timor discussions because the US 'is involved in enough problems of greater importance'. Woolcott said the US ambassador told him that if Indonesia intervened the US would hope it would do so 'effectively, quickly, and not use our equipment'.

In a follow-up cable on 18 August Woolcott reported that Suharto 'is at present firm in his attitude that Indonesia should not intervene militarily . . . at this stage. The firmness with which he holds this attitude at present has surprised and, I believed, irritated [the ministry of defence]'.

On 23 August, about a day after Fretilin established control, Woolcott cabled that Ali Murtopo told him that Suharto still opposed force, but he was being briefed on events twice daily.

Whitlam told federal Parliament on 26 August that it was Portugal's job to halt the fighting—an utterly useless legalism—and that there was no mediating or military role for Australia. Whitlam wouldn't cop Australia acting in any quasi-colonial capacity.

Indonesia now assumed Portugal's evacuation meant it had forfeited any substantial role. On 24 August, Woolcott's cable confirmed Suharto's new position: he would intervene only if Portugal 'agrees with this course' but Woolcott added that 'Indonesia probably cannot stand by for very long while killing continues'.

Woolcott then canvassed the likely scenario: Indonesian intervention without Portugal's consent. Woolcott said Suharto would 'only decide to intervene with considerable reluctance' and that Murdani promised to give Australia 'at least two hours notice'.

The Defence Department appeared to have little influence on Australia's position. But it was giving very different advice. Its thinking was contained in a 9 October advice from its future chief, Bill Pritchett, disputing the assumptions on which Woolcott and Whitlam operated.

Pritchett asserted the primacy of the defence interest with Indonesia and the department's concern that Timor might substantially impair the 30-year-old friendly bilateral relationship.

He offered a series of acute insights: 'If the Indonesians resorted to immoderate action to gain control . . . the Australian domestic reaction would probably be such as to make it very difficult for the Government to sustain cooperative policies towards Indonesia.'

Pritchett criticised the policy of integration with self-determination as inconsistent: 'What we have offered Indonesia with one hand we have sought to deny them with the other.'

Moving to his central theme, he argued that Fretilin was dominant; to achieve integration, Indonesia would 'have to dispose of Fretilin'; this would require force on a considerable scale; but 'a significant residue of opponents of Indonesia would take to the hills in guerilla operations'. So, in conclusion, Indonesia's incorporation policy was deeply flawed.

The alternative, Pritchett said, had long been argued by Defence—'Acceptance of an independent State'. It would be 'poor and weak' but would meet the call for self-determination and remove 'the Indonesian threat of force with its injurious consequences'. He admitted 'it would clearly be difficult to persuade the Indonesians to adopt it' but 'with a major effort of statesmanship' would not be 'impossible'.

Pritchett foresaw better than any adviser the doomed consequences of integration. But he surely exaggerated the prospects of getting Indonesia to change its policy so late. The invasion came in December after Fretilin's unilateral declaration of independence.

The Australian media has spent 25 years asking the wrong question. The issue is not whether Whitlam gave the green light to the invasion—the documentary evidence, so far, is that he did not.

The issue is whether a more prudent policy should have been adopted in 1974 which kept open the independence option and whether this would have prevented the August 1975 civil war which turned Suharto from dove into hawk.

The real question is whether our diplomacy could have made

independence an achievable result. Hastings believed the answer
was yes. Viviani, Willesee's aide at the time, says no.

'There are three reasons why an independent East Timor
was not achievable,' Viviani says. 'First, Suharto had decided at
an early stage that integration was his policy. His mind was set
for a long time. Second, there had to be a degree of unity in
East Timor to make independence work. But from August 1974
no party was going to prevail except by force of arms. Third,
the US position was for integration. It was the height of the
Cold War. The US would not support an independent East
Timor which it likened to a Cuba in Asia. Independence wasn't
an option because the East Timorese couldn't manage it, the
Indonesians had decided against it and the US, for different
reasons, had the same view.'

If Viviani is right, a further question follows. For 25 years,
the media has cried appeasement over East Timor—but it has
not been honest in this debate. Appeasement has a Hitlerite
derivation. Appeasement is a terrible policy precisely because a
military response was required instead.

So, if Whitlam couldn't have persuaded Suharto by diplomatic means, should Australia have gone to war over East
Timor? It is time for an honest reasoned answer to be given to
this question by the drum-beaters of the appeasement legions.

The Weekend Australian, *13–14 March 1999*

TONY BLAIR

TONY BLAIR, 43, is a new phenomenon for Britain—a young, appealing, middle-class Labour leader who is ruthless in his pursuit of victory at the coming election. You hear many complaints about him: that he has sold Labour's soul, that he won't sing songs at trade union parties, that he sent a child to an elite Catholic school, and that he is too obsessed by media image. But this is dross on the main story which is that Blair and his allies have modernised the British Labour Party, once thought to be one of the world's most hopeless cases. He understands that after eighteen years in the wilderness the Labour Party has an over-arching responsibility at the next election to win; to win on behalf of its believers and followers and, in a wider sense, on behalf of the vitality of British democracy. If winning means a re-think from top to bottom of Labour's structure, policies and tactics—and it does—then Blair has the courage. He points towards the sunlit uplands and his party follows with a mixture of greed, grumbles and gratitude.

Blair is lucky, that's the first point. British Labour, you see, underwent its own Kennedy syndrome; the night was 11 May 1994. The social democrat elite of Europe had gathered at Piccadilly. Labour had a leader, a Scot, John Smith, able and authoritative, under whom the party could either convince or delude itself that rehabilitation was at hand. It was a European gala dinner at the Park Lane Hotel, and the evening broke up amid the confidence such gatherings induce. At 8 a.m. the next morning Smith was dead. A heart attack. He had been leader for two years.

Anji Hunter was Blair's head of private office, confidante and gatekeeper, a friend from school days. She had heard the morning radio coverage of the dinner and when the doors of her office lift opened she knew at once it had to be a death. A staffer was weeping. 'I naturally thought of Tony. Then they told me, "John's dead".'

Blair's plane had just touched down at Aberdeen. His closest party colleague, Gordon Brown, rang first. British politics went into mourning. The Scots lowered their flags, even Tory ministers wept, Labour sank into grief. Blair appeared before the media, deflated, red-eyed, sombre. But politics knows no limits. A dead leader means a funeral and then a new leader.

In his heart Tony Blair knew what the death meant. Immediately. He knew in that twilight zone when he was still numb from the tragedy but with a mind that functioned rationally and on fast forward. He decided soon, very soon, that he would run. It was a natural decision. Once it was taken, he was unequivocal and unyielding.

I put to him what I had been told, that he had decided to run virtually before the body was cold. 'No, that's untrue and unfair,' he replied with emphasis. 'What happened was the moment that John died, of course, all the attention came upon who was going to be the next leader. It was impossible to escape that attention. I had to make a decision about whether I was leader or not.'

When did he first see the leadership in front of him? 'I didn't really, until John Smith died. I never thought I was going to be leader of the Labour Party.'

Tony Blair was neither the most experienced nor the most senior shadow minister. But the party and media reaction was instinctive and electric—'it must be Blair'. This was not obvious from his career; but it was a deep response to his persona. John Major had said two years before that the Labour politician he most feared was Blair, presumably confident then that he was unlikely to become leader against him. Major's prediction was correct—Blair is a tougher opponent than Smith would have been.

Death delivered Blair the leadership. The timing was perfect—three years from an election which is now imminent, facing a weary Tory government, a party torn over Europe, and a prime minister enfeebled by a grey inertia.

That Blair is lucky is important because luck is the elixir of politics. But the story tells us more—that he is hungry for power. This hunger surprised many of his colleagues at the time. Now it is so manifest it is surprising that people could have ever been surprised by it. The overwhelming impression after Smith's death was Blair's utter and immediate conviction that he was the leader and, critically, the party's vindication of that judgment. This goes to the essence of the man and the politician. So how did he do it?

After you meet Blair you know. There's a catch somewhere, but it's not obvious. He seems to be the perfect political commodity—solidly built but fit, with dark wavy hair, tanned face, relaxed body language, not just young but youthful, articulate, and a ring-of-confidence smile revealing a startling set of teeth. The smile has been seized upon by the Tories as too exaggerated, as grounds for distrust. But like everything else about him it seems natural.

In his small office towards the back of the Palace of Westminster he presents an open face. He is direct, engaging. He sits on a small lounge in shirt sleeves and tie, slightly loosened. The phone rings, staff enter, the sense of activity hovers just outside.

'He's going to be Prime Minister in a few weeks but he's still a human being,' says Shadow Cabinet member and fan Mo Mowlan. 'I mean, he's still with us. He laughs, jokes and asks you about the kids.' Yes, Blair mixes easily, but still keeps his distance. A master of comfortable detachment.

He is Oxford-educated, a barrister, devoid of roots in the union movement or working class, thoroughly middle class in his habits and lifestyle, married to a brilliant lawyer and obvious feminist, a dedicated father of three children, a churchgoer, an articulate communicator with a very clear political strategy.

What does it all mean? Essentially that he is well adjusted, not an in-bred political operative. He is the ideal candidate to win middle-class votes for Labour—to destroy the class barrier which has denied Labour the wider appeal necessary to prevail for most of this century.

Blair projects as a winner—master of the sound bite, photogenic, reassuring, clinical in image refinement, almost, one suspects, as a sixth sense. He exploits his success to multiply its impact. Beneath the friendly exterior there is a furnace of ambition and passion—the product of family background, the influence of Thatcherism and years of defeat by Tories, a Christian faith, a deep self-belief and, most likely, a touch of naivety.

My impression is of youth and freshness. Blair is devoid of that world-weary cynicism which one associates with British politics, indelibly tied to devaluations of sterling and battles with the unions. It is as though his enthusiasm is that of a man discovering things for the first time; of a politician who has only known opposition and whose psyche is innocent of the terrible compromises of power.

Two aspects of his history shape his performance—the stage and the Church. He found religion and acting before his passion for politics prevailed. In the House of Commons he is a natural actor; on his feet at Question Time he plays to the audience but possesses a touch of religious fervour. He brings a passion to his principles but he is always a pragmatist in their application. He invites comparisons with Bill Clinton. Indeed, the newspapers have mocked him for plagiarising some of the President's speeches. Both are young, attractive, intelligent leaders, but Blair has no sleaze factor, no Paula Jones, no Whitewater. The Tories have done their homework and found only blanks; the dirt file on him is thin.

Blair pledges to use the authority the party has given him. 'I think most people say I lead from the front. I think that's the only way to lead in the end. My view has always been, "Look, you've got to let the leader lead and if you don't like the way the party's being led then get another leader."'

He quickly adds: 'I've never thought that knowing your own mind means failing to listen to the minds of others.' Neat. But the conclusion is that Blair consults as a tactic.

Blair's content is radical, not in a traditional way, almost in an 'end of Labour' fashion. He has reformed the party by opening up the structures and doubled the membership since 1992, attracting an organised surge of 200 000 new members. All MPs are selected on one member, one vote—not union blocs. He has sought to eradicate what he calls the 'quasi-Marxist traditions' and return Labour to its basic values of 'improving the lot of the majority of the people'. He says the values are the same, but the means are different. He rejects State intervention and the tax/spend/nationalisation tools by which Labour has lived and worked. For him New Labour is not a marketing device; it means what it says, it's a new name for a new party.

He is almost blasé about the accusations of betrayal surrounding the party reforms he imposed and his ditching of the nationalisation platform. 'Anyone who has ever made change in a political party gets accused of betrayal,' he says. Blair knows he is in control. He is alive to the need for leaders to exert their authority: 'A few years ago people said, "You'll never change the party, they'll revolt or there'll be civil war." But we got it through and there was no civil war.'

He warms to this theme: 'Part of the problem I've had in changing the party is that a lot of the commentators define radical politics by Labour policies circa 1983, where we were ten or fifteen years ago. Well, that's just not my politics. I don't believe that's where radical change is and I don't believe that's the sort of change this country needs.' He says the 'fallacy' in the debate in America, Britain and Australia is that some 'people think if there's not this huge ideological battle to the death over the economy, then there isn't a difference in values . . . But that's just not true'.

He won't fight the old wars—he accepts the bulk of the Thatcher economic reforms, believes that the battle between capital and labour—the obsession of his party for a century—is now an anachronism, and insists that Labour deal with the needs of the community, not indulge its own fixations. He has just no time for the old-style policies, ideologies and tribalism in which Labour has wrapped itself.

But he condemns the social alienation and decay, which he says is where the Tories went wrong. He calls it a 'rampant individualism' which undermines social and family cohesion. The result is a large group of people cut off from society's mainstream, imposing a huge welfare cost, and deprived of opportunity. Old Labour would solve the problem by State paternalism, but he rejects this. His answer is to build 'a strong civic society', and a better sense of community.

Blair sees clearly not only the conclusion of the seventies— that Labour's economic intervention no longer worked—but also the lesson of the eighties—that pro-market economic liberalism is not enough. He has discussed with Clinton the President's central blunder: that after winning in 1992 as a new Democrat he then governed for two years as an old Democrat. Blair will attempt in Britain what Clinton has more recently tried in the US—to create a new synthesis between economic growth and social cohesion. This is now the great challenge; it is because he sees this so clearly that his government, if he wins, will be an international case study.

The classic example Blair offers of a nexus between social and economic issues is how the breakdown of family is linked to the breakdown of law and order. His formula is to 'be tough on crime and on the causes of crime'. He has repeatedly declared that 'Labour is the party of law and order' and pledged reforms in police, law and justice to deliver this pledge.

It is upon the altar of modernisation that Blair worships as a politician. Its essence is perspective. He has lateral vision—he sees the Labour Party from the outside as well as from the inside. This is the key to his political mind. He is neither a prisoner of its history, its tribalism nor its orthodoxies. He wants Labour to be community-receptive. He looks at Labour from the outside and makes decisions for the outsiders, the voters. He makes many references to Thatcher and I suspect her influence on him is greater than he would admit, yet he admits a lot. 'In a curious way what Thatcherism did was to change attitudes. Whether you agree or disagree with it, attitudes were changed.'

So his aim is to change attitudes. The dramatic evidence, so far, is the transformed link with the trade unions. This was the major difference between Blair and Paul Keating when they met in north Queensland in mid-1995. He acknowledges the utility of the Accord in Australia, but notes the British experience is different, with the collapse of the social contract with the unions in the seventies under the Callaghan government. He describes the relationship between Labour and the unions as one of 'no favours'. He says: 'We treat employers and trade unions equally. Each can have their say but we govern with the whole country. There's no going back over the trade union laws of the 1980s. That era is gone.' He sees the unions as a pressure group to be treated the same as any pressure group though he admits the party still retains a relationship with the trade unions which he backs.

So New Labour looks out to the community, not inwards

to the unions. His philosophy is that Labour 'must speak for the whole people'. He wants to be a unity man. No British Labour leader has ever spoken like this. Nor has an Australian Labor leader. Not Hawke; he backed consensus but he championed the Accord. In recent weeks the only living Labour prime minister, Jim Callaghan, has spoken out, warning Blair. 'I would be very opposed to breaking the relationship between the trade unions and the party,' he told the *New Statesman*. 'I suspect most party members would agree. It is instinctive in the party and movement that we should keep the link.'

It is not just Blair's content but his ethos which worries the sceptics. The *New Statesman* recalled a miners' function which the tough-minded Callaghan attended in the late seventies when, as PM, he led the sing-along with the union leaders. It is the sort of tribal bonding with the unions that is not in Blair's nature. Is Labour losing its guts and its heart? No, says Blair, adding 'emotion without reason is empty and occasionally dangerous'.

Tony Blair, born in 1953 after Elizabeth II became Queen and on the tail-end of the baby boomers, never carries his sixties adolescence as a badge of honour. His life is not typecast by that generation—there were no drugs, no Vietnam protests (just one march against the National Front) and no genuflection to libertarianism.

Blair is the product of impressive parents and a poignant family history. His father, Leo, the offspring of an affair between two regional stage performers, was farmed out as a foster child to the Blairs and saw his real mother only once more in his life. Blair was two when the family moved to Australia for four years after Leo took a post at Adelaide University. Blair's father was a self-made middle-class Briton, a true Thatcherite, converted not born. When Blair was ten his father suffered a shocking stroke. He lived, but the family adjusted downwards, and it took three years before Leo Blair could even talk again. 'On an emotional level I was suddenly made aware that nothing is permanent,' says Blair.

At Oxford he took out beautiful women, did Mick Jagger impersonations at socials and kept a distance from the rituals of politics, debates and intellectual pretence. Again, he disliked the 'system'. There was not the slightest sign that he was a future politician.

A restless Blair fell in with a group including two Australians, Geoff Gallop, now the ALP leader in the West, and a radical priest-philosopher, Peter Thomson, who exerted a profound influence. Thomson, in effect, introduced him to Christian socialism which would provide the intellectual bridge for Blair's political conversion. It was through Thomson that he read the Scottish philosopher John Macmurray, and encountered the ideas of community and social cooperation. Thomson told me: 'He saw a Christianity that was different, that was about relationships and life, not something that was private and divorced from the world.'

One of Blair's biographers, Jon Sopel, says the significance of Macmurray's philosophy is that 'it marks a shift from the Left's assumption that the State will always provide towards an emphasis on voluntary action'. This is basic to Blair's thought today.

At Oxford, Blair became both a practising Christian and an ethical socialist—scarcely a typical road to Damascus for a seventies student. Says Thomson: 'He was alive to new ideas, had a social conscience and he was intelligent.' Had he expected Blair to make the Church his career? 'I wouldn't have been surprised.'

Geoff Gallop says: 'There are two sources to Tony's political commitment. His instinct was always that Britain had to be reformed. He felt this at both school and university where he was discontented with the establishment. The second source was the social gospel. His version of Christianity became geared towards political ends and the notion that society had to be made better.'

Blair joined the Labour Party in 1975 and saw the disintegration of the Wilson and Callaghan governments. His final conclusion was that Labour must be reformed from within, a lesson he has never forgotten. When I asked him what was the main problem with the party he shot back: 'Its structures . . . The power was in the hands of small groups of activists who, with every defeat, kept saying the reason we've been defeated is because we were not far enough to the Left, which was patently absurd.'

As a serious Christian, Blair travels with a Bible in his kit, keeps his faith to himself but is determined to be a 'values' PM. He makes three points about his values campaign. First: 'I'm not preaching about personal morality.' Second: family life is too important not to be helped by governments through social, education, tax and welfare policies. Third: 'It's plain crazy for politicians to be terrorised out of talking about families . . . the family has been taboo in politics for too long.'

His conviction is that the relationship between the individual and the State must be redefined. And, again, he wants a new synthesis between freedom and responsibility. 'My view is that the welfare State can only be built in the modern society on reciprocal duties—the duty of society to give chances to those who don't have them and the duty of people to take those chances. I'm saying it's the duty of government to help single parents or young people into the workplace but it's their duty also to respond to that.'

Yet he remains elusive. Comparisons with Bob Hawke come to mind. The party entered into a compact with Hawke because it was desperate for power but Hawke changed the party forever. Was the change good or bad? Clearly, it was for the good. British Labour suspects Blair is ambitious enough to change its nature. That hurts already; it will hurt much more in office. Here, though, is the essence of Blair's appeal; it is why many people at this election, aged not just in their twenties, but in their thirties and forties, will vote Labour for the first time.

If he wins, the party will have a love–hate relationship with him; but success is an excellent antidote. When I asked one of his Shadow Cabinet backers, Mo Mowlan, whether Blair inspired affection, she replied: 'The party has a respect for him. They know he will lead them to power.' Precisely.

Blair wants to establish a new power structure for British politics. It takes a while to grasp the scope of the plans. But it seems to go like this—reform of the Labour Party, election victory, the entrenchment of a Centre-Left balance of power, and two terms of office (ten years): he notes that the party 'has never won two full terms'. So far he has made the first hurdle. Frankly, Tony Blair looks a pretty good leader for the next century.

The Australian Magazine, *15–16 March 1997*

THE INDONESIAN TRAGEDY

THE MARKETS LAY SIEGE TO SUHARTO

IT IS EIGHT days since Indonesia's President Suharto, under pressure from world leaders and the International Monetary Fund, brought down his sweeping economic reform package—but that package has failed to restore confidence and Indonesia is moving into a stage that risks a systemic breakdown.

This engulfing crisis transcends a realistic response to Jakarta's financial troubles. The issue now is essentially politics. It is a collapse of financial market confidence in the Indonesian government in general and President Suharto in particular. The 30-year authoritarian stability of the Suharto era, which has secured great material advances for Indonesia, has become its fatal flaw.

Barring a miraculous turnaround, the crisis will move to a deeper and more traumatic level. This is implicit in yesterday's exchange rate which sank at one stage to 16 000 rupiah to the US dollar, a rate which compared with about 7300 when the package was announced last Thursday amid hopes that the currency might be stabilised at about 4000 to the dollar. Such hopes last week when President Suharto was praised for his courage now seem light years away.

The deteriorating currency means that large parts of Indonesia's financial sector are insolvent and its corporate sector is bankrupt. The foreign currency debt of more than $US60 billion cannot be serviced at this exchange rate. The foreign banks will lose much of their loans. Some companies have had

90 per cent of their market capitalisation wiped out. The rupiah rate for the US dollar was around 2500 in mid-1997 before the crisis which means it has lost more than 80 per cent of its value since then and the slide at one stage yesterday was taking that beyond 85 per cent.

The next step is inevitable—the announcement of a debt moratorium or the negotiation of a massive debt restructuring. This was foreshadowed yesterday by Finance Minister Mar'ie Muhammad saying the country would help its debt-ridden companies negotiate with foreign creditors.

The future defies prediction but the questions are obvious. How much longer can President Suharto survive? Will support for him from the armed forces stay solid? At what point will the financial crisis precipitate social unrest? What might be the nature of a new regime?

In recent times there have been reports of food shortages, riots and tremors of hyper-inflation. Yet the Australian government quite properly wants to ensure that signs of trouble are not exaggerated beyond their reality. On two occasions there has been hope that the situation would stabilise—when the initial IMF package was announced in October 1997 and again last week when President Suharto agreed to reforms on a scale once unimaginable, including the breaking of special family deals, scrapping the national car project, autonomy for the central bank, deregulation of agriculture and the elimination of a series of product monopolies and subsidies.

This followed a remarkable international lobbying campaign of Suharto by America's President Bill Clinton, Japan's Prime Minister Ryutaro Hashimoto, Germany's Chancellor Helmut Kohl, Singapore's Prime Minister Goh Chok Tong, Australia's Prime Minister John Howard, Malaysian Prime Minister Dr Mahathir, Paul Keating, who spoke more frankly than any of them, and the visit of an IMF delegation including managing director Michael Camdessus and a US team led by Deputy Treasury Secretary Lawrence Summers.

Yet they failed. It is a measure of the depth of this crisis.

Foreign Minister Alexander Downer leaves for Jakarta on Sunday. It is a trip fraught with peril since Australia has only a limited influence on these events. There is, however, an important argument that Australia should put in Jakarta, the region, with the US and the IMF: the need to ensure a proper coordination of private bank debt restructuring. Advice on this matter should involve Howard as well as Treasurer Peter Costello. It is the next step in the Indonesian tragedy and the method of its execution is critical.

In retrospect, there were two flaws with last week's package. First, it should have been matched by a debt-restructuring program, a proposal which was argued to the US delegation chief Summers but not taken up. The structural reforms Suharto embraced were vital but the immediate issue is debt, debt, debt. It needs a technical solution; a restructuring is imperative.

Second, the package was derailed by Suharto's disastrous decision to secure his Research and Technology Minister, B.J. Habibie, as vice-president. Habibie is like a son to Suharto but his passion for extravagant and grand schemes meant that Suharto sent a signal to the markets that completely undermined his pledges on economic reform. Treasuries and markets around the world (except Germany, where Habibie has great friends) were horrified.

It has been obvious for some time that Suharto's nomination of a successor was integral to restore confidence. Keating raised this with him last week. But Suharto's preference for Habibie merely suggests that he cannot grasp the nature of the forces with which he is dealing.

It is a clash of two alien worlds. Nothing could be further removed from the international currency markets than the timeless atmosphere of Suharto's palace where he meets guests with a ritual politeness and ministers are always cautious in their dealings with the source of all power.

Suharto has maintained his power by refusing to develop either his political system or nominate a successor. The army still backs Suharto—but the army doesn't understand the crisis, and, as ever, there is no obvious alternative. Few nations have as much at stake in this situation as does Australia. If Suharto goes, the rupiah will rally and that's a plus. But it is far from certain that any new regime will be favourably disposed to Australia and that's our dilemma.

Indonesia is caught between the inertia of the domestic

political market and the irresistible demands of the financial markets. It is a confrontation of the new world and the old and the immediate losers will be the Indonesian people.

The Australian, *23 January 1998*

AUSTRALIA AND INDONESIA

THE INDONESIA–INTERNATIONAL Monetary Fund struggle is not just over confidence in the rupiah but centres upon a far deeper question—Indonesia's direction after its transition beyond President Suharto.

The lobbying efforts of the Howard government have been driven by long-range objectives. Australia wants Indonesia, as the dominant power in South East Asia, to keep its national unity, its pro-Western strategic outlook and faith in market capitalism (despite its flawed practices) as a model for national progress.

For Australia, these are the ultimate stakes in the crisis. The outcome will have a deep impact on Australia, our engagement with Asia and the entire region. The misconception about Indonesia's crisis is that the consequences for Australia are mainly economic. This is quite wrong.

Our economic ties with Indonesia are modest.

Before the crisis, it was our tenth largest trade partner after Germany, accounting for 3 per cent of total trade. The consequences of Indonesia's crisis for Australia are mainly political, social and strategic, a reality still largely ignored here.

There are probably two reasons for this. Our engagement with Asia has been based upon the assumption that it is now a region of opportunity, not threat, an instinct that runs surprisingly deep though it is only a generation old. Second, Australians have forgotten how events in Indonesia affect our country because, for 30 years, Suharto's New Order government has followed policies that impact so favourably upon us.

Australia's engagement with Asia didn't happen by accident. It is driven by great events: Japan's economic miracle; the rise of the Asian tiger economies; China's detente with the West; and the New Order government in Jakarta.

Australia has much invested in a continuation of Indonesian

foreign policy. Suharto's modest defence budget, an introspective military posture, regional cooperation within the Association of South East Asian Nations, trade liberalisation through
the Asia–Pacific Economic Cooperation forum and a favourable
disposition towards the US are pretty much the ideal mixture
from Australia's position. The conundrum in Australia–Indonesia
relations was captured in a lament by Paul Keating a fortnight
ago: 'The problem is that Australians who want good relations
with Jakarta are damned for supporting the Suharto Government.' Keating should know.

The problem is greater than before because Suharto's
government has outlived its time. This is why Foreign Affairs
Minister Alexander Downer says of Australia's lobbying of the
IMF for a softer Indonesian package: 'We're not in the game
of propping up or tearing down anybody. We work with the
government that Indonesia produces.'

It is easy to oppose Suharto as a militarist, a dictator, a
murderer. If it is this simple, if Suharto is merely one of the
worst of corrupt dictators, then Australia should have resisted
and opposed his rule. Of course, there would have been a
price—a hostile Australian relationship with Indonesia for
a generation. And for what purpose? A realistic assessment of
Suharto is complex. For 30 years he has run more than a
government. He has harnessed the State to his needs and sought
to substitute a development ethos for the divisive politics of the
Sukarno era. Suharto's State has been defined by authoritarianism, national unity and religious tolerance. The guarantor of
order has been the army. Suharto made political order and
economic development his twin objectives. But this compact is
close to collapse because of resentment at Suharto family corruption and denial of political rights.

At the World Bank donors' meeting in Tokyo last July,
Indonesian director Dennis de Tray offered this snapshot of the
past generation: 'There can be no doubt that Indonesia is one
of the twentieth century's great development success stories.
Three years before the World Bank first opened its Jakarta field
office in 1968, Indonesia was in a state of devastation. Its
economy had ceased to function.

'Inflation was running at more than 600 per cent per year.
At around $US50 per year, per capita income was less than half
of India's, Nigeria's or Bangladesh's.

'Three decades later, Indonesia has a record of macro-economic stability, growth and poverty reduction . . . Nearly 30 years of first-rate economic management has produced: average annual growth in excess of 7 per cent; inflation below 6 per cent; per capita income that moved beyond the $US1000 threshold more than a year ago; five times Bangladesh's, four times Nigeria's and three and a half times India's. . . . More importantly, it remains an indisputable fact that the vast majority of Indonesians shared in Indonesia's economic success.'

This is a reminder that Suharto has been a far better than average leader of a developing nation. He should be neither demonised nor lionised. But he has made three enduring blunders.

First, he has allowed his family to exploit the patronage system to an obscene extent that has generated resentment at home and infamy abroad. Second, after many thousands of deaths following Indonesia's incorporation of East Timor, Suharto failed to confront this legacy by giving the province greater autonomy and control over its political and cultural life.

Third, Suharto has refused to develop Indonesia's political system; to give expression to the rising demands of the middle class, to encourage the growth of political institutions and, above all, to organise a smooth transition to a successor.

Suharto seems to consider himself, literally, as a Javanese king and kings die in office, trying to defy their mortality.

The result, as Keating recently said, is a perception in Europe and the US of Indonesia as 'some sort of rogue State', with Suharto's Indonesia falsely compared with Mobutu's Zaire and Marcos's Philippines. It was 'noticeable how few voices exist in the US or Europe willing to speak out for Indonesia'. There are virtually none.

Indonesia has become a soft target. When I checked into my Vancouver hotel last year for the APEC meeting, I flicked on the television to watch a 45-minute program featuring North American academics talking meaningfully about Indonesia's policies of genocide and comparing Suharto with Hitler. Much of the US and British quality media campaign for Suharto's overthrow.

Do such advocates have a new president in mind?

No. Do they want a new president from the army or the

Muslim movements? Who knows? Why do they think the army would promote democracy?

The succession crisis is real. New vice-president, Dr B.J. Habibie, cannot smoothly succeed Suharto in the near term because significant army elements won't accept him, short of a deal that guarantees them power to manipulate him.

An Indonesian authority, Dr Harold Crouch from the Australian National University, says that, despite Habibie's election, 'the succession has not in fact been resolved'. Under the Constitution, the president is automatically replaced by the vice-president for the remainder of the term if he dies or is incapacitated. Yet, in the recent past, the attitude of some senior military figures has ranged from 'strong reservations about Habibie to open contempt', says Crouch.

It is easy for editorialists to call for a coup or even a revolution (a nice clean one, please, without too many deaths) but they rarely confront the real issue—the limited capacity of Indonesia to create a new political system whose legitimacy lies outside the army.

What authority will a new leader possess? Will a transition be contested? Is there a consensus on Indonesia's future direction? How will Indonesia make the transition from the army's internal security role? Given the tensions between Islam and Christianity, and scapegoating of Chinese, can a transition reduce rather than accentuate such dangers?

Indonesia needs to confront these questions soon.

Suharto's position remains strong. But his age, health and the financial crisis points to a day of reckoning. Suharto made a choice for his time—he repudiated communism, militant Islam and Western democracy as the ideology of his State. But, as Adam Schwartz wrote in his book, *A Nation in Waiting: Indonesia in the 1990s*, Indonesia 'can't afford to wait much longer' for its next step because a 'once-in-a-generation transition takes planning' and, unfortunately, little planning is yet being done. The message of the East Asia crisis is that Suharto's ideology of State-directed capitalist authoritarianism has all but exhausted its utility.

This form of governance is obsolete. It doesn't work anymore. The currency markets have a correct insight into Suharto—he doesn't really believe in the IMF reforms, but will offer concessions and then retreat. Indonesia's crisis is political because the investors and the markets have lost faith in Suharto and his system. The greatest risk is that Suharto will be replaced without reform and within Indonesia's system of military autocracy, a system that survives only by denying genuine powersharing, the hallmark of pluralism. This scenario would guarantee Indonesia's decline, growing regional tensions and a paralysis of ASEAN.

Australia's interest is for a managed transition and a new government pledged to economic growth, political liberalisation and a pro-Western disposition. It will be a lucky trifecta. The best that can probably be expected from the new IMF deal is that Indonesia muddles through, achieving a slow, uneven recovery over several years amid growing political agitation.

In Indonesia, it is a time of creating new alliances; most will slide, but some may stick. Australia has links with Islamic leaders including the ailing Abdurrahman Wahid, Amien Rais and opposition figure Megawati Sukarnoputri (whom the US especially cultivates).

But the key institution in determining the succession remains the army headed by General Wiranto, who is also Defence Minister, with Suharto's son-in-law, General Prabowo Subianto, a rising figure. Australia has close links to the military—to cut them would be to isolate us from the key force determining a successor regime.

Australia will neither advance its cause nor win many friends in Jakarta by campaigning for Suharto's fall. That would be folly. The sentiment that unites Indonesians is hostility towards outsiders who try to dictate who Indonesia's leaders should be.

Yet Indonesians increasingly know that Suharto is failing them. Unless economic recovery comes, Suharto will be forced into more repression and Australian governments will have to distance themselves from him. The transition from Keating to John Howard meant that Australia lost its personal influence over Suharto and installed instead a leader, devoid of empathy but committed to Indonesia, minus any personal bond to Suharto. The test for Australia is always an Indonesian policy governed by our national interest. The golden rule is to stay engaged. The future is a more unpredictable and turbulent Indonesia—something Australia hasn't seen for decades. It will highlight the vast differences between near neighbours.

Indonesia as a developing nation doesn't have Australia's

values regarding civil liberties, environmental protection, governmental accountability and the role of the military. Like China, it's unlikely to become a Jeffersonian democracy, though China, of course, has been a far more brutal regime than Suharto's Indonesia. By trying to bring Suharto and the IMF together, Australian policy reflects a reality and a strategy.

The reality is that we must deal with the governments that Jakarta produces. The strategy is to encourage Indonesia towards the next step in its political-economic evolution. Suharto is now the key obstacle impeding that transition.

The Weekend Australian, *11–12 April 1998*

THE CATCH IN HABIBIE'S POLICY

FIVE DAYS AGO, flying from Jakarta to Bali, Indonesia's President B.J. Habibie made the latest move in his startling solo diplomacy: to endorse in full the UN self-determination process for East Timor.

The resentment within much of the Indonesian Cabinet is now rock solid. Habibie has hijacked Indonesia to the stage where it is close to surrendering East Timor; an outcome utterly inconceivable six months ago. It is a vast policy shift for which Habibie has won virtually no credit in Australia.

The significance of the Bali summit is that it leaves John Howard dangerously dependent upon Habibie's ability to deliver a fair ballot. Yet Habibie's authority as President does not extend this far. Habibie's policy might yet end in greater bloodshed and ruin for East Timor and cripple Australia–Indonesia relations in the process.

This is because resistance to Habibie's East Timor gamble runs deep within Jakarta's elite, the Cabinet and the army. Within East Timor, the violent intimidation of the paramilitaries has generated some momentum for their 'stick with Indonesia' cause. These opponents seek to frustrate, abort or corrupt the vote on self-determination.

The limitation of the Bali meeting is the concession Habibie cannot make. Six weeks from an Indonesian election, he won't allow foreign troops into his country to keep the peace. By the way, how many leaders would?

This was always a non-negotiable condition for Habibie. The idea that Indonesia, with its long history as a Dutch colony, its fusion of nationalism and anti-colonialism and its deep pride, would tolerate the humiliation of foreign troops at this time was only ever a fantasy.

So proper security for an impartial ballot rests with Indonesia and it won't be achieved.

Howard emerged from Bali with as much as he could have got. The Prime Minister's mistake came afterwards—talking up the prospects of a safe ballot. Howard exaggerates Habibie's internal strength. The two leaders thrived at Bali—which included a 90-minute, one-on-one meeting without note-takers—but the chances are that Howard will long survive Habibie as a leader.

Much of the meeting saw a debate about the number of foreign advisers. Indonesia wanted them kept to about 40 to 60 outsiders. Australia pressed for 250 to 300. The compromise here is that the UN Secretary-General, Kofi Annan, will finalise the number and Australia is now pressing the UN to keep it high. Australians will be heavily represented in this contingent. But it will not be strong enough to have an appreciable impact.

President Habibie has given security guarantees on the ballot. These are contained in one of the annexes to the formal UN agreement. It is a tough provision that requires Indonesia to maintain order and prevent intimidation.

Howard quite sensibly relied upon this pledge and did not seek any additional document embodying this guarantee. The notion of Howard returning from Bali with a 'peace in our time' security declaration from an Indonesian president who can't deliver would have been fatal. Yet it is exactly what much of the Australian media wanted.

The private view of senior Australians involved in the Bali meeting is that the chances of getting the pro-integration militias disarmed are remote. This is a deeply pessimistic omen. The risk is that Habibie's Timor policy looks good on paper, but won't work in practice. Habibie is forcing East Timor to make a final choice now, when a much better policy would be autonomy now with a final decision on independence some years later. This was Howard's original proposal. Its merit is that it gives the Timorese a chance at reconciliation. The current situation is that Indonesia has agreed to a universal ballot, foreign police advisers, about 600 to 700 UN personnel, Red Cross and other aid groups and a re-opened Australian consulate in Dili. If the 8 August ballot endorses independence, then Habibie's policy is to effect separation from 1 January 2000.

All up, it's a huge policy reversal by a weak president in the teeth of fierce internal opposition. For Habibie's trouble, the popular media-driven Australian reaction has been a singular denigration, calls to cut Australia's relations with Jakarta and a truly bizarre campaign for Australia to wage war against the world's fourth-biggest nation as it tries to become a democracy.

Howard put the issue honestly on the table after his return from Bali. Dealing with Indonesia as a friend is the only means by which Australia has influence. Adopting a hostile approach and cutting off Jakarta will simultaneously terminate Australia's capacity to influence events or to help the East Timorese.

The murders and violence carried out by the pro-Indonesian militia make any Australian policy of engagement with Indonesia extremely hard to sustain. The limits of public support in Australia are all but exhausted. The Indonesian leaders must realise this after the Bali meeting. The statements by Labor's foreign affairs spokesman, Laurie Brereton, should be proof enough. What happens if Australians with UN badges are killed in coming months?

There are three scenarios from here: a victory for Habibie's policy, which means a vote that leads to separation from next January; a close pro-independence vote that is rejected by the new democratically elected Indonesian Assembly; and a vote against independence heavily influenced by intimidation, which Indonesia then claims as vindication of its right to East Timor. The final two scenarios promise only more trouble. But Foreign Minister Alexander Downer issued a warning to Australia when he said that as many as one in three East Timorese wanted to stay with Indonesia. That figure is probably too high—but the point is valid. It is that the real comparison is with Northern Ireland and the core trouble is the intolerant division among the East Timorese themselves. If so, there is no easy solution.

Independence leader Xanana Gusmao, still under house arrest in Jakarta, seems to be the only East Timorese leader who grasps that a settlement can only come with the majority in East Timor guaranteeing the place and security of the minority. The constant line from some pro-integration leaders that they will never accept a vote for independence only dooms Timor for another generation.

UN personnel should begin to enter East Timor within a fortnight to begin preparations for the vote. It is still not clear if the security situation will permit this. It will be the first decisive test of whether internationalising the issue can curb the violence.

For Australia the stakes are great. Our relations with Indonesia are now heavily tied up with an experimental Timor policy. This is an extremely exposed situation for Australian foreign policy and for our wider relations with Asia.

The Indonesian election is in June. Flowing from ex-President Suharto's overthrow, it will determine whether Indonesia moves towards a democratic polity or slides back into turmoil. Australia must be on the side of change and democracy in Indonesia—but this is now in jeopardy.

The Weekend Australian, *1–2 May 1999*

THE LETTER THAT SPARKED THE MELTDOWN

THE DECISIVE EARLY event that helped to trigger the August East Timor ballot along with its tragic aftermath was John Howard's December 1998 letter to Indonesia's President B.J. Habibie.

This letter was prompted by Habibie replacing President Suharto and signalling that he would accept a form of autonomy for East Timor. It meant that, for the first time in 23 years, there was a chance for an East Timor settlement.

Howard changed Australian policy in an effort to push Indonesia towards a final deal.

The Howard letter rested on four assumptions: that it was best for all parties that East Timor remain part of Indonesia; that any settlement would require a long time period and had to begin with Jakarta giving autonomy to East Timor; that further down the track (five to ten years) there should be an act of self-determination; and that an independent East Timor might be the final result.

On 19 December, Howard wrote to Habibie:

Your offer of autonomy for East Timor was a bold and clear-sighted step that has opened a window of opportunity both to achieve a peaceful settlement in East Timor and to resolve an issue that has long caused Indonesia difficulties in the international community. A settlement would enable you to put the issue behind you. It would make a substantial difference to Indonesia's standing in the world.

I want to emphasise that Australia's support for Indonesia's sovereignty is unchanged. It has been a longstanding Australian position that the interests of Australia, Indonesia and East Timor are best served by East Timor remaining part of Indonesia.

In the end, the issue can be resolved only through direct negotiations between Indonesia and East Timorese leaders . . . I would urge you to take this course, and to focus on winning acceptance for your offer from the East Timorese themselves. The best way of achieving this may be for you to enter into direct negotiations with representative leaders from East Timor, including the two East Timorese bishops and Xanana Gusmao.

On the substance of the negotiations, the advice I am receiving is that a decisive element of East Timorese opinion is insisting on an act of self-determination. If anything, their position—with a fair degree of international support—seems to be strengthening on this.

It might be worth considering, therefore, a means of addressing the East Timorese desire for an act of self-determination in a manner [that] avoids an early and final decision on the future status of the province. One way of doing this would be to build into the autonomy package a review mechanism along the lines of the Matignon Accords in New Caledonia. The Matignon Accords have enabled a compromise political solution to be implemented while deferring a referendum on the final status of New Caledonia for many years.

The successful implementation of an autonomy package with a built-in review mechanism would allow time to convince the East Timorese of the benefits of autonomy within the Indonesian Republic . . . If you see any merit in these thoughts, I would be happy to talk with you directly about them or have someone discuss them discreetly with you.

It was hard to disagree at the time with Howard's approach and it is hard to disagree in hindsight. It was time for Australia to shift policy on East Timor and, if he had not acted, there was a risk of Australia being left behind by Jakarta, the ultimate humiliation.

The key to the letter is its support for a solution over a long time. But this is the opposite of what happened with Habibie's sudden dash to a 1999 referendum.

The letter infuriated Habibie. He decided that if Australia, after supporting Indonesia for so long, believed a ballot had to be held, then it was best to hold it quickly. Why, Habibie asked, should Indonesia support East Timor for another decade, only to lose it? For Howard, the Habibie lurch to an immediate ballot was an unintended consequence of his letter. Could Habibie's response have been avoided? This is surely the critical question which historians will argue for many years.

Two points are relevant. First, if Australia had such good relations with Indonesia, why was such a dramatic shift terminating a 23-year-old policy conveyed by letter via the ambassador? Why didn't Howard or Foreign Minister Alexander Downer break the news in a face-to-face dialogue with Habibie? Why didn't Australia engage in a dialogue with Jakarta's political class to persuade them to the 'autonomy now, vote later' position? Why didn't Howard and Habibie discuss this policy change together and devise a compromise rather than deliver two jolting surprises to each other in two successive months?

Second, once Habibie announced his 1999 ballot policy, should Australia have stood its ground? A figure close to these events says: 'Australia should have stood by the policy in the Howard letter. That was the right and sensible way of getting change. Habibie's proposal was reckless and Downer had admitted before that an early ballot meant bloodshed. Australia should have tried to negotiate a ballot a few years out.'

But Howard and Downer have a strong reply. They say that once the Indonesian President had offered a ballot to East Timor, there was no practical way his stand could be reversed. On what basis could Australia argue before the international community that Habibie's policy was wrong and too dangerous? What sort of domestic backlash would Howard have faced trying to delay a ballot that offered freedom to East Timor? No politician, columnist or newspaper in Australia took this line at the time. It is the classic debate about leadership and public opinion.

The Australian, *6 October 1999*

AN UNCERTAIN FUTURE

FOR THE FIRST time in its history Australia is playing the political and military lead role in a large-scale regional operation sanctioned by the international community, the US and the region.

This is a psychological turning point in Australian foreign policy. While comparisons with Vietnam have been made the differences are far greater. This time Australia, not the US, is the leader; the action has UN Security Council support; and most of the local population endorses the intervention.

But the foreign policy challenge is daunting. The real medium-term task for Australia is to integrate an independent East Timor into a viable Australia–Indonesia relationship. That will take many years to achieve. But it should be the objective.

Australia should approach its entire commitment to East Timor with the appreciation that it needs ultimately to fit into the rebuilding of the Jakarta relationship. This will be both a moral and political dilemma. The refined message needed from the Howard government is that Australia aspires to friendly, though not special, links with Jakarta and that this is a national interest obligation.

Much will depend upon the immediate military fate of the Australian troops as they implement the UN mission of delivering security to East Timor. The chief difficulty is the game plan by the militias, backed by sections of the Indonesian army, to use West Timor as an insurgency base and the refugees they have taken across the border as de facto hostages.

For Australians there is a complex range of messages from our commitment.

First, Australia is not a regional policeman and has no role as a regional policeman. The East Timor commitment arose because Australia repudiated the role of a unilateral policeman which would have meant war with Indonesia. Australia's military role in East Timor is part of a UN coalition. The key to our future military involvement in the region lies in partnerships, alliances and UN deployments, not solo initiatives.

Second, Australia needs to avoid being forced into a choice between East Timor and Indonesia. Our task is not to support an independent East Timor against Indonesia. Our task is part of the long hard slog of reconciliation. And talk of reconciliation must begin from the start, as East Timor's leader, Xanana Gusmao, knows.

Any claims that Australia is responsible for the recent slaughter is wrong. The killing was done by Indonesians or pro-Indonesian militia. Australia is not responsible and is not guilty. It is Indonesia that must account to the international community and whose military will have to carry the onus within Indonesia for its betrayal of the nation. Australia's worst mistake would be to succumb to a new legacy of guilt, just as we embraced the falsehood that we 'lost' East Timor in 1975 and succumbed to guilt for the past generation.

Australia must somehow separate its future assistance obligations to an independent East Timor from allowing East Timor to become an Australian client State. That will be hard but it is essential. It means that the East Timor issue, as much as possible, must be internationalised. It means that in the next phase, the UN peacekeeping operation, there should be a less prominent Australian role.

Third, we need to realise there is no crisis in Australian–US relations. This may have been the appearance but it is not the reality. There have been some mishaps and mistakes. The Howard government made a double blunder. It had a seriously mistaken assessment of the post-ballot violence in East Timor and the US knows Australia made the wrong call; as a result Australia failed to alert the US earlier to the possible need for an emergency UN operation.

It is true that John Howard and Bill Clinton are not soul mates. It is true that Howard publicly criticised the US over its initially tardy response—and that criticism worked. But nobody should be surprised that the US is not sending ground forces. Why would it? The US has made a logistical, communications and support troop commitment. US diplomacy in putting the pressure on President B.J. Habibie to approve the UN force and in giving support to Australian leadership of the force, was critical. The East Timor episode is more likely to be seen as an example of the success not failure of the alliance.

Fourth, we should not delude ourselves that Jakarta's revocation of the Australia–Indonesia Security Treaty has no consequences. The treaty represented a mutual strategic decision—that Australia and Indonesia would seek their security together. Where are we now?

It can be argued the treaty was premature or shouldn't have been made before Indonesia democratised. But it can't be argued that the treaty did not represent a key strategic decision by Australia. The challenge now is to ensure that the cancellation of the treaty doesn't provoke a military rivalry between Australia and Indonesia. This is critical given there will be strained relations for some time and that Australia must boost its defence spending.

The gradual rundown in Australia's defence capability is now exposed as a national scandal. Howard pledged 4500 troops to East Timor. But Australia can't sustain this number beyond twelve months despite what the government insists. Don't forget that in the 1960s, conscription was needed to sustain a 7000–8000 force in South Vietnam. The number of combat troops Australia can sustain in the field indefinitely today is not much above 2000.

The prospect for higher defence spending has rarely been better. After so many years of anti-Indonesian hostility it is time to call the bluff of the Australian Left. Australia cannot both antagonise Indonesia and run a soft defence budget. Howard has the perfect cover to boost the defence vote—an ALP hawk, Kim Beazley, as Opposition leader and a UN operation as a justification.

The Australian, *22 September 1999*

FOOLS ON THE HILL

THIS IS A very modern and very American tragedy now being played out.

It is an impeachment that will weaken the US presidency, not strengthen it; an impeachment not demanded by the American people, and opposed by a clear majority of the people; and it is an impeachment that will be applauded around the world by America's enemies, and met with private dismay by America's friends.

The impeachment of Bill Clinton is a bewildering event, inspired by multiple demons—the puritanism within the American soul, the pulse of political greed now devouring the Republican Party and a classic Shakespearean leader with a fatal flaw or, in Clinton's case two flaws, lust and pride.

The impeachment vote is driven by political gain, not principle. This is a grand play by the Republican Party, angry and outraged by Clinton's behaviour, propelled by its righteous wing and calculating that it can extract the maximum gain by crippling Clinton, not terminating his presidency.

The House vote, 228–206 in the first instance, is a party vote. Only five Democrats voted to impeach and only five Republicans voted against. After the Senate conducts the trial, a two-thirds Senate majority is needed to remove the President and the Republicans are well short of these senators.

And they know it. Their aim is to humiliate, to degrade, and to cripple Clinton. But not to install Al Gore in the White House before 2000—with an incumbent's advantage.

Clinton has a deep responsibility for his own fate. He has

211

made three mistakes—he had illicit sex in the White House; he lied when questioned, in what most people would assume is perjury; and after the congressional elections, his pride prevented him from cutting a deal with the Republicans—admitting perjury in exchange for a vote of censure and an end to the affair.

Presumably, Clinton and his lawyers will now have to negotiate a deal along these lines with the Senate. Clinton's refusal to negotiate earlier, thereby avoiding an impeachment vote, is a true political blunder.

The military strike upon Iraq assumes a dual historical role—it illuminates US frustration at Saddam Hussein and it betrays the damage done to America's credibility. This strike will be portrayed forever as linked with Clinton's impeachment struggle, although it can be explained outside this process. The lesson for the Republicans is that you can't cripple Clinton without undermining US authority abroad.

There is a mood of madness in the mania of the anti-Clinton Republicans. As the President was impeached, so the Republican Speaker-elect, Bob Livingston, resigned because he was guilty of an extramarital affair. Clinton is still standing but the Republicans have now lost their former Speaker, Newt Gingrich, and their new Speaker, Bob Livingston. The *New York Times*/CBS poll shows the Republicans have plunged to their lowest standing for fourteen years. The poll shows that 62 per cent of Americans oppose impeachment, and that is a strong majority. The people grasp that politics has never been a place for angels.

It is totally unremarked that Australia has a deep interest in these events. The world community today needs a strong and clear-headed US. But we are being offered the opposite—a weak presidency, an embittered Congress, a fracture between the executive and the legislature, and the certainty of a growing introspective US. We will all pay for this.

The Australian, *21 December 1998*

PART V

THE CONSTITUTION, THE REPUBLIC AND THE DISMISSAL

THIS SECTION DEALS with the two great constitutional debates which have dominated the last 25 years, the Dismissal and the republic.

After the Dismissal the Labor Party was preoccupied by constitutional change to rectify the source of its 1975 humiliation. The aim was to limit the Senate's financial power and to codify the Reserve Powers. But these efforts were lost in the sand because of the failure to reach any cross-party agreement that could sustain a successful referendum. So the powers that triggered the Dismissal remained intact—with the exception of the Senate casual vacancy provision.

It was Paul Keating who initiated the 1990s debate on the republic. This was a move which surprised most of the ALP, the Coalition and the community. Keating encouraged a broad-based debate about Australian nationalism, republican models and constitutional amendments to secure the republic. He informed the Queen of his intentions and the Prince of Wales visited Australia to deliver the monarchical response.

The Coalition, divided between monarchists and republicans, promised to hold a Constitutional Convention if it won office, a handy device to conceal its internal divisions. Despite the cynics John Howard honoured this commitment and the Convention was held in old Parliament House in early 1998. It produced a republican model to be put to the people in late 1999 which, if carried, would deliver an Australian Republic effective from 1 January 2001, the centenary of Federation.

The campaign leading to the November 1999 referendum

was highlighted by a three-way split. The constitutional monarchists defended the status quo and urged a 'no' vote; republicans who supported the model urged a 'yes' vote; but the referendum was defeated by a third group—those Australians who were suspicious of the model and the politicians who promoted it, and favoured instead a directly elected president.

An unusual situation arose because the prime minister who put the referendum was campaigning against it. Given the long history of referendum failure in Australia and the split within the republican movement, the chances of a success without the weight of prime ministerial opinion were always going to be difficult.

TOWARDS THE REPUBLIC

NO POLITICAL EVENT is inevitable, but on present trends Australia is moving towards a republic. I do not see how monarchists can reverse this trend. They can check it briefly; but they can't defeat it. The defect in the monarchist campaign is obvious—they focus on the problems of a republic but they are unconvincing on the benefits of the monarchy.

Let me ask the monarchists: do they seriously believe that over the next hundred years our emotional, strategic and constitutional ties can continue with Great Britain as they are today? The truth is that when you scratch the monarchists many of them admit their system cannot endure. Many of them concede the republic is an issue of timing, not substance.

The task is to construct a broad republican coalition. That means the ALP should forget any ridiculous notion that the 'true believers' can secure a republic. The focus should be on the Liberals.

The problem the monarchists have is that the present system is an historical and constitutional construct which increasingly defies commonsense and the practical outlook of Australians. I ask you to examine the monarchy—our monarchy.

Our head of State is the Queen—not the Queen of the United Kingdom but the Queen of Australia. These two monarchies are separate. The Queen of the UK has quite different advisers from the Queen of Australia. The Crown of the UK may pursue utterly different and even contradictory policies from the Crown of Australia.

But, as we know, the person who is monarch of the UK is,

by law, also monarch of Australia. Our monarch is determined by the operation of a 200-year-old Act of Settlement passed by the British Parliament. We have a Crown of Australia—but Australians have no say whatsoever in determining our monarch. The line of succession is strictly a British affair. Our head of State isn't an Australian; doesn't live in Australia; and has only a rudimentary understanding of the nation of which she is Queen.

Not only don't we determine our head of State. Our head of State must be an Anglican—because the head of State is also head of the Church of England. Our head of State cannot be a Catholic, or a Jew, or a Muslim or an atheist. Our head of State can't marry a Catholic.

A nation that allows the decisions about the identity and appointment of its own head of State to be made totally in a foreign country always risks the possibility that it will be humiliated by outcomes it can't control. Australians have no influence, no say, no role, in determining who becomes king or queen of Australia.

Because of its intrinsic nature and because of its remoteness from Australian life, the monarchy lacks sufficient intellectual or emotional sustenance in this country. It cannot serve as a focus of our endeavours or of our aspirations. It is inappropriate as a symbol of national inspiration or improvement—and no amount of advocacy by lawyers will change this.

The royal family—and give them credit—understand this. They understand it far better than many of their Australian supporters. Earlier this year I had the opportunity to interview the Prince of Wales who revealed both a genuine attachment to Australia and a willingness to accept an Australian republic. Prince Charles revealed that during the 1980s the possibility of his appointment as governor-general had been raised. His response—he was keen but he specified to Sir Ninian Stephen one condition: there had to be unanimous political support and that was not forthcoming. So Prince Charles felt in this situation that he could not become our governor-general. Yet under the hereditary system he can still become our monarch. It is a perfect demonstration of a dysfunctional political system; that Australia has a head of State divorced from the country itself.

The evolution of Australia's constitutional system has a republic as a logical result.

It is not sufficiently recognised how far the system has evolved since Federation. In 1901 there was no Queen of Australia either in law or in fact. Australia was not an independent country; Federation did not deliver true nationhood to Australia. In a legislative, judicial and foreign policy sense Australia remained subservient to Britain.

The Federation fathers did not seek and did not achieve an independent nation. This is poorly grasped in today's debate. Alfred Deakin himself said that 'there is no pretence of claiming the power of peace or war, or of exercising power outside our territories'.

Australia's lack of independence was highlighted by our 'head of State system'. The notion of the Crown pervades the Constitution. But there is no suggestion of Australian independence under this 'head of State' system. The Queen was sovereign of Australia and many other countries. The Australian colonies federated under the Queen 'of the United Kingdom of Great Britain and Ireland'—to quote from our Constitution Act. The Queen appointed the governor-general, on the advice of United Kingdom ministers, not Australian ministers. Indeed, Australian ministers had no direct access to the Crown. The governor-general was British and his task among others, was to look after Britain's interests in Australia. It was only through him that an Australian prime minister could even communicate with the Queen.

Our 'head of State system' has been evolving since Federation. We can be certain that its evolution will continue.

Many monarchists no longer defend the monarchy. They defend what might be called our 'governor-generalate'. This argument of the monarchists concedes the fading emotional links between the Australian people and the British Crown. They argue that the governor-general, in practice, is our head of State; that the Queen has no role beyond mere ceremony; and that the governor-general as a de facto head of State demonstrates the genuine independence of Australia. I am pleased to see the monarchists put this argument—it reveals how far most of them have come. One of the most persuasive defenders of the status quo, Justice Michael Kirby, even calls Australia a 'crowned republic'—and I agree. But this is the whole point. We certainly weren't a 'crowned republic' in 1901. We have reached this stage through a subtle and sometimes subterranean process. But we have reached it. Our constitutional evolution is not going to halt suddenly at this point. Why should it? What is the argument against the final stage? Having come this far we should not be frightened of the natural and logical next step. We should not fear letting the 'stream of history' continue its course.

If the British Crown has all but ceased to have relevance for Australia then we should act on this basis. To use Michael Kirby's phrase, we should keep the 'republic' and move the 'crowned'. There's no point in being a de facto republic. This is an argument for becoming a real republic.

The republic is no nirvana; it is no guarantee of progress; it is not our top national priority. It is by no means the only constitutional reform which the nation requires. The republic should not be exaggerated beyond its real worth but, equally, its real value should not be caricatured or dismissed. That does a disservice to virtually half the population who favour a repub- lic. If Australia is to reinvent most of itself, then it will need fresh symbols, more inspiration and greater confidence. I think a republic—the right sort of republic—is an integral part of the process.

Australia was one of the first democracies. It is one of the greatest democracies and it is one of the oldest democracies. I am proud of our past and our British heritage but I don't argue that it must stand for the next century.

We don't think of Britain as being superior and once this is a reality then we won't have the British Crown as our head of State. This highlights the underlying strength of the modern republican movement. People are republicans because of their view of Australia—not because they are socialists or Irish or Catholics or hate Sir John Kerr. Once the habit of dependency is broken, it can't be put back together. Once Australia's infe- riority complex is finally cured, then we will become a republic.

There is one argument of the monarchists which is partic- ularly distasteful. It is the claim that Australia cannot move to become a republic without endangering its democracy. I recog- nise that we must get the transition right. Like the original constitution, an amended constitution won't be perfect. But let's not pretend that the present system is perfect. Let's also not pretend that the quality or survival of our democracy depends upon the Crown. It never has and it doesn't today. It depends, ultimately, on the spirit and faith and judgment of the Australian people. There are good and bad monarchies and there are good and bad republics. I would rather see Australia as a good monarchy than a bad republic. That's no choice at all. But I would prefer a good republic to a good monarchy. The idea is to advance the nation. I don't believe it is beyond the wit or intelligence of Australians, politicians, lawyers and the voting public to devise satisfactory changes to the Constitution to give effect to a good republic.

It is equally important for republicans to rebut the scare campaigns being run by the monarchists. There is one in particular—that the republic will create the grounds for a dictatorship.

The spectre of a possible drift to dictatorship in a republic was raised by the former Chief Justice Sir Harry Gibbs. The suggestion is that under the present constitution the powers of the governor-general are exercised in a tradition of impartiality associated with the Crown and that if such powers are attached to the office of president, which is a political office, then such powers will be exercised eventually for political interests of one sort or another.

In fact, a republic will create a new office of president from the political trunk of the old office of governor-general. The new office will have partly a new ethos but will also retain many characteristics from the 'governor-generalate' we now enjoy. I believe we can elect distinguished Australians to this office just as distinguished Australians in the past have been appointed as governor-general. A president does not have to be party/political. The office of president should never be party/political. If elected by two-thirds of the federal Parliament then the president won't be party/political. His powers should be broadly similar to those of the governor-general—with one exception. Under a republic, the executive power of the prime minister vis à vis the head of State will be less than now!

This can be demonstrated readily by assessing the 1975 crisis under a republican system.

Monarchists point to Sir John Kerr's intervention in 1975 to demonstrate our independence from the Queen—to support the constitutional status quo. I understand their point but they overlook the central dynamic of the crisis. It is in Sir John Kerr's book—he concealed from his prime minister his intention to dismiss. Why? Sir John tells us—he believed that to give Mr Whitlam the proper warning would have meant that the prime minister would have moved against the governor-general and the Queen would have been involved in the crisis. The governor-general was driven by his declared desire to protect the Queen. Let's get the facts right when we talk about 1975. It reveals, in fact, that the existing system is far from perfect. I point out that a president would have been in a stronger position than Kerr and would have felt no need to conceal his intent which means, of course, there would have been no dismissal but instead a resolution short of the ultimate act. Clearly, a far superior outcome.

Address to the National Press Club, April 1994

AN INTERVIEW WITH
PRINCE CHARLES

YOUR AUSTRALIA DAY *speech in Sydney was obviously an important speech. They were your own words?*
Yes.
What did you set out to do in the speech?
What I certainly set out to do was to remind people—in the wake of a particularly demoralising recession—[that] Australia has an enormous amount going for it . . . and let's remember the positive, good things which can be celebrated. And the other thing I really wanted to say was to address this whole question about the debate whether to have a republic or not, in other words, a slightly different system of government.

What I felt was necessary was to emphasise that it was up to Australians and the Australian people generally to decide which way they would like to go in the future and that having a debate was a perfectly sensible thing to do in the light of changing circumstances or whatever. That, really, was what I wanted to make clear.

The other thing I find extraordinary is the way in which the media in particular are always talking about an involvement in this country from the monarchy's point of view, as if somehow we owned the place and that to be denied the chance to be the sovereign of Australia is something terrifyingly awful.

The point that I would like to get across is that we don't own this country, we're not making money out of it or anything like that. We are merely doing what we consider to be, as a family, our duty here by the Australians. All anybody has tried to do is to help, encourage and assist. It's not as though you can make money. Then I could understand wanting to hold on to it. But it's not a question of that.

Before your visit, some people in the media actually suggested that your trip was really about stopping Australia from becoming a republic, or revising the image of the monarchy in this country. But as you've just explained, you didn't approach it that way at all.

Unfortunately, you have to live with people who make their own agendas, and they write scripts for soap operas of a continuing nature which actually bear no relation to reality. That is the difficulty.

Why did you say that you think the republican debate is actually a sign of national maturity and self-confidence?

Because I think within a democratic system it's not a bad thing at all to be able to discuss it without everybody beating each other over the head and shouting and screaming too loudly. Clearly there's always two ways of looking at things . . . you'd be jolly lucky if you had a system that everybody appreciated.

There are disadvantages and advantages to a republic, as much as there are in having a monarchy. In the end, there's got to be a debate, I suspect, to help reveal—and perhaps this will help to reveal—some of the hidden advantages and strengths of the current way of doing things.

Every so often a lot of these are taken for granted. A lot of things are unseen, under the surface. It's like the Commonwealth itself. I think of all those nations who used to make up what was called the British Empire—they have so much in common—but all these links and advantages are completely buried for the vast majority of people because they're all made up, like veins under the surface, linking associations, legal people, medical people, sporting, agricultural, every kind of aspect of life, and also ties of kinship and everything else.

One of the interesting points you made in the speech was that institutions change. The Commonwealth has changed an awful lot as an institution over several decades. You almost appeared to have offered the republicans a concession when you said that institutions in this country may well change and the people who advocate such change may actually have it right.

Clearly, everybody's looking at different ways of doing things. The New Zealanders, for instance. They voted not so very long ago to change to a system of proportional representation, which is a major step from the first past the post system. You go to Canada, and they look at things differently there. Australia and New Zealand used to be dominions—they aren't any longer; they're completely independent countries. That was a change that took place then in the institutions . . . So everybody does things in different ways.

There's no point panicking about that, or thinking it's some frightful insult or something to the Crown. By looking at it all, who knows what'll happen in twenty years' time. I don't know.

If Australia became a republic, how would that affect your relationship with Australia?

Ah, that's an interesting question. Well, I don't think it would affect it at all! As far as *I'm* concerned, as I said the other day in the speech, I have the greatest possible affection for Australia, and it's not going to make the slightest difference. As far as I'm concerned, about all this means . . . to come out here . . . I'm involved then with a country which, if that happened, would be part of the Commonwealth presumably, and I'm the eldest son of the head of the Commonwealth, and I couldn't see anything different really except that they'd still presumably take me across red traffic lights every now and then. You'd come as a visitor from a country with which Australia has very close relationships—you would come very much as a Commonwealth visitor. And I'd be able to go and visit the people I haven't been able to see. I might even be able to see all the people I haven't been able to see. And find out a damn sight more about Australia because I'd be able to do it in a private way.

So really you're quite relaxed if Australia does decide to go that way and become a republic?

Well, put it this way—I'm not going to run around in small circles, tear my hair out, boo-hoo, and throw a fit on the floor, as if somehow like a spoilt child, your toy's been taken away.

That speech you gave on Australia Day—that important speech— did that have to be cleared with Buckingham Palace or with the Queen?

Oh yes. It was all discussed in advance. Absolutely.

Was the position you took then on the republic based on advice from Mr Keating as prime minister?

(Long pause) No. But I talked to him and discussed this with him when he came to Balmoral in September. There were various discussions, and Mr Keating spoke to the Queen about it. What I was merely trying to do in that speech was to reinforce what the Queen had said should be said as a result of the meeting which she had with the Prime Minister. I certainly talked to the Prime Minister after the speech, and showed him the speech beforehand, and he appeared to be happy with it.

Is there a danger that you've disappointed or let down the monarchists in Australia?

In what way?

Simply by the comments you made. I mean, I ask that because some people might say that.

Do they believe that? I mean, I don't know that anybody does. I mean, ever since I've been coming to Australia there has been a substantial minority of people who favour a republic, and, you know, people used to say to me years ago that you ought to come out here and become governor-general and do a Lord Mountbatten, as he did in India . . . I had a lot of that.

There's always been a strong element of people who wanted the place to become a republic. And I think that those who are enthusiastic about a monarchy and what it can bring don't want to lose that. All *I'm* saying is, that if people decide eventually they want to become a republic, I'm not personally going to make a great song and dance about it. I don't know how to get this across.

The Australian, 7 *February 1994*

THE DISMISSAL
TWENTY YEARS ON

THE DISMISSAL IS the most dramatic political moment in our
history; the climax of a turbulent phase of our politics. It
is surely an insight into our character that this defining event
was overwhelmingly peaceful. Yes, there was noise, protest and
rage—but there was no blood in the streets, no sign of the army,
not even a national strike. How many nations could say as much
in a similar circumstance? I believe that while the Dismissal is
testimony to defects in our democracy, our response to it is
proof of our commitment to democracy. So, twenty years later,
how is the Dismissal seen? Let me offer several snapshots.

It is an interesting or nostalgic or forgotten issue in the
community. The rage has expired. The Labor Party recovered.
Gough Whitlam may be more popular now than at any time
since May 1974. Labor used its rage constructively; it declined
to self-destruct or to succumb to demoralised introspection. I
believe the contemporary culture of the ALP cannot be understood without reference to the Dismissal. The party abandoned
Whitlam's technique of 'crash through or crash'. It decided to
conduct its politics as ruthlessly as Malcolm Fraser did in the
early 1970s. The hallmark of the Hawke–Keating party of the
1980s was the belief that Labor should earn its legitimacy as
governing party by its performance. The contemporary ALP has
sought to occupy the Treasury benches for a sustained period,
not for a brief reformist rush before the grand alliance of the
established order could remove it.

Labor has governed for the last twelve of the twenty years
since 1975. There are many Labor parliamentarians from

227

Gareth Evans to Wayne Goss for whom the Dismissal became a central motivating event in their careers. Its influence on Paul Keating should not be underestimated. Labor channelled its rage effectively. It decided to try to control the political system which had claimed Whitlam as a victim rather than embrace a victim mentality itself.

Malcolm Fraser's actions in blocking the appropriation bills can only be understood in the context of the cultural confidence that the Menzian age had instilled in the Liberal and Country parties. It was the last gasp of the born-to-rule Liberal Party; the party that believed Labor could govern neither successfully nor for long.

It is not stretching credulity to argue that the Dismissal can even be seen as the last great event shaped by the ethos of class politics which has dominated much of our history. To many the Whitlam government was doomed because it had the socialist tag—it was committed to big spending, big government, public ownership, with many of its senior figures hostile to business and finance and its mining minister attacking the industry's leaders as 'mugs and hillbillies'. There was a distinct atmosphere of old-fashioned ideological politics in the rhetoric of Labor's opponents at the kill.

The 1975 crisis can also be interpreted partly as a consequence of profound change in the international economy which occurred in the early 1970s in the form of high levels of both inflation and unemployment which afflicted the Western democracies after the 1973 OPEC oil shock. Stagflation was the word that dominated the financial pages of the day. These conditions destroyed the utopian belief that drove Whitlam—that he could both enjoy sustained economic growth and implement his social vision. But the Coalition opposition appeared convinced that it was primarily the Labor government, not international forces, which had terminated the post-war golden age of economic growth and stability. The basis on which the Coalition blocked the 1975 budget was a restoration of the previous economic order, a commitment on which it could not deliver.

The 1975 crisis took confrontationalist politics in Australia to its zenith. Malcolm Fraser I think, was always seen as a confrontationalist politician, a legacy, partly, though not wholly, of the Dismissal. It is fascinating that in 1983 he lost to

Bob Hawke who campaigned for consensus on a platform of bringing Australians together. I would venture that the electorate today puts a premium on cooperative approaches and dislikes confrontation.

Malcolm Fraser has told me that the Liberals should look upon 1975 as an occasion for pride—but they don't. Bob Ellicott, an intellectual force in the events, identifies the difficulty for the Liberals: 'There's a feeling about, generated since, that there was some element of shame in being involved, as if it was a counter-revolutionary right-wing coup . . . As both a constitutional lawyer and a Liberal I've never had any problem with what we did.'

I suspect that the 1975 Liberal Party generation is more comfortable defending the decisions it took than are its successors in defending those decisions. For example, Reg Withers, another architect of the 1975 drama, fingers the subsequent 'guilt' legacy within the Liberal Party with his contemptuous remark that 'not one Liberal senator has caused the Labor government the slightest trouble since 1983'. I think he is a little harsh—but he has a point.

I note that Liberals as different as John Howard and Ian Macphee have said the dismissal weakened the capacity of the Fraser government. For example, Howard recalls how Fraser wanted to retain the Prices Justification Tribunal in early 1976 as a major concession to Bob Hawke and the trade unions. Macphee, a Fraser devotee, says with some justice: 'Much of the media hostility towards Fraser stemmed from the Dismissal and even his better policies were rarely presented by the media with the credit they deserved.' Fraser himself denies that the Dismissal had a detrimental effect upon his government's performance.

There were two powers exercised in 1975—the Senate's financial power and the Crown's reserve power. On these questions of power the status quo still prevails. Let me briefly look at each power.

The 1975 crisis brought to a head the contradiction in our Constitution between responsible government and federalism. The Constitution enshrined the principle of responsible government—that governments are accountable and responsible to the Lower House. Quick and Garran declare 'for better or for worse, the system of responsible government as known to the

British Constitution has been practically embedded in our federal constitution'.

But the price for federation was a Senate designed with virtually equal powers as the House of Representatives, including the power to reject appropriation. Without this political deal the colonies would not have agreed to federate. Quick and Garran describe the Senate as 'not merely a second chamber of revision and review . . . it is that, but something more than that. It is the chamber in which the states are so represented for the purpose of enabling them to maintain and protect their constitutional rights against attempted invasion'.

A number of the founding fathers knew they had implanted a contradiction at the heart of the Constitution. How could responsible government coexist with federalism? The power over appropriation meant that the Senate, if it possessed the will, could make the government responsible to it. How could governments be made and unmade in the Lower House if the Upper House could vote against supply? So it happened in 1975 that the time bomb, implanted in the Constitution from the start, was detonated.

The second area of powers concerns the residual powers of the Crown. Before 1975 many people would have denied their validity. But 1975 confirms their existence. The Governor-General dismissed the Prime Minister with an opinion from the Chief Justice that his action was constitutional.

Whitlam fell as a result of the combined exercise of the Senate's power and the Governor-General's power. Both remain intact. Not only this, but Paul Keating, in outlining his blueprint for the republic, has promised to retain the Senate's power and to preserve uncodified the reserve powers in the new office of president. That is, Labor, in its ambition for the republic, accepts the powers that destroyed Whitlam. It concludes that this is the political price to be paid for a republic.

Labor has periodically debated over the last twenty years reform of the Senate's and the Crown's powers, but it is disillusioned with these efforts, because the community is divided over the merits of the powers used in 1975, and the parties also remain divided on the issue. Therefore a referendum would not succeed.

The snapshots I have given are about how we see 1975

today. But I'd like to ask another, tougher question: How *should* we see 1975?

There were three stages to the crisis: Fraser's decision to deny supply; Whitlam's decision to remain in office; and Kerr's decision to dismiss. I want to assess each stage.

Fraser must carry the responsibility for the first step—deferring the bills in the Senate until the government agreed to a general election. Fraser justifies his action with the rhetorical question: 'Should Australia have been asked to endure another year of *that* government?' Announcing his decision on 15 October 1975 Fraser said: 'The Opposition now has no choice . . . the Labor government 1972–75 has been the most incompetent and disastrous government in the history of Australia . . . We are dealing with a chain of improprieties which constitutes one of the most extraordinary and reprehensible episodes in Australia's political history.' Fraser presented himself as a politician engaged in an act of national responsibility.

I don't believe that the judgment of history sustains Fraser's assessment. How essential was it to block supply in order to secure a change of government? Would another twelve or eighteen months of the Whitlam government, with Bill Hayden as Treasurer and Jim McClelland as Labour Minister, have produced a disastrously inferior outcome to that delivered by the first twelve or eighteen months of the Fraser–Lynch–Anthony government? I confess that I think the differences are more marginal than significant. That is, that Malcolm Fraser did not dramatically change the national direction. I would argue, though, that Fraser restored discipline to the machinery of government and confidence to the investment community.

I conclude that Fraser's claims about the necessity for a change of government at the end of 1975 are exaggerated. But Fraser's judgment of the national mood was correct—the people, if given a chance, would vote against Whitlam *en masse*.

I further conclude that while Fraser cloaked his actions in the guise of principle, the judgment of history will be that he was driven more by the quest for power and an urgency to restore the political status quo, that is, Coalition rule, than by the necessity of fundamental policy changes.

Fraser used the Senate's constitutional power—but, given

Whitlam's determination to fight, this could only be seen as an attack on the notion of responsible government and the authority of the Lower House. If Fraser had decided not to block the budget, and offered as a reason his belief in a convention that the Senate should not use its power to force the Representatives to the people, then such an action would have gone a long way to confirming or establishing such a convention which over time would have probably influenced the interpretation of Section 53. But Fraser acted as a party politician and he reflected a party-political culture. This should not surprise us. The same comment could be made of our political leaders today in relation to their own actions.

Fraser knew when he took the decision that it would lead to a parliamentary deadlock, because Whitlam had foreshadowed his intention to remain in office. Fraser defends his decision by telling me that the 1975 deadlock bears no comparison, in terms of damaging our social fabric, to the 1950s ALP split and the anti-Catholic campaigns conducted by Prime Minister Billy Hughes over the World War I referendums. It's a good point. But it begs the real issue—whether the 1975 crisis that Fraser initiated was really necessary in the national interest.

I quote Sir Garfield Barwick's account of his discussion with Sir Robert Menzies in October 1975 when Menzies, according to Barwick, said, 'The young fools are too impatient. It they give this fellow [Whitlam] enough rope he will hang himself'. I think it fair to conclude that Whitlam would have lost the next election anyway and that Fraser would have won a very significant election victory without any supply crisis and without the alienation of a significant and influential minority of the Australian community. So it might have been in Fraser's own political interests to wait.

I recognise, however, that it was hard for him to wait. The temptation was so great—given the loans affair and Rex Connor's fateful forced resignation on 14 October, virtually the very day the Opposition had to take its decision. In this sense Whitlam must bear some responsibility—the responsibility for running his government close to the ground and reducing its public support through a series of spectacular blunders. It was Whitlam's electoral weakness that attracted Fraser like a magnet. I believe that the failures of the Whitlam government must be factored into this equation. Whitlam all but invited his opposition to use the powers of the Senate against him. It is a tragedy that the first Labor government for 23 years engaged in such follies as the loans affair.

The second stage of the crisis was Whitlam's decision to remain in office and attempt, through political pressure, to force Fraser and the Senate to retreat. Whitlam's initial motive was elemental—survival itself. But Whitlam had another motive, which originated in the constitutional system.

Whitlam's stand was designed not just to save his own government; not just to thwart the triumph of the 'federalism' interpretation of the Constitution implicit in any success by Fraser. Beyond this, Whitlam intended to use the crisis triggered by Fraser to defeat the Senate in such a comprehensive manner that no future Senate would contemplate such action, and to ensure that the contradiction in the Constitution since the inauguration of the Commonwealth was finally resolved with the victory of Representatives over the Senate and of responsible government over federalism. Whitlam would become the last of the founding fathers. He would resolve the contradiction they had been unable to resolve.

Whitlam sought to achieve this by a political victory. Fraser had begun this battle but Whitlam intended to finish it. Whitlam's aspirations were clear from his speeches in the Representatives during the crisis.

There was no constitutional provision that required a prime minister, faced with the Senate's deferral of supply, to call an election. Sir John Kerr believed that Whitlam was entitled to remain in office and seek a political solution to the crisis. The Governor-General never suggested that Whitlam's action was unconstitutional at the time he launched his 'tough it out' campaign on 15 October.

There was neither a constitutional obligation nor a political convention that obliged Whitlam to call an election at this point. Whitlam argued, with considerable effect, the reverse proposition—that there was a constitutional obligation upon him to defeat the Senate's manoeuvre. This obligation arose to the extent that the concept of responsible government, as reflected in the Constitution, was being put at risk by the Coalition's tactic.

Whitlam's approach, however, was undermined by severe tactical mistakes. He assumed the reserve powers either did not exist or would not be used. He failed to persuade Sir John Kerr to his cause. He was deficient as a prime minister in the way he advised the Governor-General and as an individual in the way he related to Sir John Kerr. Whitlam left the Governor-General and everybody else with the impression that his 'tough it out' approach would be applied in the period not just before the government ran out of money but also afterwards—a situation which no responsible governor-general could tolerate. Whitlam assumed he had the option of a Senate election at any stage when, in fact, the likelihood of the Governor-General agreeing to a Senate election diminished as the crisis advanced.

In his approach the Prime Minister failed to discriminate between Fraser and Kerr. Yet he was seeking a different response from both men and therefore he should have had a different approach to them. His aim should have been to reassure Kerr and frighten Fraser. But Whitlam seems to have adopted the same approach towards everyone—a dogmatic insistence that he would never retreat—and that dogmatism only alarmed the Governor-General.

Whitlam squandered his greatest advantage—being able to advise and confide in Kerr. He never offered written advice; he never confided. His objective was obvious—to ensure that the Governor-General allowed the government the maximum possible time to bring pressure to bear upon the Senate. The key to securing more time for Whitlam was to build a trusting relationship with Kerr. Yet he hardly even tried. Whitlam did not grasp the need to win Kerr's trust. He assumed it. On 16 October Whitlam should have provided Kerr with formal written legal advice (which he never did) that the House of Representatives was not obliged to go to an election at the behest of the Senate. He should have gone to Yarralumla for a long and friendly private conversation. He should have told the Governor-General that the Solicitor-General would be made available to him for further advice at any time. He should have advised Kerr about the historic dimensions of the crisis and explained his own thinking. He should have advised that a political solution would be found to a political crisis. He should have assured Sir John that he would not be embarrassed by the government and that the government would never attempt to govern without proper parliamentary provision for supply.

This approach would have taken Kerr into Whitlam's confidence. It would have exposed Kerr to Whitlam's thinking. It would have helped to bring Kerr into Whitlam's plan. It would have established trust because Whitlam would reveal to Kerr a private strategy underlining his public strategy. It would have flattered Kerr. It would have had two lasting consequences— maximising the time that Kerr gave Whitlam to crack the Senate and helping to hold Kerr to Whitlam instead of sending him to Fraser.

Once Kerr assumed or suspected that Whitlam, in the end, would advise an election from the brink of the supply precipice, then his mind would be eased. Kerr would see Whitlam's plan—and he would not agonise about Whitlam's future moves. Once Kerr understood that his own responsibilities as governor-general under the Constitution would not be compromised by Whitlam, then he would be more tolerant of Whitlam's tactics.

But Whitlam failed to adopt any of these approaches. His tactical approach to Kerr was so faulty that it made the success of his strategy extremely difficult. Above all, Whitlam proceeded on the false assumption that he could remain in office after the exhaustion of supply or could rely upon non-parliamentary provision for supply.

The deadlock between the Senate and the Representatives, between Fraser and Whitlam, put the issue before the Governor-General. This led, finally, to the third stage, Kerr's dismissal of Whitlam.

The idea has gained currency that Kerr was a victim of two headstrong leaders, Fraser and Whitlam, neither of whom would retreat or compromise, and that, finally, he had no alternative but dismissal. I believe it is an interpretation that cannot be sustained.

The Crown and the Crown's representative will be called upon, periodically, to address a crisis. That is the nature of monarchy and the role of the sovereign; it is the role of the governor-general in Australia's system of constitutional monarchy.

The argument against Sir John Kerr is that he chose an extreme solution—dismissal of the Prime Minister without warning and with damaging consequences for his own office and the parliamentary system—when a better solution was available.

Sir John Kerr's argument that no political solution was available is not convincing. It originates in Kerr's view that his office carried little influence but an ultimate sanction. Sir John explored options for a compromise during the crisis, but he did not commit his office to this task.

There are four dimensions in which Sir John Kerr's judgment undermined a political solution: the timing of his intervention was unnecessarily premature; instead of approaching the reserve powers as a solution of 'last resort' he was attracted to their use before more orthodox processes; he failed in the Crown's obligation to warn the Prime Minister of a possible vice-regal intervention and thus to encourage Whitlam to reassess; and finally, the principle upon which he acted—that if the Prime Minister did not resign or advise a general election then he had to be dismissed—was substantiated neither by the Constitution nor by political practice. In many ways the startling point about the Dismissal is how unusual were the premises on which Kerr acted.

Sir John chose to become a constitutional innovator. I believe constitutional lawyers have obscured this reality by focusing on the validity of the two powers used—the Senate's power and the Crown's power—rather than on the circumstances of their use.

The initial basis in assessing the Dismissal is the principle on which Kerr acted. It is explained in his statement, 'A prime minister who cannot obtain supply, including money for carrying on the ordinary services of government, must either advise a general election or resign'.

It seems to me the technique used by Sir John Kerr and Sir Garfield Barwick was to construct a constitutional theory from a legal power. They said that because the Senate had the power over appropriation a government was therefore responsible to both the Senate and the House of Representatives.

It is one thing to insist that a government obstructed by a Senate motion to deny supply cannot remain in office once funds to provide for the ordinary services of government have expired. It is quite another to insist that a government denied supply by such a Senate motion has therefore lost the confidence of the Parliament and, unless it resigns or advises an election, must be dismissed.

The Kerr–Barwick theory confuses law and constitutional convention. In the process it can generate political absurdities. For example, under this constitutional theory the Senate, whose members may have been elected three and six years earlier, by blocking supply can vote no-confidence in an elected government, and force the Representatives to the people without having to face any election itself!

The Kerr–Barwick working rule is unlikely to be acceptable to the political parties, to the people or to future governors-general. Sir John's solution had the effect of undermining the position of an elected government, the notion of responsible government and the standing of the House of Representatives.

According to historical precedent, constitutional provision and political theory, the Governor-General should not have treated the deferral of supply by the Senate as a want of 'confidence' in Whitlam and therefore as grounds for a dismissal. He should have treated the situation as a test of the Senate's financial power to obstruct a government which, if persisted in to the point where funds might expire, would require a general election.

On the next issue, Sir John's defence of his timing is noticeably weak. It seems clear from his calculations and the sequence that his timing was designed to procure a general election before Christmas. He acted on the last or close to the last possible date, just as Whitlam was acting on the same date in seeking his pre-Christmas Senate election. But this was a purely administrative reason. It was not a substantial reason for the timing of such a spectacular use of the reserve powers.

Sir John says: 'I believe I had a discretion on timing. It was clear to me on 6 November that no compromise could be found . . . I had to accept what they did in the Senate and what their leader, Mr Fraser, told me they would continue to do.' The trouble with this statement is that nobody apart from Sir John had decided that there would be no political compromise. There was no reason why he 'had to accept' the advice provided him by the leader of the Opposition. These are extraordinary claims by any measure: a governor-general who is supposed to act on the advice of his prime minister asserts that he had no option but to act on the advice of the Opposition leader on an issue that involved dismissal.

There is a crucial section in Sir Garfield's 10 November opinion to Sir John. Barwick said that Kerr had to be 'satisfied' that Whitlam could not secure supply—so Kerr asserted such a condition when explaining the Dismissal. The truth is that it was impossible to be 'satisfied' about this matter on 11 November. A stranger visiting Parliament House at this time who chatted to a few politicians would have rapidly concluded that the situation was unstable and unpredictable.

Sir John's decision on timing must be set in context. He was contemplating the ultimate application of the reserve powers against a government with a majority in the Representatives, on behalf of a Senate whose resolve was unpredictable, in a manoeuvre that would split the country, damage the Crown and provoke claims that the Governor-General had been partisan.

Given this situation, it was prudent for Kerr to wait as long as possible and to be as sure as possible. Sir John had waited for 27 days; he decided that was enough. But the chance of some political settlement over the next ten days must have been at least 50 per cent. Given the issues, it is difficult but to conclude that Kerr intervened prematurely.

The third element in the critique of Sir John Kerr's actions is the Kerr–Barwick claim that the Governor-General had a 'duty' to dismiss Whitlam. This elevates the reserve powers from a last-resort solution to a more favoured priority. It implies that when a deadlock over supply cannot be easily resolved then the expected solution is an intervention by the governor-general to put the issue before the people.

Sir John approached the office as a jurist; he failed to grasp that the Crown is not a jurist. Kerr used the reserve powers to solve the crisis; he failed to understand that the reserve powers are best exercised by not being exercised—they then guarantee the influence of the Crown and it is that influence that enables the Crown to secure a political solution. He seems to have given insufficient weight to the dilemma arising from the exercise of the reserve powers. To the extent that the Crown is seen as partisan by the community, its integrity and ultimately its existence is in question.

There was an alternative to the reserve powers. It was the orthodoxy expected from the Crown or the Crown's representative—advising, warning and mediating to secure a political solution. This highlights the fourth criticism of Kerr's behaviour which, twenty years later, remains the most emotional point in the dismissal—Kerr's failure to warn, and as a consequence, the belief of Whitlam and his ministers that they were deliberately misled as part of a strategy of dismissal.

In my recent book [*November 1975*] I quote a number of people criticising the Governor-General for his failure to warn Whitlam properly—Bill Hayden, the then head of the Attorney-General's Department Sir Clarence Harders, Sir Rupert Hamer, the then Victorian Governor Sir Henry Winneke and the then NSW Governor Sir Roden Cutler.

Kerr's failure to warn has sunk deep into the culture of the Labor Party. It leads to an even more serious charge—that he deceived his ministers. It is this conviction that is the reason why Whitlam and Jim McClelland and other ministers reacted so strongly; it is the reason why Labor boycotted Kerr in such a comprehensive fashion while he remained in office.

McClelland says: 'I wouldn't have held it against Kerr if he had just been honest, if he had said to Gough, "Prime Minister, I'm in a dilemma and I might soon have no option but to dismiss you". But he didn't. Instead he planned an ambush. He did his best to deceive us and mislead us about his intentions on the reserve powers.'

One of the best examples of Kerr's technique is provided by John Wheeldon, a minister who opposed Whitlam's defiance of the Senate. Wheeldon says: 'It was at an early stage of the trouble. I was at Government House chatting to Kerr . . . He said to me, "How are we going?" It struck me at once—how are we going? When I got back to Parliament House I bumped into Jim McClelland and said to him, "Well, your friend Kerr is on side alright. We don't have to worry about him. He just said to me, 'How are we going?' " McClelland replied, "That's good. I'm just on my way to see Gough, so I'll tell him."'

This story from a minister who had been friendly towards Kerr captures the Governor-General's style. There are too many separate examples to dispute the evidence. Kerr portrayed himself as sympathetic towards Whitlam, and Whitlam concluded that Kerr was sympathetic. But Kerr did not rule out a dismissal, and Whitlam was unwise enough not to probe the Governor-General to discover his real attitude.

Sir John explains in his memoirs that he was determined to conceal that attitude. He defends himself against the charge of deception, but admits to concealment, and justifies this behaviour. Sir John acknowledges that he practised concealment against Whitlam throughout the crisis. When all the accounts given by the participants are read and re-read this looms as the extraordinary and pervasive factor. It is not about the law or the Constitution—it is about the trust between two men. Kerr distrusted Whitlam; so he declined to enter a frank dialogue.

The benchmark was set on 14 October, just before the budget was blocked, when Kerr, after two discussions with Whitlam, concluded that 'an implacable element began to appear in the Prime Minister's approach . . . From that time forward my opinion was that he was beyond the reach of any argument of mine, or even discussion'. Kerr's failure *during the crisis* to counsel or warn Whitlam was an abdication of the responsibility of the Crown's representative. The contrast is stark between Kerr's performance and Sir Paul Hasluck's doctrine of vice-regal behaviour: 'With the Prime Minister the Governor-General can be expected to talk with frankness and friendliness, to question, discuss, suggest and counsel.'

The justification advanced by the Governor-General for his behaviour was his conviction that Whitlam was prepared to sack him. Kerr felt that if Whitlam sensed that he was anything other than a 'rubber stamp', the Prime Minister would immediately approach the Palace. This is the bedrock issue. But if Kerr was seen as a 'rubber stamp' it was his own fault, which he should have corrected by being firm with Whitlam.

What should Kerr have done?

It is my view that he should have unflinchingly and courageously met his responsibility to the Crown and to the Constitution. He should have spoken frankly with his prime minister from the start. He should have warned whenever and wherever appropriate. He should have realised that, whatever his fears, there was no justification for any other behaviour. He should have demonstrated to Whitlam at the outset that he was a governor-general who would not be intimidated. He should have sought, throughout the crisis, assessments from Whitlam on his evolving plans for a solution. A situation in which the prime minister and the governor-general were informed of each other's thinking would have maximised the basis for a political compromise and minimised the grounds for misunderstanding and any resort to the reserve powers.

If his own dismissal was the price that Kerr might have to pay for honouring his responsibilities then he should have accepted that price. It was still a 'less worse' option for Australia's system of government than the one he finally took. I do not believe that Sir John would have been removed by Whitlam because the political consequences of any such attempt would have been so disastrous.

The view that Kerr should have waited and warned—thereby putting more pressure on both leaders for a compromise—is not a judgment made in retrospect; it was the conventional response. The crisis was political in its origins and nature and it required a political solution. It was Kerr's task to force Fraser and Whitlam to confront the consequences of their actions. If the Senate held, then Whitlam would have to choose between dismissal and advising an election. But Kerr was too weak in his dealings with both men and failed to put either leader under face-to-face pressure. When he found that the leaders failed to compromise between themselves he was trapped by his own interpretation of the crisis and his view of his powers into a dramatic and exaggerated intervention. Accordingly, Kerr concluded that in exercising the reserve power of dismissal he must ensure that Whitlam did not have an opportunity to consider his position and respond with a recommendation to the Palace that the Governor-General be removed.

In conclusion, I would make the following points. First, the 1975 crisis was driven very much by the three extraordinary personalities involved and their judgments and misjudgments of each other. Gough Whitlam, Malcolm Fraser and Sir John Kerr were men with defects to match their ability and ambition. We are unlikely to see their kind reappear in these positions during any future tensions.

Second, twenty years later, the crisis reveals more starkly than ever the bizarre nature of Australia's constitutional system—the prime minister can dismiss the governor-general and the governor-general can dismiss the prime minister. This is the institutional defect in our head-of-State system. It was this system which not only permitted, but which motivated a governor-general to deploy the dismissal power without warning against the prime minister while Australia's head of State, the Queen, was asleep in the Buckingham Palace bed unaware of the action being taken in the Crown's name.

The source of the problem, according to Kerr's analysis, is the governor-general's lack of tenure. In truth, it is a legacy of a monarchical system without a monarchy. If Australia had a true monarchy then the problem would not have existed, since Whitlam could not have sacked the Queen. Moreover, if Australia had been a republic the problem would not have existed, since a president would have security of tenure against removal by a prime minister. The problem was Australia's system of a governor-generalate. The Governor-General had the powers of the Queen but not the security. According to the Kerr–Barwick rule, such a system dictated a dismissal by ambush. But there will be many Australians who conclude that the Kerr–Barwick system is unsatisfactory if its logic delivers this result. But Kerr's conception of the office of governor-general proved unsatisfactory.

The crisis suggests, therefore, that the office of governor-general should be redesigned.

The decision Sir John took was that the crisis must have an exclusively Australian solution—that it was not the business of the monarch; that the monarch had no role; that the monarchy had to be protected from any involvement; that the Crown's powers were exercisable by the governor-general and that the governor-general would solve the problem. But in his desire to protect the monarchy (or to protect his own position) Sir John prejudiced the office of governor-general by rendering it partisan. That is why he had to retire early, and why his retirement was necessary to restore the office.

What Sir John proved is that Australia, in effect, is a crowned republic. The governor-general, not the monarch, exercises the Crown's power. I think an acceptance that we are a crowned republic should be the prelude to becoming a real republic.

Paul Keating's republican blueprint does not derive from 1975. The Prime Minister has been careful not to limit his republic by tying it to the Dismissal. The republic is a far broader movement. There is, of course, a narrow argument for a republic which originates within the 1975 crisis—that a president with security of tenure will have the confidence to deal openly and frankly with his prime minister. This would mean a genuine dialogue and no dismissal—unless the prime minister has a sudden compulsion to become the leader of the Opposition.

Gough Whitlam earlier this month declared that his chief interest in 1975 today is its relevance for the republic. Malcolm Fraser has recently said that a republic is inevitable. Australia is left with a fascinating constitutional hybrid—for the foreseeable future the Senate's power and the Crown's power will remain—but the latter will be vested in a presidency with security of tenure. Labor, driven by politics, has chosen to nationalise and localise the office of head of State rather than reform the powers of the office or reform the power balance between the Senate and the Representatives. The Dismissal, twenty years later, sees Australians contemplating the next stage of the evolution of our constitutional monarchy.

Hugo Wolfsohn Memorial Lecture, November 1995

THE 1998 CONSTITUTIONAL CONVENTION

THE CONVENTION AT THE HALFWAY MARK

IT HAS BEEN an Indian summer in the bush capital; dry, hot and windy off the old sheep runs, but Canberra's real Parliament House has never looked so good, reborn and alive, with all the vigour of delegates, debate, politics, deals and history in the making.

John Howard has commandeered the lovely wood-panelled PM's office from which Whitlam, Fraser and Hawke once ran the nation; Ian Sinclair sits in the old Speaker's chair like an avuncular schoolmaster; Queen's man Lloyd Waddy is a magnificent parody of a monarchical champion; Malcolm Turnbull, republican conductor, holds the spotlight to himself like a magnet always provoking loud applause and deep abuse while front, left and right are a vast collection of Australian characters once in your memory and now before your eyes—Pat O'Shane, Tim Costello, Bruce Ruxton, Steve Vizard, Geoffrey Blainey, Neville Bonner and Janet Holmes a Court.

You name it and the Constitutional Convention has got it—stuffed shirts, ratbags, intellectuals, politicians, feminists, old fogeys, larrikins, retired governors and articulate young twenties. There's lots of colour, theatre, press conferences and, for the record, a high quality of debate. This is because people care and most of them have applied their minds to the task.

Plenty of its corridors are shut and bolted, but Old Parliament House is rocking again.

Beware calling the outcome at halftime—but this convention

244

is heading towards a result. That now seems clear and it's the chief gain from Week One. Too many people have a vested interest in making this fortnight a success—John Howard, Kim Beazley and the entire republican movement, which has a floor majority.

Howard, as Turnbull said at the start, is the most important figure and his opening speech defined the parameters of the convention. Given the limitation that he's a monarchist, Howard has been a constructive force. His position is complex, evolving and misunderstood. This is the convention Howard proposed and from which he wants a republican model endorsed. Howard knows the debate has run so far that a referendum on the republic must be put. So he needs a 'clear view' on a republic model by next Friday which becomes the 1999 referendum question. Howard sees his role as honest broker of the national debate.

A deadlocked convention is a disaster. In this situation Howard has promised a national plebiscite to determine a preferred republican model. It would be messy and dangerous for all sides. Intelligent republicans grasp that Howard is offering them a golden opportunity—a referendum next year with the chance for Australia to become a republic on 1 January 2001, our birthday centenary. A new republic for a new century.

But there's a catch. Howard is a monarchist. He keeps declaring his support for the Crown because he believes that no republican model will deliver a better system of government. It must be assumed, at this stage, that Howard, while giving all Liberals a conscience vote at the referendum, will cast his own vote for the 'no' side. The referendum will lack prime ministerial imprimatur. That absence is likely to be fatal.

Howard doesn't think a 1999 referendum will be carried. This gives him two reasons for not switching to embrace a republic—it's against his beliefs and he thinks it's a loser.

Meanwhile, the convention assumed significant dimensions in the annals of the Liberal Party. The party founded by the great Ming, the party of God, Queen and Country is going republic. During the week, deputy Peter Costello, and ministers Robert Hill, Daryl Williams, Michael Woolridge and Richard Alston all declared as republicans.

Peter Reith, though undeclared, is assumed to be a republican. National Party leader, Tim Fischer, is bound by his party platform to the status quo but his heart is with a republic. Liberal premiers John Olsen (SA), Tony Rundle (Tas) and NSW Liberal leader Peter Collins are republicans. Northern Territory Chief Minister, Shane Stone, has been a champion for years of a popularly elected president. John Howard will be the last monarchist to lead the federal Liberal Party.

At the convention there are three republican camps which Tim Fischer best branded as mini, midi and maxi. By the week's end these models were being turned into a series of hybrids as republicans searched for the right compromise.

The mini is the model of Richard McGarvie, former Victorian governor in which the head of State is appointed and removed by a three-person constitutional council which replaces the Queen's role in this process. McGarvie regards most of the republic debate in this country as a dangerous shambles redeemed only by its more recent focus on his own model. Its defects run deep—it's a committee; it may start to negotiate with or advise a PM; it may divide internally; it will be a target of political pressure; it may become a weak institution with no tradition in our culture.

It is the model Howard dislikes least, the model which former chief monarchist, Tony Abbott, endorsed on Wednesday as a tactic since if Australia becomes a republic he wants the minimum possible change. Red-blooded republicans dismiss this model with contempt. It keeps appointment of any president, probably called governor-general, within the privacy of the PM's office.

The question being canvassed in King's Hall on Thursday was whether monarchists would king-make the McGarvie model by tactical voting. Probably not. It's hard to see how it gets the numbers anyway and monarchist boss, the formidable Kerry Jones, insisted that monarchists would vote as a bloc against all republic models. Yet cracks are apparent and Tony Abbott's name was mud this week among his former friends for being a sensible pragmatist.

The easy target for abuse this week was Malcolm Turnbull, spearhead of midi model—the ARM–ALP orthodoxy endorsed by the Keating cabinet in 1995 with a president elected by a two-thirds majority of a joint sitting of federal Parliament.

The paradox is that Turnbull was quite prepared to compromise on substantive issues. He wants a bipartisan referendum campaign for the republic with the Liberal Party 'in' not 'out'.

But the so-called 'true' republicans, the champions of the popular election, were angry at Turnbull's reluctance to make a leap their way. It was a difference, frankly, between professionals and amateurs. Turnbull spent years with the Keating government devising a republican model. Most 'true' republicans, by contrast, hadn't done their homework. Venting their frustration on Turnbull was easy but futile. The split is between those realists in the Labor Party and the Australian Republican Movement who seek a constitutional change merely to have an Australian as head of State instead of the Queen; and those so-called 'true' republicans who want the republic to be politically uplifting and spiritually enlightening such that it cures the dark side of Australian democracy and of ourselves.

The realists are represented by those professionals, Kim Beazley, Gareth Evans, Malcolm Turnbull and Neville Wran, the ALP and ARM leaders. The pitch was in Turnbull's opening speech with his reminder that at the 1988 Bicentennial celebrations at Sydney Cove the main speech was given, not by an Australian, but by Prince Charles. Turnbull asked: was there no Australian who could safely handle a pair of scissors? The goal for which the ARM had fought was that 'Australia's head of State should be an Australian citizen representing Australian values living in Australia chosen by and answerable to Australians'.

This is the slogan—that any Australian can rise to become his nation's head of State. It is a simple, emotional and powerful appeal—though the details aren't.

But the 'true' republicans speak another language. They aren't happy or convinced by the ARM's elitism or minimalist model in which the president is elected not by the people but by a two-thirds majority of federal Parliament. They see this as a sop, a sell-out, a fix, a contempt of the people and an utter failure to realise the potential of the republic.

Those backing an elected president include the Clem Jones Queensland team, the Real Republic Victorians that include Tim Costello and Moira Rayner with backing from that great larrikin, Phil Cleary, Paddy O'Brien from the West, the Ted Mack NSW group, Pat O'Shane—all of whom polled well in the elected vote for delegates. This list is far from exclusive and the 'true' republicans aren't a unified group.

In her speech, Rayner warned that 'no minimalist model, no cautious compromise' will capture the people. The convention was 'a once-in-a-lifetime chance to build a new Constitution' and a thoroughly democratic Australia. Rayner moved unsuccessfully on the opening day that the convention address at length a charter of rights, the recognition of the indigenous people, the accountability of government to the people and a new preamble to the Constitution. She repudiated 'powerful white men' parcelling out rights, declared that 'we must surpass our own caution or it will defeat us' and quoted Thomas Jefferson that constitutions must be reviewed every 30 years to stay relevant.

Mack savaged the existing system. Not for him the merit of our democracy. He attacked a Constitution which 'encourages continuing careerism, cronyism and corruption', an 'endless Balkanised legal and bureaucratic' war where 'public policy is constantly distorted and accountability avoided'. This Constitution was 'a patently obsolete hybrid' and produced 'an undemocratic, massively expensive, moribund political-administrative structure'.

The Mack answer, amazingly, is to adopt the American model, or at least its best features, and throw out the Westminster system.

The mantra of the 'true' republicans is to make the people sovereign; their rhetoric feeds popular prejudice with the accuracy of the best market researchers; and, above all, most are short on detail. Their position is founded on a contradiction—they say direct election is the model most likely to prevail—yet, in most cases, this model means a radical change, which almost certainly points to a crushing referendum defeat.

The Weekend Australian, 7–8 *February 1998*

NOT YET TIME FOR A DIRECT ELECTED PRESIDENT

THE REPUBLICAN CAUSE is coupled with a community perception that the republic must address voter alienation from politics and not just create an Australian as head of State.

This is why support for a popularly elected president runs

deep. The people want to reclaim ownership of the political system from distant Canberra. The conundrum for republicans, however, is that an embrace of the poll-driven popularly elected model may only see the current high levels of support for this model evaporate come referendum day.

It is also apparent republicans are split between the bigger and smaller States, with NSW and Victoria more disposed to the parliamentary election of the president, while ALP leaders Peter Beattie (Queensland), Geoff Gallop (Western Australia) and Mike Rann (South Australia) are convinced popular election is essential for a republic.

The polls document support for popular election. So what, exactly, are the problems with this model and why is it likely to be rejected?

Here is a short list.

First, the synthesis of the office of governor-general, with its immense constitutional powers, with a popular election mandate creates a powerful political office. The president becomes a new and influential politician. The prime minister has no defined constitutional powers and is not mentioned in the Constitution; nor is the prime minister directly elected.

The conclusion is inescapable—unless the constitutional powers of the president are limited then direct election will create a new political system. It will mean a new and powerful politician in Canberra living at Yarralumla (far more magnificent than the Lodge); this would represent an even greater centralisation of power in Canberra; it would institutionalise rivalry and conflict within the heart of executive power; it would create vast possibility for conflict—a Labor president with a Liberal prime minister or vice versa; it would limit the scope of the prime minister, no doubt, but creating a divided executive (in addition to a divided Commonwealth legislature) is hardly an improvement in our governance.

(Some champions of direct election say they want a radical change either to the US or French systems. That's fine. But they don't explain why on earth Australians will throw out the baby with the bath water and embrace such systems. Other direct-election adherents are plain dishonest and pretend direct election won't alter the existing system.)

Second, it is the direct election process that guarantees the politicisation of the office of president. On what basis do candidates campaign? The quality of ceremony? The appropriate presidential attire? What a joke. They will campaign for advantage against each other on the basis of public policy issues—Aboriginal reconciliation, Wik, tax, Asianisation, multiculturalism, the GST. In the current context why wouldn't Hanson or a fellow traveller nominate?

It's true the popular election model produced on Monday is a valiant effort to keep the presidential contest non-partisan by requiring the three candidates for popular election to be vetted and approved by a two-thirds majority of Parliament. Even if this produces non-party figures, they will still be politicians because, by definition, they seek a popular mandate for public office. That's what being a politician is all about.

Third, by making the president a popularly elected and political position, the traditional governor-general's role as a unifying and impartial status above politics is destroyed. The election, in fact, buries this tradition. In the current system, the governor-general can unify by action, rhetoric and behaviour. Under a popular election a majority of the population (yes, a majority) will probably vote against the successful candidate. If there are three candidates with preferential voting, as proposed in the Monday model, there's a good chance the winner won't have 50 per cent of the primary vote. But why only three candidates? Why not four or five or six? If so, at each stage the winner's share of the primary vote is smaller and smaller. What price a unifying role?

The fourth problem is that popular election means the president's powers must be fully codified and limited in order to achieve a non-executive office. This is legally possible but appears an insurmountable political task.

Given that the Senate has co-equal powers with the House of Representatives, a deadlock between the Houses is a likely occasion for resort to the presidential umpire. These powers, used by Sir John Kerr in 1975, aren't codified. The task of codification means either the Senate's supply power is effectively checked or eliminated (which neither the non-Labor parties nor the smaller States will accept) or the president's powers to dismiss a PM during a deadlock must be confirmed (which the entire ALP rejects).

This issue has been debated for 22 years since 1975. There is no political agreement. None is in sight. If the president is elected, the powers must be clear but if the 1975 issue can't be solved, then codification isn't possible and the elected model can't work.

Many insist that only public election can carry a republican model. Interesting. This model will be opposed en masse by the Howard government, the Liberal and National parties, the non-Labor States, key figures within the federal ALP, most constitutional lawyers and, inevitably, a fair slice of the media. Its day has not yet come.

The Australian, *11 February 1998*

RESULT OF THE VOTE

THE DEFEAT OF the republic exposes Australia as two different societies—a confident, educated, city-based middle class
and a pessimistic, urban and rural battler constituency hostile
to the 1990s change agenda.

This schism is not just an insuperable obstacle to a republic.
It is far more serious—a threat to a cohesive and successful
Australia as it tries to adapt to the globalised economy of the
new millennium.

The republic referendum, beaten 55 per cent to 45 per cent,
leaves Australia in a constitutional twilight zone where it is
detached from any real monarchical faith but unable to negotiate a republican future.

The republic will now be removed from the formal political
agenda of the Howard government. The Prime Minister has
achieved his two immediate aims: defeat of the republic and
preventing his government from being wrecked on the issue.
Kim Beazley, who campaigned strongly for a cause he knew was
lost, will now cut back Labor's republican profile. Beazley says
a Labor government elected in 2001 would conduct a plebiscite
on the principle of monarchy-versus-republic, likely to be put
at the 2004 election, as the first in three steps to reactivate the
process. If you think this sounds difficult, you're dead right.
Another referendum is many years or even decades away.

The way forward must involve a serious debate about a
directly elected president option. This means, at the early stage,
deciding whether the model should be a US-style executive
presidency or a directly elected non-executive, non-political
presidency that is impartial. After this principle is decided, the

hard part—devising the model—can begin. But it will be a more contentious debate with no guarantees about progress.

The picture of a divided Australia leaps from this weekend's result. This is a new class division that transcends the Liberal–Labor divide. Rich blue-ribbon Liberal seats voted for the republic along with the Labor inner city and ethnic heartland. The no vote was highest in the poorer seats dominated by blue-collar, rural workers and pensioners.

This was not a vote for the Queen; it was not just a vote against the republic on offer; it was, at a deeper level, a vote of distrust in the political class and its agenda of 1990s reform by people who simply said the republic was not a core issue for them.

The Howard battlers who defected from Keating Labor in 1996 and who voted for Pauline Hanson in 1998 turned out for the No vote at this referendum. Where will they go next?

The irony of the Kerry Jones-led monarchist campaign is that she declared Australia to have the best system of government in the world while she systematically set about undermining it with her campaign against politicians as a class.

John Howard will interpret this result as a vindication of his stance and his judgment. The Howard prime ministership will be defined by this result since his role was probably decisive. So how will this play out for Howard? Will the voters reward Howard or will they reject his brand of leadership as being too negative for the new century?

Deputy leader Peter Costello is a sure winner from this process. Costello has campaigned in an effective and mature fashion. He has offered an alternative vision to that of Howard along with a younger, fresher image.

Three judgments are to be made on this referendum. First, it was a near miracle to even get the referendum under a Howard government. Second, given the scare campaign, the great republican split over direct election and the opposition of the prime minister, the Yes campaign did well to win 45 per cent. Third, this was the right model to be put now. It won most support from the Constitutional Convention and it was the model best able to attract backing from both conservative Liberals and some of the radical direct electionists. The vote is now over, but the serious debate about direct election has hardly begun.

The Australian, *8 November 1999*

PART VI

IMMIGRATION AND MULTICULTURALISM

As Australia grew into a more tolerant society it lost its faith in immigration. This connection is not necessarily cause and effect but the link can hardly be overlooked.

Immigration is probably the most successful and important initiative of Australia's first century as a nation. It is a feature of Australia that has drawn worldwide attention and it is the key to our social pluralism. But during the 1990s there has been a collapse in support for immigration and a decline in its national interest rationale.

Why exactly should Australia persevere with large-scale immigration? Fewer Australians can offer a clear and confident answer to this question. Fewer politicians are prepared to champion immigration while many are dedicated to a far smaller program. On immigration, John Howard is the most sceptical prime minister since the inauguration of the program more than 50 years ago.

There are many reasons for this sentiment—a generation of high unemployment, fear that immigration accentuates environmental degradation, the fashion of lower population growth to enhance quality of life, the collapse of the 'populate or perish' ideology and fear that immigration is dominated by domestic politics and the ethnic lobbies rather than the national interest.

From the start politicians have manipulated public opinion to achieve their immigration goals. The launch of the program by the Chifley government with Arthur Calwell as our first Immigration Minister remains an act of political audacity. It was made possible only by Japan's wartime threat to Australia, the

257

consensus for a post-war national development, the reassurance a Labor government gave the trade unions on jobs, the insistence that British immigrants would dominate the intake (not kept) and Calwell's personal crusade not just to maintain White Australia but to argue that a post-war immigration program was the key to making Australia strong enough to stay white (a false proposition).

The 1966 Cabinet papers document the ongoing political manipulation at the heart of immigration. They reveal the reform of the White Australia Policy was a process of subterfuge. The dilemma facing the prime minister, Harold Holt, was to reconcile his belief in reform with the need to reassure the Australian public that reform wouldn't change its society. The ALP, half fooled and half fooling itself, joined this illusion.

Australia's historical skill on immigration has been to maintain a bipartisan approach across the political parties. This was Pauline Hanson's complaint in the 1990s when she said the big decisions on immigration had never been put before the people. That is because the parties have usually agreed rather than divided on immigration. However, the threat to the program in the 1990s runs deep. It is driven by a combination of economic and social factors that constitute a challenge for Australia as an ongoing immigrant nation.

The final article in this section deals with the private debate within the Howard government about the slogan of multiculturalism. Howard declined to use the word for much of his prime ministership. Ultimately, however, he was not prepared to ditch it. In its April 1999 report the National Multicultural Advisory Council recommended continued support for what it officially called 'Australian multiculturalism'. The report was accepted by the Prime Minister, but the debate in the community is far from over.

THE DISGUISED DEATH OF WHITE AUSTRALIA

THE 1966 CABINET papers show that just 30 years ago the only way the White Australia Policy could be substantially modified was by denying the real scope of the change.

A reading of the Cabinet papers and parliamentary debate highlights how recent is Australia's non-discriminatory immigration policy and how the basic 1966 change came through stealth, not as a decision about principle.

It was the liberalisation made by the Holt Cabinet on 2 March 1966 that is often described as the major watering down of the White Australia Policy.

Yet there was no suggestion made by anybody at the time, not Prime Minister Harold Holt, nor the agent for reform, Immigration Minister Hubert Opperman, and certainly not the Labor Party Opposition that Australia was embracing a non-discriminatory immigration policy.

This is because the move away from the White Australia Policy was evolutionary. The 1966 decision still left in place important discriminations against non-Europeans. Indeed, the Cabinet even rejected two recommendations in Opperman's submission.

The documents show that the liberalisation was only possible because of the assurances given by the Minister and written into the words of the Cabinet decision that basic policy was not being changed and, in particular, that the decision would not lead to any large increase in the number of Asians or non-Europeans entering Australia.

The papers also raise the possibility that Opperman—who

had brought forward unsuccessfully a similar Cabinet proposal in 1964—was prepared to be more liberal in his interpretation of the new rules than either his colleagues or the Parliament realised.

The timing suggests the departure of Sir Robert Menzies was relevant. Opperman wrote to Holt on 15 February 1966, a month after Holt became prime minister, proposing his submission.

Opperman wanted to build upon the decade-old decisions of the mid-1950s that had allowed entry to a small number of 'distinguished and highly qualified' Asians. He proposed that non-Europeans enter on the same status as other immigrants and that the procedure be broadened to enable selection on individual merit. Opperman's submission stressed that the fundamental policy of 'social homogeneity is not in question'.

The previous year the ALP had removed the words 'White Australia' from its platform. It had substituted instead the need to avoid 'difficult social and economic problems which may follow from an influx of peoples having different standards of living, traditions and cultures'.

Holt himself had stressed that the system was no longer a White Australia Policy but a restricted immigration policy.

The Prime Minister offered an insight into the reasons for the change when he told the media off the record that 'we have all felt that the policy has suffered by virtue of some of the cases which have hit the front pages of the press in Asia . . . I would hope that we can avoid situations of that sort in future'.

A strong note on Opperman's submission by a deputy secretary of the Prime Minister's Department, Sir Peter Lawler, exposed the real issues: 'Public and international criticism of the present policy is advanced as the principal reason for change. The practical consequences of the proposals must be the admission of more non-Europeans, particularly Chinese, for permanent residence . . . Admission of greater numbers would obviously erode the long-standing policy . . . If the changes could be administered so as not to increase the numbers admitted, the hopes of non-Europeans, already raised, would be dashed. If on the other hand greater numbers are allowed in, this will serve to whet appetites and spur on those seeking a complete dismantling of the policy.'

(Lawler also said that the previous year the number of non-Europeans for permanent residence was about 350 and that 'neither the trend nor the figures are negligible.') Lawler's analysis of the dilemma was correct. The Cabinet was playing with mirrors pretending that the change was one of administration, not principle. Once begun, the liberalisation would lead over time to a major change in policy. The fascinating question is which politicians grasped this and which, for various reasons, insisted that little was really happening.

In his announcement the Minister said that non-European entry would be 'somewhat greater' than before. But Labor's Immigration spokesman, Fred Daly, was persuaded by Opperman that the reform was minor. In the debate on 24 March, Daly said: 'We accept the assurance given by the minister that there is to be no departure from the accepted and established principles of our immigration policy.'

Daly said that Labor's support was subject to Opperman's assurances—that wealth would not be a basis for Asian entry; that non-Europeans would not be approved to meet general labour shortages; that there would be no large-scale entry of workers from Asia; that professionals would only be approved when Australians were not available for the job.

The Cabinet had insisted upon such assurances. So Opperman could confidently give them to the ALP.

Many Labor speakers, including Daly, said that Australia had avoided the racial problems of nations such as Great Britain, the United States, Malaya, Singapore, Fiji and South Africa, among others. (The non-European immigration to Britain received much unfavourable attention.)

Other ALP speakers such as Charles Jones declared that, 'I am opposed completely and unreservedly to any migration other than European migration', while Frank Stewart said that it was not a sin 'to be white or . . . for a white nation to want to retain a predominantly white population'. Both backed the reforms on the same basis as their Labor colleague from the West, Fred Colland, who said that on his interpretation there would not be any 'really significant' change to the policy. Kim Beazley (snr), though, had a different view, saying the change 'ends the administrative practice of drawing the line at race'.

The decision left much discretion to the Minister. Opperman had circulated a one-page document to the Cabinet, separate to the submission, giving examples of the non-Europeans who would be given entry in greater numbers.

They included people with technical skills, proficiency in arts and sciences, professionals to fill undermanned areas, specialists who had spent time here, businessmen and others whose character made their residence here feasible.

On 4 March, two days after the Cabinet decision, the ever-alert assistant secretary in the Prime Minister's Department, Geoff Yeend, wrote a memo pointing out that Opperman's examples were 'a far more expansive view' of the changes than sketched in his Cabinet submission.

The Australian, *1 January 1997*

IMMIGRATION IN RETREAT

AUSTRALIA'S IMMIGRATION PROGRAM has entered a new, reduced and apprehensive era which poses questions not just about immigration but about the nation's future.

Stubbornly high levels of unemployment, scepticism about multiculturalism and a decoupling of immigration and the national interest mean that the intake, and the very idea of Australia as an immigrant society, is in retreat. The paradox is that Australia remains one of the world's most successful immigrant nations.

Since 1945 when the great immigration program was inaugurated, Australia has had a government-sponsored annual intake that has played a decisive role in the political, economic and social transformation of the nation. A total of 5.5 million people have arrived. This accounts for half our population growth. In Australia today about one person in four was born overseas.

Immigration affects people directly—at work, shopping, sport, school, prayer. It generates powerful emotions. Public support for the program is essential. There is no doubt that Australia's absorption of millions of new arrivals over the past 50 years—marked by high intermarriage among people of different origin—has been one of our great achievements and an example worthy of more international attention than it has won.

Australia took about 1.1 million immigrants in the 1980s compared with about 960 000 in the 1970s, 1.3 million in the 1960s and about 1.4 million from the late 1940s and through the 1950s.

A snapshot of the 1995–96 intake reveals that immigrants come from more than 150 countries with the major sources being New Zealand (12 per cent), the United Kingdom (11 per cent), China (11 per cent), Hong Kong (5 per cent) and India (4 per cent).

The program has been underpinned by a broad bipartisanship across the major parties. The defining principles have been national sovereignty—that Australia must control its own program—public acceptance that Australia will benefit from a larger population, a belief that immigration ultimately contributes to economic and social wellbeing, an acceptance of humanitarian responsibilities and, for the past 30 years, the principle of racial non-discrimination.

After the election of the Howard government last year the size of the program was trimmed back to 86 000 from Labor's last figure of 99 000—though 86 000 is higher than Labor's recession year intakes—with a rebalancing from family to skilled migration.

Announcing the changes the new Immigration Minister, Philip Ruddock, issued a public warning: 'Community confidence in the program has reached an all-time low.' This is confirmed by recent public opinion polls. The most serious sign of the depth of the problem was a Newspoll published in *The Australian* last October which revealed that support for higher immigration was virtually non-existent.

Only 2 per cent wanted more immigrants while 71 per cent said immigration was too high (which included 52 per cent saying it was 'a lot too high'), with 20 per cent saying the level was about right. The survey found a relationship between attitude and income—the lower the income the more negative was sentiment towards immigration.

Ruddock's modest changes were designed to 'restore confidence in immigration'. But Ruddock, a cautious and sensitive minister long familiar with the issues, admits that it won't be easy to shift opinion and stresses that 'there isn't a great deal of room to move'.

Immigration has drifted, gradually but relentlessly, into a new era. Attitudes towards the program are shaped by our unnecessarily high unemployment levels, rising concerns about the environment, pervasive doubts about the future value of immigration and a bedrock concern in parts of the community about multiculturalism.

The Pauline Hanson phenomenon last year should send an unmistakable message about the crisis facing immigration.

The message for policy from Hanson is twofold. First, that the program has become too divorced for too many people from practical gain and benefit. This is not just a perception; it is a reality. It dictates reforms to the program that need to be rigorous and publicised. Second, Hanson represents a message to leadership to renew resolutely the idea of a non-discriminatory immigration program as a non-negotiable element of Australian polity integral to our society, security and prosperity for today and tomorrow.

Asked about the erosion of public support, Ruddock replies: 'I don't think it has eroded. But it's never been strong.'

Ruddock believes governments must be responsive to community opinion because 'if you do not have broad community support for the program itself then it's very difficult to introduce people into that environment and expect they'll settle in'.

This is where the challenge begins. The truth is that the Newspoll figures suggest a turning point for the immigration program. Ruddock has identified a series of new directions which, in different ways, are designed to re-establish a connection between immigration and the national interest.

The first is that critical measure—the numbers. He favours a fairly tight intake (certainly compared with the 100 000-plus for six consecutive years under the ALP before the program was trimmed in the early 1990s). For the Howard government's second year the intake is likely to be around the mid-80 000s again or even lower. Yet Ruddock also rejects the 'flat earth' outlook of the Australian Democrats and their many backers who want zero net migration.

Ruddock points out that this means taking only 28 000 people to get a net zero—but 'you've got 12 000 refugees, 14 000 free movements from New Zealand, young Australians marrying people from abroad and all sorts of expectations about family reunion. So I've not found anybody who thinks we can deliver a net zero outcome.'

The message is that Australia's migrant tradition and practices are ingrained. We will continue as an immigrant nation.

The high intake days are gone for the time being—but the program remains a fixture.

The government's second change relates to composition, notably, to give more weight to skilled migrants making a transparent economic contribution. Ruddock claims that when Labor cut the program it cut the skilled category.

'A properly structured immigration program can deliver new job opportunities for Australia,' Ruddock says. 'But a program that doesn't have the right composition can add significantly to long-term unemployment.'

Arguments against immigration on economic grounds are 'flawed' provided a government manages the program wisely. Ruddock says that unemployment for skilled migrants is at or below the general jobless rate—but for other migrants it is double. The conclusion is that the program needs a powerful economic focus geared to the labour market. This was the original intention.

From this flows a third series of changes some of which have faced stiff opposition in the Senate: limits on family reunion eligibility (with Ruddock saying that the family stream took up an excessive 70 per cent of the program under Labor); a greater weight to English language as an element in evaluating skill factors; a two-year post-arrival delay on a series of welfare benefits for migrants; and a priority accorded to applications where the sponsor is an Australian citizen to recognise the value of commitment to this nation.

The overall aim is manifest—to allow the government to exercise a greater control over the intake in the national interest.

But what is Ruddock's real purpose? Is it merely to restore confidence in immigration? Or is the purpose to restore confidence as a mechanism to achieving a bigger program? He answers cautiously: 'In my view it [the changes] will significantly restore confidence to the point where we may well be able to sustain a larger program than we have. But I would not assert this as an objective.'

On current trends Australia's population will be about 23 million and stable in 25–35 years time. This is not a target. It is the projection from the Bureau of Statistics based on a decline in natural population increase and the assumption that immigration remains at the present level. Ruddock raises the figure to stimulate debate.

You can look at this in two ways—either be horrified that Australia must accommodate another five million or bemoan the certainty that under this scenario Australia will become more marginalised, less influential and a subject of increasing criticism for occupying a continent with a very small, mainly white population accepting only a limited number of migrants in the selfish cause of its own living and environmental standards.

There must be serious doubts whether this result is compatible with Australian sovereignty.

Immigration has shaped our fate over the past half century. The size, nature and quality of the program will be just as vital in the next half century. Don't be misled by the pessimists, the prejudiced and the zero populationists.

The Weekend Australian, *3–4 May 1997*

MULTICULTURALISM, CAN THE SLOGAN ENDURE?

I F JOHN HOWARD wants to address the social fractures that he exploits to win votes, then he should decide whether our behavioural paradigms—multiculturalism and reconciliation—need to be redefined or scrapped.

The polls suggest that the community is disturbed about ethnic issues, with hostility towards Asians, immigration, multiculturalism, native title and Aboriginal reconciliation.

Recent detailed surveys by both Liberal and Labor parties show that Howard's shift from the Keating orthodoxy on these issues is exactly where public opinion lies. Once people see the Prime Minister championing our traditional identity, rejecting any Asianisation of Australia, criticising and cutting immigration, procrastinating over putting Pauline Hanson last on the Liberal ticket and insisting that today's generation should feel no guilt about past injustice towards Aborigines, then it should be no surprise that such positions are seized with greater public assertion and growing support.

But Howard cannot keep running against Paul Keating's agenda. Sooner or later, by actions and words, he must define with less ambiguity his social philosophy.

This is most difficult in the domain of Aboriginal reconciliation, where a backlash against Keating's approach has deepened with Howard; he has created an association between reconciliation and white guilt—a fatal political link. Howard has pledged himself to the word reconciliation but discredited its meaning.

It is, however, far easier for the government to move on

multiculturalism. This has always been defective as a settlement philosophy because there is no universal grasp of its meaning. A national objective that is neither understood nor supported cannot survive. It is time for multiculturalism—as a slogan—to be scrapped in order to salvage its reality. Australia needs a better statement of national intention that encourages support for ethnic diversity.

In a little-noticed statement on 30 June, Immigration Minister Philip Ruddock reconstituted the National Multicultural Advisory Council and gave it sweeping terms of reference. In effect, Ruddock has asked the new 15-member council, headed by the chief of Fujitsu, Neville Roach, to reassess the entire agenda of multiculturalism—principles, policy and implementation. He wants a blueprint for the next decade. Significantly, Ruddock said he wanted a report designed to ensure 'that cultural diversity is a unifying force for Australia'. The committee is filled with eminent Australians, many of them from ethnic backgrounds. Its report will become a landmark for the Howard government's social policies and Australia's future path towards ethnic diversity.

When I asked Ruddock whether multiculturalism would remain the defining slogan, he replied: 'I'll tell you in a year or two.' He correctly said that this was not a new debate for the nation.

An effort to come to grips with national symbols after exhaustive consultation was made in the 1994 report from the Centenary of Federation Advisory Committee chaired by former Victorian premier Joan Kirner. Phillip Adams, who served on the CFAC, says the feedback on what it meant to be an Australian fell under two broad categories. He says: 'There was an identification with the landscape, a groping to link our vistas with democracy. A searching for a spiritual link with the land. The other responses emphasised Australia as a country of the "fair go", with proud relevance to "tolerance" demonstrated by multiculturalism.'

Yet on the first page of its report, the committee moved away from multiculturalism as a vision to offer an entirely new synthesis between unity and diversity. It said: 'The motto of 1901 was: "One people, one destiny". For 2001 it must be: "Many cultures, one Australia".'

The report explained: 'Core values must be consolidated and

celebrated. Only then can they be used as the building blocks for the new century. Australia can be a world leader in terms of achieving cohesion in diversity.'

This declaration had echoes of an earlier report, the 1988 Fitzgerald report, which said: 'Immigration must be a two way commitment between the immigrant and Australian society . . . Multiculturalism does not appear to have been a persuasive vehicle for analysis and community education about the beneficial social impact of immigration.'

The report concluded that 'the philosophy of multiculturalism is not widely understood and the uninformed ensuing debate is damaging the cause it seeks to serve'.

That was a warning; it was eight years before Hanson's arrival.

The Hawke government, partly in response to Fitzgerald, then produced a National Agenda for a Multicultural Australia based upon the work of the Advisory Council on Multicultural Affairs, headed by Sir James Gobbo. This 1989 document was decisive. It defined multiculturalism in a careful and balanced way. It championed a right to ethnic and cultural heritage, but only within a framework of loyalty and obligation towards Australian unity.

Ruddock recalls: 'The opposition at the time looked at that definition and affirmed it. And today John Howard will tell you that if that's what we mean by multiculturalism, then the Howard government has absolutely no problem with it. Just no problem.'

But there is a problem. It is that this definition—with its exact balance of rights and responsibilities—is not what most people mean by multiculturalism. The work by Gobbo (now Victoria's Governor) and his committee was excellent. But the people don't have this concept of multiculturalism, this careful sculptured balance.

Ruddock continues the story: 'What happened is that the fiercest political advocates of multiculturalism would go out and read the first three dimensions to people. They'd tell audiences: "This is what it means. You're entitled to a job, you're entitled to every benefit from the Australian community that anybody else gets, and you're entitled to your past." But the other half—the commitment to Australia—never got a look-in.

'Part of the problem with the term "multiculturalism" is

that some people think there's one law for ethnics, that they can keep their culture but they don't have to be committed to Australia, that they're not treated the same way by the courts and so on.

'There was an underlying fear, in fact, of the way it was being promoted. We only got half of the agenda. If the term multiculturalism is used properly—and the definition is on the table—then it occasions no difficulty for anybody.'

Ruddock won't pre-empt his own review body. 'Multiculturalism is there at the moment,' he says. 'And I've got an obligation to ensure that it is understood.'

If you are under the delusion that multiculturalism is understood, then listen to the nation's leading researcher, Hugh Mackay. 'It's a term which has never had a comfortable currency in this country,' he says. 'It sounds like a bureaucratic invention and social engineering. People think it sounds like something that's been imposed upon us. It is seen more as a fragmentation of culture, lots of little subcultures, without coalescing.

'But the response to multiracial is different. If you say "multiracial", then people don't miss a beat. But the word people love is "cosmopolitan". It sounds exciting and when you say it people swell up with pride. Cosmopolitan sounds like something we achieved, not something that was imposed upon us. With multiculturalism, I keep getting a sense of unease whenever it's mentioned.'

One of the intellectual architects of multiculturalism, Professor Jerzy Zubrzycki, a member of Ruddock's new committee, recently said: 'We need to consider whether continued use of the term multiculturalism is not a deterrent to the acceptance of an ideology that seeks the pursuit of justice, fairness, civility and decency for all Australians, regardless of their ethnic or racial background.

'Certainly, we need to employ the adjectival derivation "multicultural" to describe the demographic reality of Australia at the end of the second millennium. But the clumsy, pompous, polysyllabic noun multiculturalism—adopted from the Canadians and incorrectly associated in the public mind exclusively with ethnic groups, has outlived its purpose . . . we need another term.'

It is important to get the national definitions right. If the symbols and directions aren't right, then policies won't be right and public support will never solidify.

There are two defects with multiculturalism as a national symbol—the term is still not understood, so the task now is probably hopeless; it is widely seen as a policy for Australians from ethnic minority backgrounds, but not all Australians.

The Kirner committee's 'Many cultures, one Australia' offers a way forward. It is a synthesis between unity and diversity, given equal weight in a slogan whose meaning is obvious, supportable and aspirational. The centenary of Federation is the time to orchestrate a significant change. But there is a better position than the Kirner committee's notion of many separate cultures that can be moulded into one nation.

A far better choice is '2001: Many races, one culture'. This definition has three merits—it declares our destiny as a multiracial and diverse society; it declares our unity and repudiates any fragmentation into a nation of tribes; and it projects towards a new civilisation since the evolving culture is neither Asian nor European but a unique Australian creation.

The Weekend Australian, *30–31 August 1997*

PART VII

THE YEAR 2000

NATIONAL DISGRACE

JOHN HOWARD AND Kim Beazley have failed themselves, their parties and the country.

The Australian people are the victims of a conspiracy— a betrayal by the political class against the best interests of the nation. It has been a long time since Federal politics saw the combination of such a flawed prime minister as John Howard and such a weak Opposition leader as Kim Beazley. This is the most obvious feature of our politics. The source of the problem is the same in each case, yet there is a national conspiracy to deny the obvious.

Within a few weeks, Howard has managed to spook his own government. The collapse in its voting support is totally self-inflicted. The Labor Party rarely lands a political punch on Howard. The truth is that Howard is the most knee-jerk, poll reactive, populist prime minister in the past 50 years. He has turned the leadership virtue of listening to community reaction into a desperate overreaction to transitory opinion inflamed by tabloid headlines and talkback jocks. National Textiles was an accident just waiting to happen. The defect lies in Howard's approach to politics.

His opponent, Beazley, heading towards his fifth year as ALP leader, has failed to tell the Labor Party or the country what his leadership represents and what direction he plans for Australia's future. Labor seems to be locked into a defensive mind-set, so confident it can win the next election on Howard's flaws that it seems incapable, so far, of devising bold new policy. The entire country knows what Labor plans for the historic

2000 year—a relentless negative campaign against the GST, a tax it intends to keep. This is political fraud on a grand scale.

Globalisation presents harsh new problems for political leaders. But Howard and Beazley are failing the test. Australia's situation is bizarre. We enjoy our strongest economic expansion of the century. Our Reserve Bank governor, Ian Macfarlane, says that the 1990s growth cycle has run for nearly nine full years and our average gross domestic product growth rate in this period has been 4.1 per cent as opposed to 3.6 per cent in the US. We have outpaced the US miracle. Yet any visitor touched by the media-driven political debate in the past few weeks would conclude only that Australia is in the depths of a national crisis.

This crisis lies in our own heads and hearts. The 1990s have delivered a prosperity and peace rare in our history. The benefits have not been evenly spread but the overwhelming majority of people are better off. Yet aggravation fed on fallacy is the staple of political dialogue. Howard's greatest communications failure is his inability to make Australians feel content or proud or unified or reconciled to their lives, their challenges and their good fortune. It isn't because he doesn't try but his efforts rarely succeed.

Howard's big problem is not just the GST. It is also his failure to articulate a post-GST policy or offer a convincing view of what his second-term prime ministership is about. What is Howard's second-term agenda outside the GST and Telstra privatisation? This is a government short on political nourishment, vision and emotional empathy, and the entire community senses this.

The real issue raised by National Textiles is whether Howard's dual identity as an economic reformer and a political populist has reached its point of exhaustion. He has been all things to all men for too long.

Howard keeps telling his MPs to hold their nerve over the GST, but then he panics over the Coalition's loss of support in the bush and regions. It is obvious that the Federal government has been psyched out by the Kennett government's dramatic loss of support in the Victorian countryside.

Howard's National Textiles fiasco had four dimensions. He undermined any sense of a coherent strategy to handle the problems of the bush and the regions; he embraced bad policy—

use of taxpayer funds for employees hurt by company failure; he offered a special deal for one group of workers, thereby inspiring hostility from other groups; and his impulsive reaction blinded his judgement, so that he failed to perceive the conflict of interest situation arising from the directorship of his brother, Stan.

Nobody who knows John Howard would believe his motive in the National Textiles bailout was to save Stan Howard's neck. His motive was closer to home—to save his political neck. But Howard's over-reaction has a lasting consequence—he has completely blurred the boundaries between a good and a bad policy government. In so doing, he ruins his best political asset and his advantage over Labor. It is proof that economic reform and political populism don't work—a proposition that Howard has never accepted as PM and, I believe, never will.

Polls show upwards of two-thirds of Australians either oppose the GST reform or think they will be worse off. But most people will be better off—the July package cuts tax on many goods, boosts exports, cuts income tax and increases welfare payments in a hefty overall net tax cut. There is a huge disconnection between perception and reality. Why? The answer lies in the Coalition's administrative ineptitude and Australia's political culture.

Howard's economic policies—tax reform, industrial reform and privatisation—are designed to reap the advantages of globalisation. Yet his populist rhetoric largely confirms the world view of the talkback jocks that globalisation is an evil. Howard is trapped into a communication with the Australia people via radio jocks hostile to his reform philosophy.

The rise of radio and the decline of newspapers and television as political agents is central to our changing political culture. Howard thinks the radio jocks are his friends, but they are really his enemies. Radio gives the politicians a voice, but it devours them and multiplies the culture of complaint. The rationale of the radio jocks is to de-legitimise the political class and blame the politicians for any social ill, real or imagined, so that their own authority and ratings are enhanced. It is likely that if Howard went a month without appearing on talkback radio, the Coalition's poll ratings would improve.

Howard, a born fighter, recovered in parliament this week because he managed to finger Labor's great defect—the ALP runs off an anti-globalisation fear agenda devoid of any policy solutions. The Beazley ALP, thus far, lives off the politics of complaint, but it is trapped in a time capsule on policy.

The Coalition got traction this week when Howard exposed Beazley's stance on National Textiles and Treasurer Peter Costello taunted the Opposition leader over his refusal to abolish the GST. The issue was the same on both counts—what does Labor stand for?

Beazley, in some ways, is a more serious populist than Howard. The textile industry in Australia has been the recipient of cartloads of money, protection and assistance for decades. It has been a bottomless pit for many hundreds of millions of dollars of taxpayers' money. Yet Beazley's solution, announced on the National Textiles picket line on February 8, was to declare: 'It is absolutely vital to this region that this factory is kept open. If you care, John Howard . . . you will be at the cabinet today saying: "We have got to now put in place the economic underpinnings of keeping that factory open."'

Here is the Labor Party of 2000. It wears its heart on its sleeve and it preaches the worst form of economic hoax—that governments should be bailing out failed inefficient firms and that this is a solution to economic change. It is a reversion to the pre–1980 bad old days; a huge leap into the past. It is the stand of a party that has learned nothing and forgotten everything. If there is one lesson that Australia's political class should have learned, it is the folly of propping up failed firms with more taxpayers' money in the name of workers and families. Such bailouts don't work and they are a fraud upon the people in whose names they are invoked. Even worse, the impression must arise that Labor has little ability to handle the problems of the age.

There is a serious question to be posed about the Labor Party today: Is the ALP capable of governing Australia in the age of globalisation?

Labor has yet to show the answer is yes. This should be the main task of its policy review now under way. The party needs to address this question, not just frighten the horses. The point is reinforced by its stand on the GST. Labor is running an enormous anti-GST scare, assisted by a series of Howard government blunders. But there's a catch—Labor intends to keep the GST. No, this isn't a joke; it's the truth.

Shadow Treasurer Simon Crean outlined the Opposition's position this week: 'If it were possible to stop the GST in the lead-up to its implementation, we would. But, as much as we dislike the tax, by the time of the next election these inter-linkages and relationships will be in place. By then it will not be possible to unscramble the GST egg. We can, however, ease its worst effects. We can make it less unfair. That is what Labor [is] committed to doing.'

So the Labor Party will campaign for the next 12 months against a tax that it intends to keep. In this sense, Labor's high-profile campaign is a con job. The ALP, of course, doesn't have to keep the GST. If the GST were half as bad as Labor pretends, then Labor would abolish it. But Labor won't because the GST is too advantageous a reform for any Federal govern-ment. The trade-off Labor faces will be whether to significantly roll back the GST or keep most of the tax in place and use its revenue for health and education programs.

For years, social democratic parties in Europe have funded their grand public sector programs off their indirect tax base. The Labor Party in Australia, no doubt, will do the same.

When will Labor release the full details of what modifications it plans to the GST? Crean says: 'The full extent of these problems will only emerge after the GST has been in place for some time. We cannot tell you how we will lift the burden until we know how much money is available and who it is going to hit. We will not know either of those things until the tax has been operating for some time.'

What does this mean? It probably means that Labor wants to delay the release of its tax policy until about three or four weeks from voting day, maybe in November 2001.

What has happened in Australia is that the downside of globalisation dominates. In a deeper sense, Australia just doesn't get the politics of globalisation. Our leaders can't manage the new politics necessary to get good policy and carry people with them. There is a danger in Australia that the political class will become a menace to the national changes necessary to make globalisation work.

The need is for a new strategic role for government, which must become less of an executive and more of a facilitator. Overseas, this is often called the Third Way. The Third Way is based upon a recognition that the First Way—social solutions by state intervention—won't suffice anymore. It is based on a recognition that the Second Way—solutions based upon individual wealth and economic libertarianism—won't suffice anymore. A new synthesis is required. To rewrite Bill Clinton's 1992 slogan: 'It's the society, stupid.' Howard's reform agenda is too narrowly economic and Beazley's agenda is too old-fashioned.

There are two starting points: first, an honest dialogue between the leaders and the community—and Australia doesn't have this; and, second, an understanding that policies of social inclusion are the absolute requirement for the successful society today.

Good leaders bring out the best in the character of their people, not the worst. This is an issue over which John Curtin agonised at great length during World War II and it is critical to his greatness.

Howard faces a test this year when Aboriginal reconciliation reaches its climax. The people want leadership that unites, binds and repairs, not leadership that divides unnecessarily. The Coalition doesn't get this point but the leader who follows policies of social inclusion wins more political space for his economic reforms and wins a society that feels better about itself.

The Weekend Australian, *19 February 2000*

INDEX